Novations

STRATEGIES FOR CAREER MANAGEMENT

Gene W. Dalton
Paul H. Thompson

Scott, Foresman and Company
Glenview, Illinois   London

ISBN 0-673-18181-2

Copyright © 1986 Gene W. Dalton and Paul H. Thompson.
All Rights Reserved.
Printed in the United States of America.

8—KPF—90 89

Library of Congress Cataloging in Publication Data

Dalton, Gene W.
  Novations : strategies for career management.

  Bibliography: p.
  Includes index.
  1. Organizational behavior.   2. Psychology,
Industrial.   3. Level of aspiration.   I. Thompson,
Paul, 1938–   II. Title.
HD58.7.D35   1986   650.1'4   85-14635
ISBN 0-673-18181-2

To the hundreds of professionals and their managers whose willingness to share their experiences and organizations made this research possible.

Preface

During the years when we were examining the data on what we and others were calling the "obsolescence" of engineers and other professionals, we made a promise to ourselves. We often reaffirmed that pledge during the hundreds of interviews we had with accountants, scientists, engineers, professors, systems designers, bankers, and managers. Many felt frustrated, angry, puzzled, and even betrayed by the things that were happening to them in organizations. The promise we made to ourselves during those years was that if we were able to find anything that would help these people better understand the organizational processes with which they were grappling, we would share it with them. We would not publish our findings where only our colleagues in organizational studies would read them, nor restrict them to management journals. We would write something that would at least be available to every "knowledge worker," to every person who had spent years in a school or university learning a profession and then tried to use that professional training in a complex organization—which no one at the school or university had prepared them to understand. This book is an attempt to fulfill that promise.

We were not able to find any talisman that would assure that every capable, hard-working professional would find a satisfying career in organizations. We did not find a simple way to transform all organizations into places where professionals and managers would no longer feel "stuck," or "owned" by their bosses, or angry that their efforts could seem so little appreciated.

What we did find, however, was a way to understand how careers in organizations unfold. From the hundreds of interviews, we were able to extract at least one way of explaining why some professionals were highly valued by their organizations throughout their careers, while others, apparently equally bright and well-trained, received progressively lower performance ratings with every passing year.

We were able to arrive at a way of viewing organizations that "makes sense" of many of the seeming paradoxes in career development. We found a way of portraying careers that, when presented to professionals and managers in organizations, draws silent nods and comments like, "Yes, that's the way things work around here." After presenting our career stages model to a group of professionals, we have each had a scientist (or financial analyst, accountant, or engineer) say, "I only wish someone had shown me that 10 years ago." Conversely, our description of organizational careers has seemed so intuitively familiar to many successful and experienced professionals and managers that they often anticipated what we were going to say or gave us examples of the stages, blocks, or novations we were trying to describe. One manager, for example, said to us, "I have moved from: managing my manager . . . to managing myself . . . to managing others . . . to managing the organization."

A highly respected professional in an engineering consulting division of a large chemical company told us:

> Your career stages model parallels what I have come to describe as the levels of problem-solving that our people move through on their way toward becoming what I consider to be a first-rate consultant:
>
> I. Inexperienced or ineffective consultants have a set of "tools" or techniques in their repertoire and, whether they realize it or not, look for problems where they can apply those tools.
> II. Consultants begin to be genuinely helpful when they start to listen to the client and focus on the solution to the client's problem, using whatever tools are needed.
> III. Consultants become even more helpful when they learn to help clients explore whether or not they are working on the right problem.
> IV. The most effective consultants—and we have very few of these—are those who are broad enough in their thinking to question whether or not the right system is being addressed. They are able to ask whether a problem is actually a technical one, or whether it might more usefully be conceived of as an organizational or a political problem. Are we going to be able to attack the problem more usefully, they ask, by working at it technically, by reexamining organizational policies, or by working with governmental bodies and trade associations to get more rational legislation or agency rulings?

We have also provided managers and professionals a new language with which to discuss careers and performance. Each of the authors has had the experience, after presenting the material on career stages to a group of managers, of having one of them say, "Can I get a copy of your overheads on career stages? (See Figures I.5 and I.6 on pages 8 and 9 in this book.) I have to hold a performance appraisal with one of my people next week, and I want to use it to help me explain what I have been trying to say to him [or her] for the last year."

Our former colleague, Paul Lawrence, once told us that a good theory is one that is obvious—once it is stated. We would like to think that our model of careers has at least some of that quality of "obviousness" to the readers of this book.

To whom, then, do we recommend this book? First, to professionals and managers working in organizations. It has been our primary aim to present our model clearly and understandably to those who are trying to build careers in these complex amalgams of systems, which we call organizations. Our central purpose has been to give them another way of thinking about their careers that will increase their ability to make informed choices.

Second, we commend this book to the spouses of professionals and managers. We believe it will help them understand the experiences their spouses relate to them as well as the organizations in which those experiences take place.

Third, we believe this book will be useful to students who plan to enter organizations—and to their professors. Students who have learned how to debug a circuit design, calculate a funds flow analysis, or prepare a good legal brief may still be poorly prepared for organizational life. They also need a clear way of thinking about how to manage their relationships and an understanding of the functions organizations will expect them to perform. Those who are preparing to be nurses, engineers, salesmen, accountants, systems designers, lawyers, and financial analysts would do well to have a map in their minds of the organizational milieu into which they will enter. They may not feel the urgency for this map that those already in organizations feel, but we have found repeatedly that the careers of these students are significantly, and often almost irretrievably, determined by the way they conduct themselves in the first few months on the job.

Fourth, we believe that it is important that line managers and human resource specialists understand the findings and ideas in this book. As we point out in the last chapter, a number of organizations have found that our research has significant implications for the way organizations are managed and structured.

Finally, this book is important to us as a means of communicating our ideas and findings to those who share with us an interest in the study of organizations and careers. We value their respect and welcome the discipline of their criticism.

Gene W. Dalton
Paul H. Thompson

PROVO, UTAH

Acknowledgments

How do we acknowledge the debts that we have accumulated over the many years that have led up to the publication of this book? It is impossible to recognize them all, but there are a few that we cannot fail to mention.

We must acknowledge our debt to our parents, Dell and Rachel Dalton, and Harold and Elda Thompson, who taught us that understanding comes only through hard, patient effort—but that it is worth the price.

We would like to recognize the strong influence Fritz Roethlisberger played in attracting us to the study of the individual in the organization. Fritz's infectious and intense curiosity has influenced all our work since meeting him. We have also both been strongly influenced and benefited by our association with Paul Lawrence.

The senior author would also like to recognize the great influence Abraham Zaleznik and Louis B. Barnes played in introducing him to the study of careers of professionals in organizations. During those early years, the first author was also indelibly changed by Robert J. Wolf, who cared deeply about the lives and careers of those with whom he worked. The support and encouragement of Bob Livernash as we moved into the investigation that eventually resulted in this book will never be forgotten.

We would like to express our gratitude to the hundreds of professionals and managers who have discussed their careers, their experiences, and their ideas with us. If anything has given us the energy to continue our work, it has been the privilege of working with these men and women who care about the quality of the work they do, the people with whom they work, and about making their organizations places where competence and integrity are valued.

In conducting the studies described in this book, we were aided by the strong support and insight of a number of managers and professionals who helped make it possible for us to gather the data needed. We would like to express our gratitude to Keith Laws, Ray Mayhew, Wally Decker, Harold Johnson, Don Roberts, Veigh Nielsen, Bill Sackett, and Ann Lewis.

Another group that has helped advance our work and allowed us to share our findings with others has been the editors of the *Harvard Business Review*,

Organizational Dynamics, and the *IEEE Spectrum.* We have particularly appreciated the support and counsel of David Ewing and the late Bill Dowling.

Several people helped us gather data, garner insights from the data, and write up drafts of the material gathered. We want to gratefully acknowledge the contributions of Richard Kopelman, Peter Graves, Chris Meek, Ian Wilson, Kerry Patterson, Gary Jewkes, Norman Hill, Lee Perry, Mary Kay Stout, Owen Cherrington, Amy Bennett Johnson, Jeff Dyer, Robin Zenger Baker, and Kurt Sandholtz. We should like to make separate note of the contribution of Ray Price in helping us to draft the first article describing the career stages model.

During several years while we were conducting this study, we had the good fortune of meeting with a group of other researchers who were also looking at various aspects of careers in organizations. We gained much from these meetings and remain particularly indebted to Edgar Schein, Brooklyn Derr, Michael Driver, Lotte Bailyn, Paul Evans, Fernando Bartolome, John Van Maanen, David Kolb, Don Wolfe, Jim Clawson, and Meryl Louis.

We have been greatly aided by financial and other forms of support provided us by the Brigham Young University School of Management and the Harvard Business School for the conduct of the research, which later led to the writing of this book. The Office of Naval Research helped provide funding for meeting with colleagues from other universities to discuss research on careers in organizations. Although none of the gift funds from the 3M Foundation, Jan Ertezek, or Henry Marcheski went to support this research directly, they have supported the growing research program at the Brigham Young University School of Management, and we want to gratefully acknowledge that support.

We have appreciated the support received from our colleagues at the School of Management, both in the conduct of the research and in the writing of this book. We acknowledge the help Alan Wilkins and J. Bonner Ritchie have extended to us by reading specific chapters of this book and offering suggestions for improvement. Over the past few years, we have benefited greatly by discussing many of the ideas that appear in this book with David Cherrington, Stephen Covey, Gibb Dyer, William G. Dyer, Kirk Hart, Reba Keele, Kate Kirkham, Weldon Moffitt, and Warner Woodworth.

Our two associates, William Marek and Norman Smallwood, have significantly contributed to our understanding by demonstrating to us and to others the practical implications of the ideas in this book for the management and design of organizations.

We are deeply indebted to Lisa Casper, Karen Zobell, and Jill Madsen for their competent and cheerful help in preparing and reproducing the manuscript. The chapters that follow are significantly more understandable and readable because of the competent and thoughtful editing of Carrie Sandholtz, Susan Eliason, and Laura Cutler.

Finally, and most importantly, we want to express our deepest gratitude to our wives, Bonnie Dalton and Carolyn Thompson. Not only have they assumed untold responsibilities for us and shown astonishing patience during the years of late nights and weekends we have devoted to this study, but their herculean effort in getting the final manuscript ready for the publisher was an act of love—and relief.

But in spite of all the generous help we have received from others, we reserve and deserve responsibility for those parts of the book that contain errors, omissions, and oversights.

Gene W. Dalton
Paul H. Thompson

PROVO, UTAH

Contents

Novations
STRATEGIES FOR CAREER MANAGEMENT

Introduction

This book is about professionals in organizations. There are over 27 million of these knowledge workers in the United States. They already make up a quarter of the work force and are growing faster than any other segment. Their initial training was as engineers, scientists, accountants, MBAs, and so on, and they have spent their lives as employees in complex organizations dependent in large part on their professional skills.

These professionals have often been told how critical they are to the future of the organizations in which they work—and to the nation's economy. In spite of having entered into organizational life with high expectations, many find themselves confused, frustrated, and angry. They complain about feeling "stuck"; they mutter about "politics"; they are bewildered by seeing others no more technically capable than themselves getting assignments, influence, and positions that they desire. Most importantly, they find themselves in a world they do not fully understand—a world for which their formal education did not prepare them. These feelings do not go away as the years go by; they get worse. Older professionals are even more likely than their young associates to find themselves plateaued, under-utilized, and unappreciated. This book has been written to help professionals understand why this is happening to them and what they can do about it.

Several million managers have the responsibility of managing, utilizing, and developing these professionals. They are asked to give these people performance evaluations, assignments, and counseling. The managers feel the responsibility of helping these professionals make sense of what is happening to them, in order that they might be more effective in their work and in the management of their careers. In some cases, of course, this is relatively easy to do. More often, however, it is difficult, and may even be compounded by the fact that the managers themselves are not sure what is happening in their own careers.

The way careers unfold is a mystery to most people, especially to those individuals who are trying to build careers in a bewildering organizational world. Part of the mystery, however, comes from the fact that the majority of us have inadequate or misleading ways of thinking about organizations and careers. The careers of professionally trained employees in organizations do not proceed in straightforward or linear pathways. They develop in distinct and, in some ways, discontinuous stages. Paradoxically, some of the very activities and orientations that make for success at one stage hinder movement into the next stage unless they are abandoned.

Two ideas are central to understand the careers of professionals: career stages and novations.

1. *Career Stages:* Several years ago we wrote an article entitled, "The Four Stages of Professional Careers"(1). It presented the thesis that there are different stages in careers, and that different activities, skills, and relationships are required to be successful in each stage. We found that not all professionals move through all the stages. A majority of the professionals in the firms that we studied had not moved beyond the first two stages.

   Moving from one stage to the next requires successful performance within the stage an individual has already attained. It also requires a complex process of obtaining the trust and support of other key people to begin performing the tasks and entering into the relationships inherent in the next stage. It was the effort to understand the complex processes involved in moving from one stage to another that led us to the concept of "novations."

2. *Novations:* The word "novation" is a legal term with a long history in English and American jurisprudence. It is unfamiliar to most people outside the legal profession, but better than any other word in the English language, the word "novation" describes the complex process that provides the key to understanding the way individual careers unfold in today's organizations. The dictionary defines the term as " . . . the substitution of a new obligation or contract for an old one by the mutual agreement of all parties concerned(2). We found that changing relationships are critical in moving from one stage to the next. But to make such a move, individuals must renegotiate a new set of obligations and expectations with all those around them. Delicate as these mutual negotiations are, they are compounded by the need to make psychological shifts with new self-perceptions, new self-expectations, and adjustments to new pressures. Novations proceed with such seeming naturalness for some people that few people around them even take note of the changes. But the majority of professionals have a very different experience. They often feel stymied and frustrated in their careers. These are the ones who fail to understand and successfully carry out novations. We describe in this book what we have learned about novations, how some individuals successfully carry them out, and how others fail in that effort.

CAREER INTEREST

First, let us note the rising competition professionals in organizations face, and how we came to study stages and novations.

RISING COMPETITION

Even though the need for professionals is growing, there are several trends that have increased the competition for good assignments and advancements.

The first trend is the boom in education. The percent of the workforce today that is college educated is twice what it was two decades ago (3). A million seniors graduate from college each year(4). Over 35,000 attorneys finished law school in 1983(5). The number of persons completing an MBA degree each year has increased from 5,000 to 50,000 over the past 20 years(6). Some trend-watchers fear that the growth in the educated population will not be matched by an increase in challenging and fulfilling jobs. James O'Toole, author of *Work, Learning and the American Future,* warns:

> No industrialized nation has been able to produce an adequate number of jobs that provide the status, and require the skills and educational levels, that their work forces are achieving(7).

The bulge in the population entering early adulthood is another factor. The number of people between 35 and 44 will continue to grow by one million per year during the 1980s. By 1990, nearly one-third of the population will be between 25 and 44 years old. This is the age when most professionals expect to move into more responsible and visible positions. Sheer numbers make this very difficult. Furthermore, analysts project that the number of people aged 15 to 25 will drop by seven million between 1980 and 1990(8). This means fewer new employees for the professionals of today to manage in the next decade.

Another factor creating greater competition for assignments and promotions is the increasing number of professionally trained women. The number of women professionals jumped to nearly seven million in 1980, up from fewer than three million in 1960(9). Most analysts project a similar increase in the two decades following 1980.

Finally, the recession in the early 1980s began a trend in American corporations toward reducing the number of middle managers. Executives began to worry that their companies were top-heavy in administration and choking in red tape. They shortened lines of reporting and cut managerial positions. *Business Week* described a "cut in middle management staffs of old-line companies, ranging, for example, from 20% at Firestone and Crown Zellerbach to 40% at Chrysler. . . ." Executives streamlined marketing, strategic planning, and finance functions (traditionally the realm of the young MBA) to create more flexible organizations. As a result, there are "fewer rungs on the ladder, fewer footholds on each rung" (10). This means a constriction of the once-plentiful opportunities for corporate advancement, just at a time when more people are competing for these opportunities.

AGE AND PERFORMANCE

Our interest in the careers of professionals in organizations did not derive from trends in national demographics. It emerged from a study on performance measures that we began as professors at the Harvard Business School in the late 1960s. We became intrigued when we found that the average performance ratings of design engineers rose steadily for each age group until ages 30 to 35, then declined steadily for each subsequent age group until retirement. This relationship between age and performance is portrayed in Figure I.1.

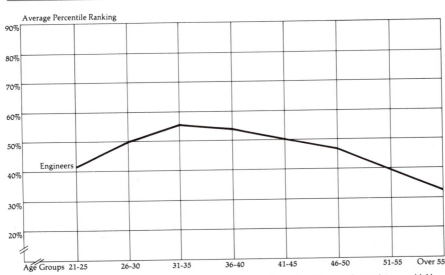

FIGURE I.1 Age and performance: managers' evaluations of engineers (11).

4

Average Performance Rankings

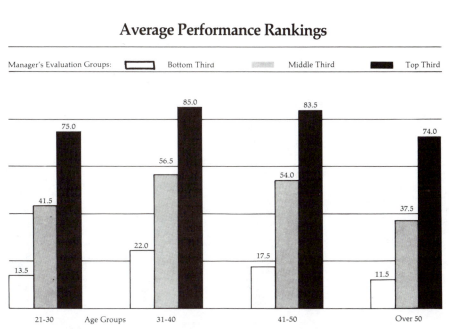

FIGURE I.2   Average performance rankings of top, middle, and bottom thirds of four age groups of design engineers(12). (From Paul H. Thompson, Gene W. Dalton, and Richard Kopelman, "But What Have You Done for Me Lately—The Boss," IEEE Spectrum (October 1974), pp. 85–89. (c) 1974 IEEE.) NOTE: Each engineer's performance ranking came from a comparison against all engineers in the firm regardless of age. Thus, the average rating of the top third of the engineers over age 50, for example, is an average of the performance rankings of the individuals in this group compared against engineers of all ages.

Fascinated by these data, we launched an extensive study of over 2,000 design engineers in 6 companies, asking: "Why the long steady decline?" and "Do professionals become obsolete like machines?" One finding that interested us greatly and changed the focus of our studies emerged when we examined the overall performance rankings of engineers divided into four age groups (12). (See Figure I.2.)

We found that the difference in performance rankings *within* the age groups was greater than *between* age groups! There were a significant number of design engineers in their 40s, 50s, and 60s who were ranked as high performers. What distinguished these engineers who continued to be highly rated from those who did not? We checked to see if they took more company-sponsored or college courses. They did not. But they *did* have different kinds of job assignments. (Figure I.3.) Those who had high performance ratings also had more complex job assignments,

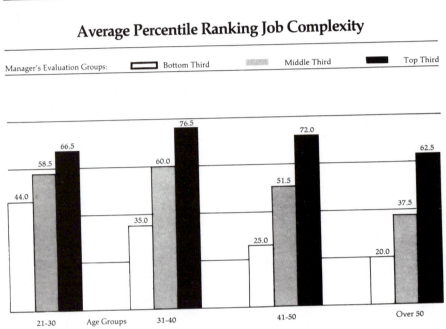

Average Percentile Ranking Job Complexity

Manager's Evaluation Groups: ☐ Bottom Third ▨ Middle Third ■ Top Third

FIGURE 1.3 Average job complexity rankings(13). (From Paul H. Thompson, Gene W. Dalton, and Richard Kopelman. "But What Have You Done for Me Lately—The Boss," IEEE Spectrum (October 1974), pp. 85–89. (c) 1974 IEEE.)

requiring the use of judgment, skill, and technical knowledge rather than just routine work. And the difference between the complexity of the jobs of the high performers versus low performers increased with age. These data about job complexity gave us a significant clue, but we didn't fully understand the implications at the time. We continued to pursue the question: "What distinguishes those professionally trained employees who continue to be highly rated from those who do not?"

To answer this question, we interviewed 550 professionally trained employees: 155 scientists in 4 laboratories, 268 engineers in 4 organizations, 52 accountants in 3 firms, and 75 professors in 3 universities. Our subjects were selected to give us representative samples of high- and low-rated performers. We began by simply asking them to describe their own careers and those of their fellow professionals. "What," we asked them, "characterizes the high performers you know?" Their responses were coded and then compared with the way the high-rated and the low-rated performers described their own careers.

Our early analysis yielded only frustration. Each promising uniformity exhibited too many contradictions. Each new hypothesis failed to find support in the data. It was only when we began to look at the effect of time that a clear pattern began to emerge. High performers early in their careers were performing different functions from high performers at mid-career. And both these groups were different from high performers late in their careers.

As we investigated further, it became increasingly clear that there are four distinct stages in a professionally trained employee's career. These stages derive from the needs of organizations to have certain functions performed well by individuals who are competent, well trained, and who have earned from others the trust that allows them to perform these functions. Each stage differs from other stages in the tasks individuals are expected to perform, in the types of relationships they form, and in the psychological adjustments they must make. Figure I.4 sketches some of the central features of each stage.

In Stage I, individuals work under the direction of others as apprentices, helping and learning from one or more mentors. In Stage II, they demonstrate their competence as independent contributors. In Stage III, they broaden and act as a mentor for others. Those in Stage IV provide direction for the organization. Figures I.5 and I.6 provide an overview of the way an individual in each of the four stages might be described by a careful observer. It is important to realize that although the stages are distinct on important dimensions, there are elements in each stage that

Central Activities, Relationships and Psychological Issues in Four Career Stages

	Stage I	Stage II	Stage III	Stage IV
Central activity	Helping Learning Following directions	Independent contributor	Training Interfacing	Shaping the direction of the organization
Primary relationship	Apprentice	Colleagues	Mentor	Sponsor
Major psychological issues	Dependence	Independence	Assuming responsibility for others	Exercising power

FIGURE I.4 Central features of the four stages (14).

Characteristics of Career Stages

Stage I

Works under the supervision and direction of a more senior professional in the field

Work is never entirely his or her own but assignments are given that are a portion of a larger project or activity being overseen by a senior professional

Lacks experience and status in organization

Is expected to willingly accept supervision and direction

Is expected to do most of the detailed and routine work on a project

Is expected to exercise "directed" creativity and initiative

Learns to perform well under pressure and accomplish a task within the time budgeted

Stage II

Goes into depth in one problem or technical area

Assumes responsibility for a definable portion of the project, process, or clients

Works independently and produces significant results

Develops credibility and a reputation

Relies less on supervisor or mentor for answers, develops more of his or her own resources to solve problems

Increases in confidence and ability

FIGURE I.5

are present in each of the other stages, although in a different form. Our description of each stage focuses on the issues that differentiate one stage from the next.

Since our understanding of these stages came from a quest to find what distinguishes high performers from others, we expected to find that individuals who had moved through several of these stages would be relatively highly rated. Conversely, we expected that individuals who had remained in early stages were likely to be low-rated. We went to the managers of groups of about 50 to 80 professionals, and asked them if they knew all the professionals and supervisors below them well enough to describe the work each was doing and how well he or she was performing it. Usually they said they did. If the manager said no, we went to the next management level below. We explained the four stages, showing the manager a sheet of paper similar to Figures I.5 and I.6 and asked the manager to describe each of the professionals and managers under his or her supervision in terms of these stages. We gave the managers a deck of 3×5 cards with the names of each person on a card and asked the manager to place them in four piles representing the four stages. The concept and categories seemed comfortable to the managers and were close to the way they already thought about their people. If a manager stated that someone was transitioning between one stage and the next, we asked the manager to place the individual in the stage that most closely described the individual's role at the present time.

We then compared the stages into which individuals had been placed with their current performance ratings. As expected, those described as being in later stages had higher average performance ratings than those in earlier stages. But some very interesting additional patterns emerged when we plotted the relationship between the stages into which individuals were placed and their performance rankings. The patterns were quite similar in each organization where we plotted this relationship. Figures I.7 through I.10 present the scatterplots of age and performance for each stage in one research and development organization (15). The vertical line in all the scatterplots represents the average age of all the engineers and scientists in the organization; the horizontal line represents the average performance ranking for the total population. A triangle indicates an individual holding a managerial or supervisory position.

The scatterplots in Figures I.7 through I.10 reveal a number of significant patterns:

- Not all those described by their managers as being in Stage I are young: their average age is 39! Most individuals in Stage I have relatively low ratings; but note that the older a person is, the lower the rating.
- A similar pattern is evident in Stage II. There are a number of young per-

Characteristics of Career Stages

Stage III
Involved enough in his or her own work to make significant technical contributions but begins working in more than one area

Greater breadth of technical skills and application of those skills

Stimulates others through ideas and information

Involved in developing people in one or more of the following ways:
a. acts as an idea leader for a small group
b. serves as a mentor to younger professionals
c. assumes a formal supervisory position

Deals with the outside to benefit others in organizations, i.e. working out relationships with client organizations, developing new business, etc.

Stage IV
Provides direction for the organization by:
a. "mapping" the organization's environment to highlight opportunities and dangers
b. focusing activities in areas of "distinctive competence"
c. managing the process by which decisions are made

Exercises formal and informal power to:
a. initiate action and influence decisions
b. obtain resources and approvals

Represents the organization:
a. to individuals and groups at different levels inside the organization
b. to individuals and institutions outside the organization

Sponsors promising individuals to test and prepare them for key roles in the organization

FIGURE I.6

9

Stage I—Scatterplot of Age and Performance

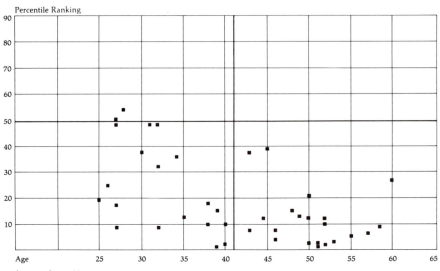

Percentile Ranking

Age

Average Age = 39
Average Performance Ranking = 17th Percentile
■ Nonmanagers = 100%

FIGURE I.7 Stage I.

Stage II—Scatterplot of Age and Performance

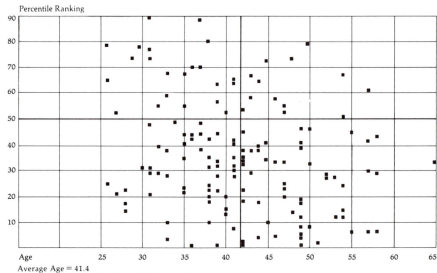

Percentile Ranking

Age

Average Age = 41.4
Average Performance Ranking = 34th Percentile
■ Nonmanagers = 100%

FIGURE I.8 Stage II.

Stage III—Scatterplot of Age and Performance

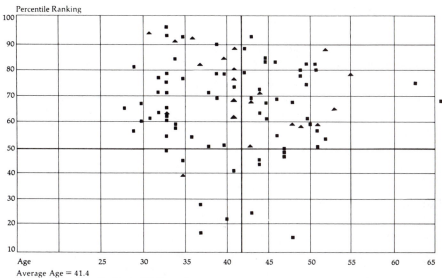

Age
Average Age = 41.4
Average Performance Ranking = 65th Percentile
■ Nonmanagers = 76%
▲ Managers = 24%

FIGURE I.9 Stage III.

Stage IV—Scatterplot of Age and Performance

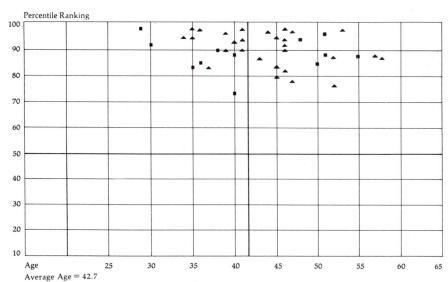

Age
Average Age = 42.7
Average Performance Ranking = 89th Percentile
■ Nonmanagers = 28%
▲ Managers = 72%

FIGURE I.10 Stage IV.

11

formers in Stage II with high ratings, but relatively few high ratings among Stage II people over 40 years of age.

- Only in Stage III do we see any significant number of people over 40 with above-average performance ratings. Note also that the average age of people in Stage III is the same as in Stage II—41 years old.
- It is only in Stage IV that we find uniformly high ratings. Note also that the average age of those in Stage IV is only 42. The average age over all 4 stages only varies by 3 years!

The patterns in the scatterplots in this research and development organization were typical of other organizations studied, except in one way. Organizations differed greatly in the extent to which nonmanagers played Stage III and Stage IV roles. In this particular research and development organization, 77 percent of the people described by their managers as being in Stage III were nonmanagers and 30 percent of those in Stage IV were nonmanagers. But these percentages varied greatly between organizations. In many organizations, even research and development organizations, there were no nonmanagers performing Stage III or IV roles. The reasons for these differences will be examined later in the book.

CAREER STAGES AND ORGANIZATIONAL NEEDS

The strong relationship between career stages and performance ratings is not surprising. Each flows from a basic fact about organizations. In order for organizations to maintain their viability, they need to have certain functions performed well. All functions are important, but some are more highly valued than others. Some functions can be performed by someone with little experience in the organization or industry; some can only be performed by someone with a deep understanding of the organization, its task, and its competitive environment. Some functions, if performed poorly, cause minor and temporary problems; other functions, poorly performed, cause major and long-lasting harm. Some functions can be performed adequately by most professionals with minimum training in the appropriate field; other functions require a combination of relatively rare gifts and abilities. The four stages represent clusters of functions that are progressively more highly valued by those whose task it is to evaluate and reward others on behalf of the organization. Thus, if one person is performing Stage I functions very well and another person is performing Stage IV functions very well, the performance of the person in Stage IV will be more highly valued because the functions are more highly valued.

We realize, in making this statement, that we run the risk of being seen as parroting the obvious. But we have met so many professionals in organizations that act as if they did not understand this little truism, we are willing to risk the embarrassment of belaboring what may seem patently obvious to some readers. It is our observation that one of the reasons so many individuals do not appear to understand the point being made here is that they don't think in terms of organizational needs. They do not focus on the functions that must be performed in order for the *organization* to survive and grow. However, those who have been selected to act on behalf of the organization and to evaluate the performance of others are explicitly asked to think in those terms. The most common criterion used to compare the performance of professionals and managers is, "value of the individual's contribution to the organization during this period." We believe that the contribution of the stages model is that it helps individuals to focus on organizational needs and on the functions valued by organizations. We are convinced that such a focus is far more helpful in explaining and understanding the problems and questions of building long-term careers than looking at interpersonal style, individual drive, or personal aggressiveness, etc.

STREAMS MORE THAN STRUCTURES

The stages model alone, helpful as it is, has the disadvantage of conveying a static quality to a rapidly changing phenomenon. Because organizations have a continuous flow of people moving through them and because the environment is always making new demands on the organization, there is a constant need for individuals to deal with new tasks, perform new roles, and provide new leadership. Those who step forward and capably address these needs are usually recognized as having an enhanced or continuing value to the organization. Over time, those who fail to fill these needs are judged as having relatively less value.

To step forward and perform needed functions, however, is not a simple process. Not only must individuals recognize the needs, they must have the skills to perform the new activities. They must also have gained the confidence of others in the organization so they will be permitted to perform new activities and be accepted in new roles. In addition, these individuals must make the personal internal adjustments necessary to leave rewarding roles, activities, and established relationships in order to step into the more unfamiliar and unknown.

A novation from one stage to the next begins before any explicit or formal change occurs; it is more an informal renegotiation of expectations, obligations, and relationships that takes place as individuals move from one stage to another. Individuals must:

1. Demonstrate some new capabilities and attributes required by a new role.
2. Obtain the trust of those who will be critical in helping them get the opportunity and cooperation necessary to perform well in the new role.

Often, the formal transfer or promotion on the organizational chart, if it ever comes, follows, rather than precedes, the critical informal novation from one stage to another.

These changes often take place so naturally, so easily, that they are sometimes imperceptible to the casual observer. But they can also be difficult and frustrating to both the professional and those with whom he or she works.

HIERARCHIES, OBSOLESCENCE, AND STAGES

We believe that the career-stages model and the concept of novations can help readers in several ways. These ideas can provide readers with a new way to look at the organization in which they work, at their own careers, and the careers of those with whom they work. Our ability to understand and to deal effectively with the world around us is both limited by and enhanced by the models, the concepts, the metaphors we have with which to examine that world. The concepts of stages and novations also provide us with a new way to talk with one another about careers. Frequently, when we have presented these ideas to managers, we have had one or two managers ask for a Xerox copy of Figures I.5 and I.6, so they could use them to provide a language for talking with subordinates during performance appraisal interviews.

We have found that many professionals and their managers are hobbled in their behavior by having too few ways of thinking about careers and organizations. Moreover, the models they do have are too limited to take into account some of the important things they see going on around them.

Too many individuals we have met have had little else but the pyramidal model of organizations and careers with which to make sense of the rich, buzzing, blooming confusion around them. They know that the hierarchical organization charts and promotion lists they have in their desks are important, but realize that these charts miss much of the complexity they experience in their working relationships. When organizations have tried to parallel the pyramidal organization charts with "dual career" ladders, they have often found themselves unable to portray or achieve what they had in mind.

The "obsolescence" model of careers, with its neat "half-life" calculations of an individual's worth as an up-to-date professional, has provided a persuasive metaphor to justify funding for continuing education (an outcome we generally applaud). The obsolescence model, however, carries with it an implied solution to the problem it was designed to highlight. The solution, obviously, is to update and reeducate professionals, restoring them to the state they were in when they came out of school. Continuing education can be valuable in its own right, but it has been far from a panacea for those wishing to build viable careers in organizations. In fact, the data from our studies failed to show that the high-rated performers were any more likely to have taken continuing education courses than the low performers.

It is our observation that the pyramidal and obsolescence models, alone, are just not rich enough to give individuals the intellectual tools they need to understand the complex organizational world that they inhabit.

PREVIEW OF WHAT FOLLOWS

In the chapters that follow, we will be looking in more detail at the functions performed and the relationships of individuals in each stage. But more than anything, we'll be sharing with the reader the frustration, discouragement, and anger of the hundreds of "knowledge workers" we interviewed who could not understand what was happening to them. These include bright young MBAs in the first painfully discouraging months on the job, CPAs who make partner at age 35 and wonder where to go next, and 45-year-old engineers, feeling stuck in routine jobs, and swearing they will never let their children become engineers. For, paradoxically, it is by looking at those having problems making novations that we learn most about this complex process. It is by looking at some individuals failing and others succeeding that we begin to appreciate how often the blocks to progress stem from our own passivity or misreading of organizational life. Chapter 1 describes the transition into Stage I and the pitfalls that prevent many professionals from performing well in this stage. We look at the way reciprocity develops and deteriorates between apprentices and mentors.

Chapter 2 focuses on the renegotiation of responsibility that lies at the heart of the novation into Stage II. We look at the paradox of professionals working for independence, then finding themselves immobilized when they find themselves responsible for their own output and for managing their own time and relationships.

Chapter 3 begins with a look at the factors that block people from moving successfully into what we have come to call the mentor stage. Taking responsibility for others' work raises additional problems and requires new skills. Chapter 4 reexamines the reciprocity between mentor and apprentice and explores what many writers and training programs ignore—that mentoring is deeply imbedded in work performance. Chapter 5 examines the rewards and dilemmas of moving into Stage III. The rewards include influence, status, job security, and the opportunity to help others develop. The dilemmas include feeling "caught in the middle" between upper management and subordinates and dealing with constantly conflicting demands on one's time.

The next section begins with a discussion in Chapter 6 of how much those we actually observed in Stage IV differ from the stereotypes in our society of those who direct organizations. They were not all chief executive officers or "businessmen." None were "one-minute managers"; in fact, some were not managers at all. We take a close look at Stage IV nonmanagers and the kinds of organizations where they are found. Chapters 7 through 10 explore the four major functions performed by those in Stage IV:

- Providing direction for the organization (Chapter 7).
- Exercising the power necessary to assure that vital tasks are accomplished (Chapter 8).
- Representing the organization to important individuals and groups inside and outside the organization (Chapter 9).
- Sponsoring and developing individuals to play key future roles in the organization (Chapter 10).

Some readers of an early manuscript of this book read Stage IV chapters first, then chapters pertaining to Stages III, II, and I, in that order. They felt it was more interesting and helped them understand the material better to read it in that order. If some readers choose to look first at Stage IV, they at least have the encouragement of the few early readers who tried it and liked it.

In the final two chapters, we examine the implications of stages and novations for individuals and then for organizations. In Chapter 11, "A Different Drummer," we acknowledge that by looking at what makes a person highly valued in an organization, we have looked at only a limited part of that person's life. While being valued for what one does at work is important, it is far from everything. There are those who make deliberate decisions that they know will limit the assignments, evaluations, and rewards they receive at work. Many do so in order to be able to devote more time and attention to other areas of their life that they may value more, such as family, humanitarian and religious service, or personal independence; or, to the pursuit of what the Greeks called one's "daimon," a personal destiny rooted in the exercise of one's unique capabilities.

Chapter 12 examines the implications of this study for organizations, and those who manage and structure them. It is not inevitable that so many of these talented and highly trained people should feel stuck, underutilized, and powerless. Too many of our assumptions and practices used in organizations today were designed to manage semi-skilled manual laborers. We challenge the reader to rethink how an organization should be managed whose products are new knowledge and creative thought.

In the Appendix, we have included a questionnaire about career-stage activities. It is designed to provide information to assist the reader in determining his or her own career-stage level.

One final word. The number of minorities and women in the organizations we studied was small, particularly in Stages III and IV. But, as we shall point out in the chapters that follow, the networks that we describe are part of the reason for these small numbers. As the work force in our society continues to change, however, much more will be learned about the similarities and differences of the career strategies of a diverse work force. Our model of careers is not normative, but descriptive; not how things should happen in organizations, but how they do happen. Those who want to change things must start with a solid understanding of what is described herein.

Stage 1

Apprentice

After only eight months on the job, George Landen was looking for a way out. Not that he was incompetent—he had graduated near the top of his MBA class at a leading business school, been heavily recruited, and had finally accepted a position with one of the Big Eight accounting firms. A successful career had seemed the inevitable next step.

But Landen's short career in public accounting had been more painful than successful. When asked what had gone wrong, Landen shrugged his shoulders. "I guess it's the work itself," he sighed. "You can't get into depth on any problem. Deadlines are so tight that all your work ends up being pretty superficial. I guess that's what they want, but it drives me crazy."

Questioned about his performance, Landen's fellow workers told a different story. Said one, "Landen's technical competence is impeccable, but he's too quiet—he keeps to himself. It's almost impossible for him to handle his clients and colleagues effectively. If he could break out of his shell, things might be different. But as it is now, I'm afraid that management wouldn't be the least bit sorry to see him go."

When TechLabs hired Paul Anders, his research supervisor felt that it was one of the best decisions the company had ever made. Not only was Anders extremely bright, but he had recently completed his doctoral work at a highly respected university where his faculty advisor was acknowledged worldwide as a leader in his field. The recommendation he gave Anders was among the highest he had ever given a student. Impressed by Anders' outstanding academic record, the supervisor felt confident that the young Ph.D. could handle the high pressure environment of TechLabs' research organization.

Within a few months, however, the supervisor's optimism began to wane. The projects to which Anders had been assigned were progressing slowly and inefficiently. Time deadlines and budget constraints were routinely exceeded, making Anders' work a sore spot for the entire division.

Puzzled, the supervisor increased his support of Anders' projects, going out of his way to encourage the young scientist. But Anders' performance continued to decline. As the supervisor's efforts intensified, Anders began to miss work, ostensibly because of illness. Within 3 months, his performance had deteriorated to the point that the supervisor terminated his employment.

The transition from school to the world of work has never been an easy one, but for many young professionals—such as Landen and Anders in the above examples—it can be particularly problematic. Nearly all face difficult and often painful adjustments. "I wish I could understand it," lamented the laboratory director of a large research organization. "We bring in about a dozen of the best young people we can find each year. Two years later, seven or eight are contributing. The rest flounder for a while, then end up leaving the lab."

This research director's situation is by no means unique. Most large companies admit to losing over half of their college recruits within the first 5 years on the job. A high rate of turnover among "first job" professionals has come to be accepted—almost expected—by both new employees and their employers. And turnover is only one symptom of the difficulty of the transition. In our interviews, we talked with hundreds of professionals who were still with the organization that had originally hired them. More often than not, they agreed that the early years of their careers had been awkward and frustrating—regardless of how well they had done in school.

For many professionals, this transition is the beginning of a relatively short but important stage in their careers; most spend a relatively small fraction of their worklife (2 to 5 years) in Stage I. Others, however, remain in Stage I throughout their professional lives. For this reason, our discussion of Stage I will focus on two distinct but interrelated areas: "getting started," the initial novation from school to work; and "developing competence," the effective Stage I apprentice.

GETTING STARTED

Despite the differences between being a student and being an employed professional, the two roles do not seem radically dissimilar. In fact, when asked to describe the typical Stage I employee, professionals in a variety of fields came up with the following list of characteristics:

- Works under and is expected to accept willingly the direction and supervision of a senior professional in the field.

- Seldom works independently but is given assignments that are portions of a larger project or activity.
- Usually does most of the detailed or routine work on a project.
- Is allowed to exercise "directed" creativity and initiative.
- Is expected to perform well under pressure.
- Lacks credibility and status in the organization.

Many of these traits would characterize a student at least as well as they describe a newly hired professional; on the surface, the activities and expectations associated with Stage I certainly do not appear to be overwhelming. Why, then, the difficulty many experience in making the transition? Our interviews highlighted three specific problems.

The first was articulated by a manager in a large national bank:

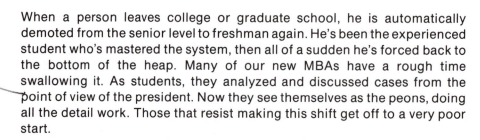

> When a person leaves college or graduate school, he is automatically demoted from the senior level to freshman again. He's been the experienced student who's mastered the system, then all of a sudden he's forced back to the bottom of the heap. Many of our new MBAs have a rough time swallowing it. As students, they analyzed and discussed cases from the point of view of the president. Now they see themselves as the peons, doing all the detail work. Those that resist making this shift get off to a very poor start.

This comment vividly illustrates one of the major adjustments faced by new professionals: the abrupt and near-total loss of hard-earned status. For an ambitious MBA, such a loss can be particularly difficult to reconcile. Yet even for graduates in technical fields, the "first job" experience may require a massive reorientation of their self-concept. As a supervisor in a research and development lab observed:

> People have trouble in Stage I until they realize that everything they learned in school doesn't make them an expert. After all those years at the university, they still have to learn to apply their knowledge. We have a new Ph.D. who's struggling right now. He's "book smart" but needs to develop judgment and maturity.

Closely related to this movement from senior to freshman is the second problem: impatience. Many students look forward to their first job as a kind of emancipation from the slavery of student life. Confined by rigid graduation requirements, tired of the demands of professors, they long for the freedom they believe their profession will provide. It is easy to understand their disillusionment when, as someone's subordinate, they again find themselves in a dependent relationship. Describing his first year, a physicist at a reputable research laboratory indicated:

> My first year here was a real trial. I had an excellent record in graduate school and was anxious to get to work, to make a contribution. For a whole year, no one gave the slightest attention to my suggestions. I was mad as hell—on the verge of leaving—when I finally realized that I didn't yet understand the complexity of the problem we were working on. Now I try to take time with the newcomers, to help them understand the dilemma of that first year.

In the professional world, independence is rarely instantaneous. Impatience can torture the young scientist, engineer, or businessperson who has plans of working on his or her own. It can also make unbearable the quantity of routine work expected of beginning professionals.

The third problem has to do with the very nature of "higher education." By the time they graduate, most future professionals have been through a rigorous academic program, providing them with highly developed and specialized skills. While such technical training is indispensable, it is by itself incomplete. Alluding to this inadequacy, one manager commented:

> In some ways, a college engineering program is poor preparation for an engineering career. In college, students work alone and are graded individually. Any collaboration is usually considered cheating. In an engineering firm, on the other hand, teamwork is essential. Projects are evaluated as team efforts. School hasn't prepared them for that.

Shifting from a competitive to a cooperative environment requires social and interpersonal skills that are often inadvertently ignored, if not deliberately avoided, in the standard preprofessional curricula (1). This problem is certainly nothing new. Elton Mayo made the following incisive observation over 40 years ago:

> We have failed to train students in the study of social situations; we have thought that first-class technical training was sufficient in a modern and mechanical age. As a consequence we are technically competent as no other age in history has been; and we combine this with our utter social incompetence(2).

The inability to work with others does more than hamper teamwork among colleagues; it can also severely limit the effectiveness of client relations, as illustrated by the story of the dissatisfied accountant at the beginning of this chapter. "Being able to develop and maintain a good relationship with clients is almost more important than technical skill," a partner in an accounting firm told us. "Unfortunately," he continued, "accounting students are used to working with numbers instead of people."

This is not to discredit the educational system, but rather to recognize that even the most thorough academic program cannot offer complete, comprehensive preparation for every occupational situation. Such a recognition is invaluable, if only to keep the problems, frustrations, and adjustments of the transition from taking a young professional by surprise. Knowing what to expect, however, is only the first step towards a successful novation into Stage I. Our interviews identified a second step that is perhaps the most crucial: finding a mentor.

MENTORS

In Book II of *The Odyssey,* Homer introduces a character named Mentor, an old friend and advisor of Odysseus, King of Ithaca. Before leaving for the Trojan War, Odysseus entrusts Mentor with the care of his household and the education of his only son, Telemachus. Wise and loyal, Mentor never betrays the King's trust, even though the King, having been gone for over 20 years, is presumed dead by the majority of the Ithacans(3).

From this specific origin in Greek mythology, the word "mentor" evolved into a general term for any wise and trusted counselor. Recently, the word has been more narrowly defined but more widely accepted as a result of Daniel Levinson's work on adult life cycles. Levinson describes the mentor's role as follows:

> A good mentor is an admixture of good father and good friend. . . . [He is] a transitional figure who invites and welcomes a young man into the adult world. He serves as guide, teacher and sponsor. He represents skill, knowledge, virtue, accomplishment—the superior qualities a young man hopes someday to acquire. He gives his blessing to the novice and his Dream (4).

In our interviews at one large research organization, we asked the scientists and engineers whether they had had a mentor early in their careers. Sixty-five percent responded positively—and these sixty-five percent were given significantly higher performance ratings than their mentorless peers. Why? As Levinson indicates, a mentor can help the green professional in a number of ways. We will focus on four that are particularly critical.

TRAINING

As has already been illustrated, a Ph.D., MBA, or B.S. degree does not automatically provide comprehensive preparation for a career. There is a great deal more to learn once the college graduate accepts his or her first job. Although some organizations have formal training programs designed to fill this gap, most new professionals—having recently completed 4 to 8 years of formal training—resist the idea of yet another training period. As a consequence, the informal training provided by a mentor has a number of built-in advantages. Referring to these advantages, a young scientist explained:

> Early on, one of my co-workers took enough of an interest in me to teach me the dos and don'ts of the profession. He was pretty damned exacting—he hated sloppy work, but never rejected it without explaining why it was unacceptable. He told me there was a right way and a wrong way of doing things, then showed me the consequences of each approach. He's also the one who finally taught me how to study; somehow, I'd missed that in college.

In other words, a mentor can provide the type of one-on-one education that is uncommon in a university, benefiting not only the apprentice but the organization as a whole.

KNOWLEDGE OF THE INFORMAL SYSTEM

An essential ingredient in beginning professional activity is an understanding of how to get things done through the informal system. An organization is more like a living organism than a machine: one cannot find out how it works by reading organization charts, policy and procedure manuals, etc. Only another person who understands the "system" can teach the new employee to negotiate its idiosyncracies. This includes details like obtaining supplies, travel reimbursements, and support services, as well as the vital processes of securing resources, endorsement, and funding for new projects. A mentor's knowledge and influence can be especially helpful in this latter activity.

CHALLENGING JOB ASSIGNMENTS

"My job's a bore," complained one MBA who was recently graduated. "All I do is basic financial analysis. Any high school kid with average intelligence and a pocket calculator could handle most of this stuff with no problem."

Like this MBA, many graduates complain that their first job assignments are routine, unstimulating, even stupefying. While this phenomenon is often part of a dues-paying process that we will explore in the next section, it can be mitigated—if not eliminated—by having a good mentor. One young researcher praised his mentor for having sensitively guided his professional progress:

> I owe an awful lot to Val Cutler for the expertise I've developed. He did more than explain things to me and give me hints to improve my work. He actually gave me some of *his own* assignments to work on—important things that he didn't have time for. He would outline my responsibilities, then I'd take off on my own. Gradually, he gave me more and more. He always had time to help but wasn't constantly looking over my shoulder.

Most established professionals have more work than they can handle alone. They are usually willing to share that work with an eager apprentice, provided the apprentice proves capable and responsible. Helping someone get started on fruitful research in a promising area can lead to the beginning of a life's work. Assigning an engineer to work on a project that will utilize the latest technology, for example, will help assure his or her being a valued resource to the firm over the next few years. Offering an assignment to handle a large or difficult loan account brings an opportunity to demonstrate one's ability and a sense of achievement obtainable in almost no other way.

A part of a mentor's job assigning function is, of course, to help assure that apprentices aren't placed in assignments so far over their heads that they are likely to fail completely and injure their reputations. The mentor has to be willing to trust his or her subordinate who must, in turn, be able to trust the mentor's judgment of how much they are ready to handle. A manager who had the reputation for developing strong people was described by one of his peers as having a very good feel for this balance:

> Hank Stoddard runs his unit the way he runs his family. He has a very clear model of what he's doing. It's a bar mitzvah process. "You're going to be a good man. When you're ready, I'll pass the baton to you. You'd better work hard because I'm going to hand the thing to you the minute you're ready and not one minute later. But don't hesitate either, because I won't hand it to you until you're ready." Then one day he says, "Today you're a man!" It's a fascinating thing to watch.

On President Reagan's desk sits a sign that reportedly reads, "You can do a lot of good in this world if you don't care who gets the credit." While such a philosophy is refreshingly selfless, blind adherence to it could be Stage I suicide. In order to receive rewards in the organization—salary increases, stimulating assignments, promotions—new employees must get some of the credit for their work. The decision-makers in the organization need to know that they are making a positive contribution. The odds are small that a recently hired graduate, insulated beneath two or three layers of hierarchy, will be sufficiently visible on his or her own. An influential mentor can be invaluable. Commenting on his mentor's help, a young accountant in a larger manufacturing firm remarked:

> I hadn't been here too long before my boss put me in a position where I could work most of the time on my own. This often involved reporting directly to the controller and the plant manager. My boss did this deliberately to give me exposure. He would brief me before each report to make sure I knew what I was doing, but I always gave the reports on my own. He even had me make a quarterly presentation to the corporate controller.

This accountant had an unusually supportive mentor who not only provided the opportunity for visibility at high levels, but instructed him on how to handle himself in such situations. This kind of opportunity has benefits that extend beyond Stage I—it allows the apprentice to develop contacts vital to his or her long-term career progression. Ordinarily, no one person decides the fate of others in an organization; even the chief executive officer needs the support of certain critical people if he or she is to make an important assignment workable in the long run. This is even more true at lower levels in the organization.

Eugene Jennings makes an interesting distinction among four types of superiors. The first type, he asserts, are evaluators, including all the superiors, lateral and vertical, who are in a position to evaluate someone's performance. In the second category are nominators, those who stand well enough with their peers and superiors to be asked to recommend individuals for promotions and assignments. The third set are sponsors, or nominators who are different in one minor respect: they are respected enough by the authority set that the latter will think twice before the sponsors' recommendations are rejected. Finally, there are promoters, or those who have authority to formally place professionals. While someone may be a promoter in one part of the organization and a nominator at another level, a person in Stage III is more likely to be categorized within the first two types than the last two. Jennings' categories clearly indicate that a Stage III professional can best reward good performance by making it visible to important others (5).

How does he or she go about it? Obviously, one method is to tell other people when good performance is turned in. There is certainly opportunity for this recognition in the review sessions that are held in most professional organizations. But testimonials are far more believable when there are other witnesses, and when the judges have had a chance to see for themselves. Consequently, effective mentors seek opportunities for their people to make presentations themselves. They look for assignments that will give their apprentices high visibility and contact with sponsors (the mentor's sponsors, particularly).

To summarize, then, a mentor can be instrumental in aiding the young professional in the areas of training, gaining mastery of the informal system, receiving challenging job assignments, and being noticed by superiors. Given these advantages, it is initially surprising that such a large number of professionals—over one-third in the above-mentioned organization—fails to find mentors. The reasons for this failure are instructive, however, and deserve further discussion.

First, mentors are scarce in many organizations. In addition, the number of apprentices that one can work with effectively rarely exceeds two or three. In a rapidly expanding organization with a limited number of senior people, this creates a radically lopsided mentor/apprentice ratio. We found one such ratio in a high-tech firm that had mushroomed in its early years. Exploring a new technology, they had no choice but to hire recent graduates—experienced people were all but unavailable. A physicist that started with this organization in its formative years reminisced, "I didn't have anyone remotely resembling a mentor because there just plain weren't enough to go around. The new guys like me had to nose around looking for opportunities, then start working on them."

Second, there are certain groups of employees for whom mentors seem to be disproportionately scarce, regardless of their overall availability in the organization. One organization we studied had 10 women professionals, ranging in age from 23 to 50. All ten were rated by their managers as still in Stage I. Admittedly, this was an extreme case; but for women, the situation was not particularly favorable anywhere. A woman physicist explained:

> Men won't enter into a mentor relationship with a woman. As a result, you miss out. I noticed it when I first started here. Conversations with me were different. Sure, they talk to you, but not like they talk to the guys—not about lab policy, not about the way the system works, or how you get ahead. You know, chitchat instead of physics. They didn't take me seriously—at least,

that's what I felt. Maybe they didn't mean to exclude me, but they somehow never got around to telling me how or where to publish. One of my colleagues, a black, could really relate. They wouldn't tell him the things that were important.

Our information on male minorities is sketchy, but the data on women clearly identify difficulty in finding a mentor as a major roadblock in their career path.

We encountered a third explanation for the failure to find a mentor, which was somewhat surprising. There are evidently some professionals who either do not *need* or do not *want* mentors. Of the former group, we discovered a few examples supporting the assertion that "exceptional people create exceptions." Supervisors at a large research laboratory singled out Jerry Hunt, one of their top physicists, as a "self-made" success. We asked him about his transition into the profession:

> For 6 weeks I was in Stage Zero, just milling around the place. For Stage I, I looked over Don Lefevris' shoulder for a couple of months. Then I worked beside him for another 2 months. That was Stage II. He'd hide out in my office and write these ultra-complex computer programs. I watched him for a while—a lot more closely than he suspected. Then I started to write; then I took over. I learned the rest on my own.

This comment exudes confidence—almost braggadocio—but it is well-deserved confidence, according to superiors. They described Hunt's work as "an enormous contribution, not only to our lab's reputation but to the field in general." Research and development organizations do not have a monopoly on these "exceptions," of course; in any profession there are a handful of individuals whose native intelligence, confidence, and/or savvy reduce their dependence on outside guidance and support. These few seem to succeed not only without the organization's help—but sometimes *in spite of* the organization's hindrance.

More abundant, however, are individuals whose psychological need for independence is so strong that they cannot handle the role of the apprentice. This is a potentially serious handicap. Consider the following case:

> As manager of the chemistry department of a renowned laboratory, Art Maloney could hardly be called a failure. But his career had been plagued by disputes with supervisors. He'd resigned from several important projects after butting heads with the boss. "I had my share of false starts," he admitted, "but a mentor was out of the question. I'll be damned if I was going to let *anybody* tell me what to do." In retrospect, Maloney conceded that he might have been more productive if someone had told him about the factors that were important in building a career—or rather, if he'd listened.

29

Thus, a stubborn insistence on independence can preclude the development of a workable mentor/apprentice relationship.

Our discussion of these "exceptions"—the Jerry Hunts and the Art Maloneys—further highlights the mentor's importance. But we rarely hear young professionals asking, "Why find a mentor?" The overwhelming question is, "How?" Any attempt to answer this question involves an interesting paradox. Our research confirms what common sense would seem to dictate: that the mentor is far more likely to do the selecting than to be selected. In other words, encouraging a new hire to find a mentor is uncomfortably like telling an orphan to locate a set of parents to adopt him: not an impossible task, but one that usually works the other way around—when it works at all.

Such a comparison is more metaphorical than accurate, however; in a majority of cases, new employees have some influence—perhaps more than they realize—in determining the people with whom they will work. Even greater is their influence over the *type* or *quality* of professional relationships that they develop, emphasized in the next section of this chapter.

A logical starting point in the search for a mentor is the formal organization itself. One obvious strategy is to trace the hierarchy up one notch. Supervisors often perform a number of mentor functions. With up to ten people reporting to them, however, most supervisors do not have time to play the role of mentor to all of their subordinates—even if they have the ability to do so. Yet even when time demands are not an issue, interpersonal clashes may be: not everyone hits it off with his or her boss. What are the relevant criteria in seeking a mentor other than the formal supervisor? Using the stages model, a good mentor is a person performing at a competent level in Stage III. Although a later chapter will treat Stage III in depth, a quick look at the mentor's role from the apprentice's point of view will be enlightening.

Ideally, the new employee would select a mentor with the following characteristics:

- Technical competence
- Teaching ability
- Knowledge of the informal system
- Emotional maturity
- Influence with decision-makers

Few people, however, meet all of these specifications. Those who come closest are sure to be extremely busy.

This conflict between competence and availability can be frustratingly circular. In any professional organization, competent senior employees have enormous demands on their time and energy. Not only do many young employees want to work with them, but they are given more than their share of challenging assignments. They can thus use all the help they can get. But here the problem doubles back on itself: while these potential mentors need help, they do not have time to bring many new employees up to a level at which they can contribute significantly. Many young professionals complain about this dilemma. For some, it is a situation they have faced since the early days of their graduate program. Dan Lubben, a nuclear engineer at a large west coast research institution, remarked with some bitterness:

> My Ph.D. advisor was a little too prestigious. When he wasn't attending conferences, he was up to his ears in his own projects—keeping up his precious reputation. Sure, his name looked good on my dissertation, but I had to turn to other graduate students for the bulk of the help on my project.

There are several ways of dealing with the dilemma. One option is to seek out a person who is good but not famous. With solid skills but no burden of reputation to carry, he or she will have plenty (but not too much) to do—hence, overcommitment will not preclude mentorship.

A second, more specific approach is for the new employee to team up with a promising young professional making the novation from Stage II to Stage III—and thus looking for his or her first apprentice. This prospective mentor is presumably skilled, experienced—but not yet overloaded. In addition, the new mentor's incentive to provide good training is built-in: a capable, well-prepared apprentice reflects favorably on the mentor. The symbiotic nature of the resulting relationship is well illustrated by the experience of Max Weenig and Ron Bentley:

> Near the end of the first year of his MBA program, Max Weenig began looking for summer employment. He contacted Ron Bentley, a partner in a small consulting firm, who hired him for the summer. The two worked well together, developing a close friendship. When Weenig graduated, Bentley was the first person he contacted. Bentley, in the meantime, had been hired as the controller of a large manufacturing firm. He was looking for competent people he could trust—Weenig was a natural. After about a year on the job, Weenig was made supervisor of one of the largest departments in the controller's organization. A few years later, Bentley accepted a position as assistant secretary in a department of the federal government. Again, he needed people. He invited Weenig to fill a key staff slot. The two enjoyed a long and productive relationship before their career paths eventually separated.

Weenig was Bentley's first apprentice, and together they moved into excellent opportunities in three different organizations.

A third strategy is to join an existing team as apprentice to the apprentice, becoming what could be called the "third generation" in the relationship. This course of action is not risk free, but its advantages are numerous, as seen in the following case:

> Howard Brown was a senior professor in the research institute of a large university. With his national reputation, he played a crucial role in generating research funds, dealing with sponsors, making presentations at conferences, etc. Mike Nelson, his junior colleague, was a project leader on two or three major studies that Brown had brought to the institute, thus beginning the transition to Stage III. Andrew Kearns, a Ph.D. candidate, was the third generation in the team.
>
> The trio was extremely productive, publishing a number of articles and books in their field. Role differentiation presented no problem. Brown had contacts and could drum up resources, but he was too busy for mentoring. Nelson, the middleman, was in charge of locating research sites, designing questionnaires, and coaching Kearns on a day-to-day basis. Kearns did most of the detail work in data collection and analysis. Their working relationship lasted, in one capacity or another, for over 15 years.

We have deliberately avoided presenting these strategies as foolproof. Regarding the second case, for instance, it is unfortunately true that there are not enough high-potential professionals to go around. And in the third example, it may well be that "two's company, three's a crowd": personality conflicts are more likely to surface in a threesome, as are rivalries between the two junior members. To consider these strategies "solutions," then, is to miss the mark; rather, they are intended as a survey (by no means exhaustive) of alternatives open to young professionals in their search for mentors.

But what if the search is futile? What if none of the alternatives succeeds? In emphasizing the importance of mentors, we may have inadvertently fostered the impression that a person who does not want or cannot find a mentor is doomed to a maladjusted working life. This is simply not true. There are at least two major sources of Stage I support available to all professionals: peers and nonprofessionals.

PEER SUPPORT

Careers are too often viewed in terms of a race or game in which individuals compete against everyone else in the organization. This view is particularly prevalent among those roughly the same age or those that started with the organization at about the same time. Perhaps an outgrowth of a competitive educational system and a sports-oriented society, the attitude can nonetheless be personally damaging, as well as organizationally dysfunctional. A chemical engineer commented:

> As a student, you can learn a lot from your peers. They're working on the same problems you are, so you are really in a position to help each other. The same holds true on the job. It's kind of a mutual reinforcement. You all have areas of overlap, but you also have different strengths. Besides, it's more convenient to discuss ideas and problems with your peers than it is to find your supervisor.

Although most professionals enter the working world with certain standard skills, their respective strengths and weaknesses vary widely. Collectively, they form a broad pool of resources. And as the chemical engineer indicates above, drawing on these resources is generally more "convenient" than consulting with the supervisor. Convenience, however, is not the sole motivation for going to peers rather than the supervisor for help. Supervisors are required to evaluate the performance of their subordinates. A subordinate that repeatedly brings his or her problems to the supervisor runs the risk of becoming a nuisance or, worse, appearing incompetent. Such a reputation would obviously have a strong negative correlation with salary increases, job assignments, promotions, and other rewards. Thus, it is at times genuinely advantageous for new employees to take at least some of their questions to peers.

Another benefit of solid peer contacts is the network of associates that they provide. In a previous example, we saw how Dan Lubben turned to his fellow graduate students for help on his dissertation project. One friend in particular turned out to be unexpectedly instrumental. As Lubben explained:

> During the last year of my doctoral program, I started sending out resumes. The year before, an acquaintance of mine, Mike Koski, had graduated and been hired by [one of the top west coast research labs]. I'd been interested in working at the place, but I didn't send them a resume. Instead, I sent a few to Mike and asked him to take them around to people personally, saying something like, "I've worked with this guy and he's good." Well, they flew me out for interviews and hired me as soon as I graduated.

Lubben's supervisors told us how impressed they had been with the way his resume was delivered to them. "It was a creative approach," they said. "It stood out. We knew right away we wanted to interview him."

Earlier in this chapter we identified "knowledge of the informal system" as one of the areas in which mentors can be most helpful to young professionals. In many cases, however, peers with a year or two more experience in the organization can be just as helpful. A business school professor described the importance of this sort of help as he began his career:

> In my first job as a research assistant, I had no idea where to begin. I'd just finished my MBA and my faculty advisor was gone for the summer. Luckily, there was a guy around that was a couple years ahead of me—John Grant— who showed me the ropes. He knew a lot of people at school and how to get things done: things like which secretaries to go to in the typing pool to get a rush job out on time or how to get a travel advance. He told me that no one would bother me if I spent $15 a day for meals, but above that, my expense report would raise some eyebrows. I learned a lot from him in the 3 months we shared an office.

Experiences of this kind are not uncommon among young professionals. It was a peer relationship similar to this one that proved crucial at the outset of Jerry Hunt's highly successful "mentorless" career. These data suggest that productive peer relationships should be almost as high a priority as mentor/apprentice relationships—and for the Stage I professional, the former are far more controllable than the latter.

SUPPORT FROM NONPROFESSIONALS

"Feel free to talk to me whenever you have a question, but if you really need to know what's going on around here, ask Karen, the department secretary." This is regular advice from a department chairman to graduate students at a large university, and it points to a key issue. Support people are often long-service employees with stores of inside information. They may know how the informal system works better than anyone else in the organization—but their information is not free for the asking. Some young professionals take their academic background or degree too seriously; they feel uncomfortable working with less educated people. A computer architect with a Masters Degree in Electrical Engineering described his group's secretary in these terms: "She's an airhead—definitely not too intelligent. She went to the tech [a local technical college]. You know what kind of people go to the tech, don't you?" Such extreme cases may be rare, but the attitude—often couched in humor—can get professionals into trouble. It is not difficult to imagine the secretary withholding valuable information from this engineer.

Information is not the only critical variable, however. Condescending professionals apparently do not realize that support people can have great impact on their productivity. Consider the following situation:

Phil and Stan were part-time instructors hired by the business school of a large university. Phil attempted to maintain what he considered "appropriate social distance" between himself and the support people in the department. He rarely had a conversation with a secretary except to "order" her to type some material and "have it ready by tomorrow at 9 A.M." More often than not, the secretary was "unable" to get the work done on time. Having little patience for such "sloth," Phil took his frustration to the department chairman. But for Phil, the secretary's output remained unchanged the rest of the year.

Stan, on the other hand, took time to get to know the secretaries in the office and frequently spent a few minutes "socializing." His friendship seemed genuine, not patronizing. In one conversation, he discovered that the secretaries liked a certain kind of donut. From then on, whenever he brought them a large typing assignment it was accompanied by a donut for each. His typing was nearly always done on time and with very few errors. Professionals like Phil tend to alienate not only secretaries, but technicians, draftsmen, programmers, and other support personnel. In doing so, they pay a heavy price. Ego preservation at the expense of productive relationships is costly. Nonprofessionals can offer a wealth of services and information to the new employee who treats them as important contributors rather than second-class citizens.

DEVELOPING COMPETENCE

To this point, our emphasis has been primarily on relationships with mentors, peers, and nonprofessionals, all of whom are vital to a smooth transition into the world of work. We now shift our focus to an area of equal importance to the Stage I professional: competent performance.

MANAGEMENT DEFINITIONS OF COMPETENCE

When asked to list the qualities of successful Stage I professionals, one manager we interviewed responded without hesitation, "First, they have to be technically sound and, in general, competent. We take that for granted." The statement is hardly a startling revelation. Indeed, many young professionals seem to take their own technical competence for granted, almost as if it were conferred along with their diploma at graduation. Our research indicates, however, that managers usually define competence much more comprehensively than do recent college graduates. In the manager's eyes, competence encompasses not only specialized university training but a variety of complex and, in some respects, contradictory attributes, which the effective subordinate is expected to possess.

ACCURACY

The first of these attributes is technical accuracy. In the extreme, this is the ability to do flawless detail work—and do it without complaint. As mentioned above, Stage I assignments are typically routine, even dull. One manager commented:

> There's a lot of nonglamour work to be done between the time a project is conceived and its actual implementation. The person in Stage I is most likely to be stuck with it. I like a subordinate who recognizes that someone has to do the detail stuff and doesn't gripe about it.

Despite the dullness, accurate detail work is of crucial importance to the organization. No corporation wants to send correction notices to tens of thousands of stockholders because of an error in its quarterly report; no construction firm wants a lawsuit because a structural engineer miscalculated stress factors in a building design; and no company wants to recall food products because of incorrect ingredient labeling. Failure to double-check facts and figures, whether from carelessness or lack of interest, can result in a reputation that is hard to erase.

> Karl Sondrup graduated with an MBA from a prestigious business school and accepted a job with a noted Washington, D.C., consulting firm. One of his first assignments involved the routine checking of other people's calculations on a project the firm was doing for the Department of Defense. As Sondrup recalled, "A partner in the consulting firm was presenting our findings to a group of high-ranking military officials at the Pentagon. In the middle of the meeting, one of the generals found an error in the figures—a misplaced decimal point, causing the estimates to be off by $90,000,000. When the partner got back from the meeting, I caught hell. 'I don't like looking bad in front of the generals,' he said."

Accuracy, then, is paramount. And yet, most managers deem it unwise for first-job professionals to get bogged down in detail work. Said one:

> We don't want our people to merely take an assignment, go back to their calculators, and start crunching numbers. We need people who will ask intelligent questions about why we're using that particular approach to the problem. We don't want automatons.

BROAD PERSPECTIVE

Implicit in this manager's comment is a warning against the adoption of a restricted, narrow perspective. While effective subordinates concentrate on the quality of their own work, they need to see beyond the immediate numbers, beyond the limited task, to the larger framework of which they are a part. The importance of such a view increases as the Stage I professional begins the transition to Stage II— the topic of the next chapter. There is one aspect of the broad perspective, however, which merits further discussion here.

Most human beings (and many managers) suffer from a mild sort of egocentrism, in the form of a "Do it right: do it my way" philosophy. This philosophy is clearly seen in the following definition of "a good subordinate," given by a manager in a large national bank:

> A good subordinate is one who thinks of the things I would do before I do them. This means that he or she tries to adopt my perspective and look at things from my position in the organization, not just his or her own.

Thus, young professionals that can incorporate the boss's point of view into a "broad perspective" not only see their own tasks differently, but also have a standard against which to evaluate their own ideas and actions.

DISCIPLINE

A third attribute that managers associate with competence is discipline. As illustrated by the example of Paul Anders, cited at the start of this chapter, employees who consistently fail to meet deadlines can create severe problems for supervisors. Equally frustrating, however, are those who constantly begin but never finish projects—even in the absence of time constraints. A division leader in a research laboratory described one of the division's computer scientists in these terms:

> Ray's an exceptional software designer—brilliant, really—but he jumps around too much from one job to another. He never stays on one thing long enough to push it through to the end.

A manager at another firm referred to this phenomenon as "the shotgun approach," adding that, "we prefer high-powered rifles to shotguns."

These "rifles" need to be on target, however. Managers tend to give poor ratings to employees that are highly proficient at completing projects of low importance. As one manager explained:

> Some of our new hires work like the dickens on small, definable tasks—you know, things they can finish in a matter of hours or days. They stay away from major projects until, at the end of the year, the high-priority assignments have either not been completed or they've been done by someone

else. It's like they invest their time where they think they'll find sure and easy success. No wonder their performance appraisals are not exactly glowing.

The manager's comment highlights the conflicting nature of demands faced by Stage I professionals: expected on the one hand to be disciplined and productive, they are at the same time supposed to contribute significantly to important and often difficult projects. This dilemma and the "detail work versus broad perspective" issue already mentioned suggest that the process of developing competence as a Stage I apprentice is anything but cut-and-dried. There was one area, however, in which we found universal agreement among managers: the importance of doing well on first assignments.

FIRST ASSIGNMENTS

As threadbare as is the adage that states, "You never get a second chance to make a good first impression," it is nevertheless valid in the world of the newly hired professional. Those who work hard and do well on their first projects develop credibility that can lead to favorable future assignments, salary increases, and visibility. A manager in an accounting firm remarked:

> I tell people to do the best work they can on their first job, and after that, their reputation will be a big help to their career. Early success is a hell of a lot better than success later on. If they do a lousy job on their first assignment, it'll be tough to get them another opportunity. Managers want only the best people to work on their projects.

This is not to say that careers are inevitably ruined by a single mistake, nor that early success guarantees long-term achievement. History is replete with stories of both phenomenal recovery and colossal underachievement. Our point here is that if a young professional wants to be seen as a "winner" by management, high performance on the first assignment is invaluable. In the words of a successful accountant:

> I learned a couple of key lessons on my first assignment. The first was to put in all the effort that you can, taking a real interest in what you're doing, going the extra mile. The second was to do it right. My supervisor said, "If you make a mistake on your first draft, that's no problem. But if you make a mistake on the final draft, then you've got troubles."

INITIATIVE

Although the above comment reemphasizes the importance of accuracy, it also points to another issue of vital importance to the would-be "effective" apprentice. In outlining the traits of the Stage I employee, managers in various professions mentioned the exercise of "directed" creativity and initiative. This ability to do more than required, to be resourceful and innovative, is directly related to first-job success. One manager wearily described the minimal effort of some subordinates:

> I have people coming back to me all the time saying they couldn't do what I'd asked because of such-and-such or so-and-so. They may call a guy, and he's sick or on vacation or something else. But they never seem to ask themselves "Is there any other way to get the needed information?" They just go through the motions and then report back, thinking that I'll accept their good intentions as a substitute for what I need.

Determining when to take initiative—and how much to take—can be a touchy business, however. According to one author, there are five levels of initiative that an individual can exercise in relation to the boss:

1. Wait until told what to do.
2. Ask what to do.
3. Recommend what to do.
4. Act, but report action immediately.
5. Act independently, reporting the action routinely (6).

On some matters, the boss may want the subordinate to operate on level five, whereas on other matters level two would be preferred. Rather than play a guessing game, the most successful young professionals we interviewed had clarified their supervisor's expectations. Either by open discussion with their supervisor or by careful observation, they had learned what was expected of them.

ASKING FOR HELP

Like taking initiative, asking for help can be a sensitive issue for both managers and subordinates. Some bosses want to be deeply involved in a project. They use requests for help as opportunities to train inexperienced newcomers to the organization. Other bosses are concerned only with the final product and do not want to be bothered by frequent questions. As one bank manager put it:

Some subordinates will take an assignment, work as hard on it as possible, then come back to you when they get stuck or when it's completed. Others start coming back to you from day one, pestering you, trying to get you to do their work for them. People in the second group don't do very well in our bank.

Here again, the Stage I professional is responsible for judging when to petition assistance and when not to. The goal is not to totally avoid asking for help, but rather to discern between problems requiring the boss's attention and those that may be handled alone or with the aid of peers. Indispensable to this type of discernment is an analysis of the risks involved. A promising young accountant outlined his strategy for seeking advice from his supervisor:

My boss had high expectations for me when he hired me. In trying to live up to them, I adopted a policy of taking risks—not gambles, but calculated risks. If it was a high-risk decision, I always consulted the boss, avoiding full personal responsibility for the outcome. But if the job was not overly risky or not of central importance, I'd go it alone, not wasting my boss's time with the details. I assumed it was important to look out for my boss's welfare, not just my own. If I could make him look good or make his job easier, less time-consuming, then it would benefit me as well. I didn't try to cover my errors, though—when I made a bad decision, my boss was the first to know.

This strategy worked well for the accountant. His mentor rewarded him by spending extra time with him, giving him valuable training, and providing him with opportunities to make presentations to higher-level managers in the firm. The result was a genuinely reciprocal relationship, both individuals benefiting from their association with the other. Indeed, since most effective superior/subordinate relationships are characterized by this sense of mutual benefit, the concept of reciprocity merits further discussion and illustration.

RECIPROCITY

In this section, we have explored a number of attributes of competence, as defined by managers whose emphasis is understandably on performance. Accuracy, initiative, and discipline are directly performance-related. Reciprocity, however, requires the cultivation of two qualities that are more relationship-based: communication and trust.

COMMUNICATION

The information flowing between superior and subordinate is the lifeblood of reciprocal relationships. Unfortunately, many young professionals tend to the extremes: either flooding their supervisors with information or reducing the flow to a mere trickle. Both approaches are equally damaging. In criticizing the first approach, for example, managers point out that they have neither the time nor the desire to know all that the subordinate knows about a particular situation. If they did, the subordinate would be expendable. Effective subordinates learn to keep the boss informed on *appropriate* matters only. One rule of thumb suggested by managers is to supply information about the progress being made on particular projects, withholding details of the step-by-step activities behind that progress.

More thorny is the issue of filtering out negative information. Eager to impress, or perhaps naively assuming management omniscience, new professionals often fail to call attention to problems, mistakes, or misjudgments. Some individuals may feel that they do not have all the relevant facts in the situation, and thus say nothing. Whatever the reason for it, restricting the passage of "bad news" almost invariably does more harm than good. Managers need negative as well as positive information.

On the other side of the coin, many young professionals feel neglected or ignored by their supervisors. They often interpret a lack of communication or infrequent contact as evidence that the manager considers their performance sub-par. In reality, the boss may simply be swamped with responsibilities and commitments of his or her own. For this reason, differing expectations about frequency of contact and the amount of time spent together can be a major sore spot in a superior/subordinate relationship. In the experience of successful Stage I professionals, we noticed a variety of techniques used in deciding how often and how long to meet, including:

- Getting together whenever something came up. (These contacts could be initiated by the superior or the subordinate.)
- Setting up another appointment at the end of each session together.
- Establishing regular meetings (e.g., Wednesday at 9 A.M.).

Any of these plans can be effective, as long as it represents a joint agreement between supervisor and apprentice.

TRUST

If information is the lifeblood of reciprocity, mutual trust is its foundation. Difficult to define in the abstract, trust can perhaps be more usefully discussed by focusing on specific conditions favorable to its development. E. E. Jennings identified four of these conditions: accessibility, availability, predictability, and loyalty (4). We will use these terms not as strict definitions of the "prerequisites" to trust, but as approximate labels for categories of trust-generating phenomena observed in the organizations we studied.

The first condition is *accessibility,* meaning open-mindedness and free exchange of ideas. In a reciprocal relationship, both parties must demonstrate that they value each other's ideas. Subordinates that show little respect for the boss's ideas will receive little trust in return, and even less support for their own ideas. This does *not* mean that the two people always have to agree with one another. In Jennings' words, "The minimum requirement of trust in this sense is that the subordinate respects new and different ideas enough to think them through carefully and energetically." (7)

Although Jennings singles out the subordinate, acceptance of and respect for ideas must work in both directions. While at a large computer electronics firm, we interviewed a capable young MBA who had had an extremely inaccessible manager. As the MBA related the story:

> The guy [his manager] was a real prima donna. He couldn't stand anyone else's ideas, no matter how obviously superior they were to his own. My guess is that he felt threatened. Anyway, after a few blow-ups, I was finally transferred out of his division to a new position where the boss let me try doing some things my own way. I reduced his workload by about 50%, and he returned the favor by letting me write my own assignments, even my own raises.

A second variable in the development of reciprocity is *availability,* characterized by both parties being available physically, mentally, and emotionally when the other is under pressure. Since managers generally bear most of the pressures, subordinates are typically expected to supply the lion's share of the support—a fact that at first seems to violate the balance implied by reciprocity. In a truly reciprocal relationship, however, this apparent lopsidedness is compensated in other ways. Consider the following case:

> A professor in a research-oriented university was under pressure to complete several projects with tight deadlines. As a result, one of the graduate students began to protest, claiming that the professor was not spending sufficient time with him on his research. Another student took a different approach. In a meeting with the professor, he said: "With all the irons you've got in the fire, I know you're under a lot of pressure right now. This article we're working on isn't really pressing—it can wait. If I could be of help on any of your projects, I've got some extra time and would be willing to pitch in and contribute any way I can."

The second student was invited to work on two projects, thereby gaining valuable training and experience. In addition, he received exceptionally favorable letters of recommendation upon graduating. Thus, by being available, he helped not only his boss but himself as well.

Predictability is the third condition in Jennings' terminology. Managers do not like surprises that embarrass them or make them look bad. An accounting manager underscored the importance of this factor:

> I was recently supervising some tax work with one of our clients. I assigned a fairly routine but important part of the project to a new member of the team. He kept saying, "I can do it." Each time I checked, he'd say "I'll get it done— don't worry." Well, when I went out to the job on Friday night, his part of the project was not done. We had to make a major adjustment that night in order to meet a filing deadline. The client had gone to Las Vegas for the weekend and was pretty damned upset when we called him. You can bet I don't take that accountant's word anymore on important matters.

Predictability goes beyond mere dependability, however, to include a sort of faith in the subordinate's good judgment and taste. Managers need to know that those under them will handle delicate administrative circumstances with tact and thoroughness. If young professionals demonstrate early in Stage I that they can preserve customer relationships—even on sensitive projects—they will free the manager to pursue other duties and responsibilities. If on the other hand subordinates jeopardize relationships with customers, they will be less trusted in the future and therefore of less value to the boss.

Jennings labels the fourth condition loyalty. Managers are not likely to trust a subordinate with important information unless they feel certain that the information will not be used to further the subordinate's career at their expense. But loyalty must also be considered in a broader context. There are times when loyalty to an immediate superior involves disloyalty to the organization or to society. Such situations are fraught with inner conflict and, at times, compromise. One highly effective subordinate outlined his strategy for dealing with questions of divided loyalty:

> I'm not a "yes" man. I know the importance of speaking up and saying what's on my mind. But I'm also aware that other people in the organization may have a better perspective than I do. So I follow this formula: I argue forcefully *one time* for my position. Then, if my boss does not accept my recommendation, I try to make his decision an effective one through my support and commitment. That is, of course, unless I feel a conflict with my personal values.

43

The final qualification in the above statement is an important one. Notwithstanding the emphasis we have placed on becoming an effective subordinate, there are some things that are far more important than being loyal to (and hence trusted by) a manager of dubious values. Young professionals are in the long run better off if they understand their own values and adhere to them—even if it means running into conflict with the boss or losing a job. In the context of the first career stage, this issue has far-reaching implications. First, in the presence of serious questions about a senior colleague's integrity or ethics, mentor/apprentice relationships should be approached with caution. Second, with the advent of irreconcilable differences of values in existing superior/subordinate relationships, the young professional should not hesitate to look for another assignment or position. Loyalty requires commitment and cannot be given lightly.

In summary, then, the development of competence as a Stage I apprentice involves a variety of skills and abilities, many of which may not be immediately obvious to the young professional. Best-seller lists have historically been dominated by books suggesting that the way to "get ahead" in organizations is to wear the right clothes, join the right country club, use the right language (both body and verbal), or graduate from the right school. These factors may help some individuals in some organizations, but our research has indicated that managers are much more impressed by such qualities as accuracy, initiative, discipline, and breadth of perspective.

In addition, we have shown the importance of reciprocity in establishing productive mentor/apprentice relationships. Dependent on appropriate communication and mutual trust, relationships of this sort approach a level of collegiality more typical of Stage II than of Stage I. Thus, the fully competent apprentice is, in theory, prepared to make the novation into the next career stage—a move to which we now turn our attention.

Stage II

2

Independent Contributor

One day you are an apprentice, and everyone's pet; the next, you are coldly expected to deliver. There is never sufficient warning that the second day is coming.

MIGNON MCLAUGHLIN, *The Neurotic's Notebook* (1)

When most people think of a "professional," they picture a person in Stage II—an accountant doing an audit, an engineer designing a piece of equipment, a banker making a loan. Statistics indicate that this is not a misconception. In each of the organizations we studied, 40 to 50 percent of the professional employees were categorized by their managers as being in Stage II. More significant than the sheer number of Stage II professionals, however, is the critical nature of their tasks. Chemical companies need top-notch chemists in their labs in order to develop new products. Banks require competent loan officers to avoid serious financial difficulty. CPA firms count on reliable auditors to keep clients and stockholders satisfied. All of these are typically Stage II roles.

For this reason, most professionals look forward to the independence and challenge of their own projects, clients, or areas of responsibility. As Stage II professionals, they feel that they will be able to begin making meaningful contributions to the organization. A smooth transition into Stage II, however, is far from automatic. And once the transition is made, poor performance in this stage can mean below-average salaries, boring job assignments, and, eventually, frustration and bitterness. In this chapter, then, we will describe in detail the activities of Stage II, focusing on both the problems people encounter in becoming first-rate professionals and the decisions they must make at this point in their careers.

TRANSITION INTO STAGE II

PORTRAIT OF STAGE II PROFESSIONAL

After analyzing hundreds of interviews, we identified four central characteristics of Stage II professionals. First, they *assume responsibility for a definable portion of the project, process, or clients.* While most Stage I professionals do much of the detail work, the move into Stage II requires that they assume primary responsibility for specific clients or a discrete part of the project. A management accountant described this transition in his career:

> As a junior I was assigned to limited parts of each project. I decided early on that I didn't want to do that my whole career, so I started putting in a little extra effort. I not only did my best on the part assigned to me, I did all I could to learn about the entire project. Once management saw that I could talk intelligently about the total project, I was advanced to a senior position and given responsibility for the whole thing.

Second, they *work with relative independence.* This does not mean that Stage II professionals are instantly allowed to work on their own. The essence of organization is the coordination of an individual's activities with the activities of others. But in Stage II, employees are no longer closely supervised. A young financial analyst had this to say about his transition into Stage II:

> After about a year-and-a-half with the company, I pretty well knew the ropes, so they put me in charge of monitoring the procurement accounts. Before this time, whenever someone from another department came in with a question, I had to check with my supervisor before making a decision. Now that I'm in charge of the accounts, I deal with their questions—and make most of the decisions myself.

Closely related to this reduced supervision is the third characteristic: people in Stage II *manage more of their own time.* Time clocks disappear and supervisors quit checking on individual subordinates every week, let alone every day or every hour. This is both a reward and a problem. A manager in a large bank remarked:

> A critical quality for our loan officers is versatility. They need to be able to keep ten balls in the air at one time. It requires setting priorities. So many of our young officers get working on one project and forget everything else. Then they get a phone call from an important customer, and they can't deal

with it because they are immersed in something else. The big challenge is to manage a host of different things at once.

Beyond Stage I, few professionals have the luxury of being able to devote all of their attention to one specific activity over an extended period of time. Most are involved in several different projects simultaneously. The challenges of time management can pose a threat to continued professional development.

Finally, Stage II professionals *develop credibility and a reputation for competent work*. Independence and increased responsibility are usually granted as they become accepted as reputable professionals. Recognition of their competence often spreads beyond their own department to other parts of the organization—in some cases, even to clients and others outside the organization. A marketing specialist described this sort of growth in his reputation:

> About a year ago, I noticed that I was beginning to develop some real credibility with the people in new product development and sales. The ones that used to challenge my figures—asking me if I really knew what the hell I was talking about—started asking for my advice instead.

Given these characteristics, it is not immediately apparent why professionals would have difficulty moving into Stage II—and at first glance, the statistics indeed seem to indicate that the transition into Stage II is not a particularly formidable obstacle. We asked managers in six organizations to categorize their subordinates in terms of the four career stages, with the following results:

Percentage of Total Professionals in Each Stage	
Stage I	13.4
Stage II	46.2
Stage III	29.3
Stage IV	11.1
Total	100.0%

As expected, Stage II contained the largest percentage of employees. When we analyzed these data by age, however, we had our biggest surprise: Stage I professionals ranged in age from 21 to 60, *with a mean age of 38.* We were told that some of those currently in Stage I had been in Stage II—some even in Stage III—but had moved (or been moved) back into Stage I. Others, of course, had never made the transition into Stage II. What went wrong? Our analysis pointed to a number of factors that merit individual consideration.

BLOCKS TO MOVING INTO STAGE II

ADJUSTING TO INDEPENDENCE

As indicated above, Stage II performance is characterized by the exercise of increased independence. By age 25, most have had a great deal of training in being dependent but precious little preparation for real independence. From the first grade through graduate school, the student's task is to find out what the teacher wants, then do it. On the first job, the game is practically unchanged. A successful transition into Stage II requires that individuals transcend the dependence acquired in school and first-job settings.

This is no easy process. Independence includes responsibility for developing original ideas, for setting individual standards of performance, and for relying on personal judgment in decision-making. One young physicist's experience in making this shift is instructive:

> Since my early days at the laboratory, I'd always worked with Chuck Robinson on research projects. It took 3 years before I had the confidence to submit a proposal on my own. But, even with my own project, I never made a decision or wrote a final draft without consulting Robinson. When he took a 6-month assignment in Kwajalein, I was paralyzed. I couldn't do a thing for about 4 months. Eventually, I figured out that I could get the opinions of other people in the department and make a decision using their inputs. It was a major discovery for me to realize that I didn't need a boss to approve my decisions.

This physicist's "discovery" illustrates an important point: Stage I personnel are often capable of operating independently, but fail to do so only because they have never *had* to. Such failures are at times linked to the influence of a mentor. As emphasized in the previous chapter, the development of a productive mentor/apprentice relationship is the key to a smooth transition *into* Stage I. Interestingly, a successful transition *out of* Stage I often hinges on the effective abandonment or redefinition of these same relationships.

A mentor benefits greatly from having a competent, experienced apprentice. Apprentices typically do the majority of the less desirable work. In addition, they represent the investment of significant amounts of the mentor's time and energy. If the mentor and apprentice have worked well together, they have no doubt been fairly productive. Considering these factors, it is understandable that mentors are often reluctant to lose such valuable helpers. This reluctance, however, can inhibit the subordinate's career development. One mechanical engineer stayed with the same supervisor for 8 years, eventually ending the relationship on a sour note:

> My first project engineer taught me all about basic engineering, the importance of considering cost factors, and how to do design work. I don't want to sound ungrateful—he really helped me get a good start. But it got to be a little overbearing. I mean, I was to the point where I didn't need all that hand-holding. I felt like he was stifling my growth, not giving me the freedom to do it myself, but he wouldn't change. It really started to get on my nerves, but I couldn't see any way out of it without leaving the company. My division leader heard that I was looking for a job in other companies and called me in to talk about it. When he found out what the real issue was, he transferred me, and the problem was solved.

This engineer's sense of being trapped or stifled is typical of the strong emotions that can surface in the process of leaving a mentor. These feelings are often complex mixtures of gratitude and resentment and are, thus, difficult for the individuals to discuss openly. This can place undue strain on the existing relationship. Clearly, there comes a time when it is in the interest of both parties to establish new ties and to be exposed to different people and ideas. A chemist described his transition away from his mentor as an uncomfortable, but necessary, process:

> I worked with Gerald Farmer for 5 or 6 years. He was a superb teacher, and I learned a lot from him—but he had this habit of never completing projects. So after a while, our work together bogged down. I was anxious to publish some of our results, so I wrote the first draft of a paper and gave it to him to polish up. I never saw it again. He evidently got interested in something else and forgot all about it. So then I wrote an internal paper, reporting some of the work, and put only my name on it. Our division leader called me in and asked, "Don't you want to put Farmer's name on it too?" I said, "No, he hasn't done a damned thing on this for 2 years." The division leader supported my decision. That one act signalled that Farmer and I had finally gone our separate ways.

Despite the adversarial overtones of the last two examples, we are *not* advocating a sort of "stick it to your mentor" strategy of career advancement. On the contrary, the avoidance of hard feelings is advisable whenever possible. An influential and supportive mentor can be of tremendous aid to the young professional's career. Our point is simply that the process of adjusting to the increased independence of Stage II can be problematic and painful.

LACK OF TECHNICAL SKILLS

The possession of specific skills is a must for Stage II professionals. Although some advance to this point in their careers with technical inadequacies, our research suggests that professionals unable to overcome this handicap are unlikely to do well in Stage II. A manager in an international bank described the unfortunate experience of Ted Barker, a young "fast track" bank officer:

> Ted Barker was 27 years old when he was hired. He had an MBA from a prestigious business school. He was bright and articulate and moved very fast. In three years, he was promoted to vice president and placed in charge of consumer banking in Brazil—a very important assignment. Two years later he had been fired. He'd moved so fast that he knew almost nothing about the technical work of the bank. He didn't know what was going on in his organization. He didn't even know what questions to ask. His department seemed to be having a few problems, and when senior management began to dig into it, they found *serious* problems. The mutual fund had fraud troubles, and the credit card system was losing bundles of money. It wasn't that Barker was dishonest—he just didn't know how to check on his subordinates to protect the bank's interest. There was a series of problems that he didn't know about and hadn't brought under control, so they fired him.

LACK OF CONFIDENCE

A majority of the respondents to our inquiry used the word "confidence" when they described people in Stage II. While it may be easier to have confidence if one is competent technically, competence is neither a necessary nor a sufficient condition for the development of confidence. We heard numerous stories of young accountants, bankers, and engineers who had a great deal of self-confidence but lacked the technical skills to back it up and, as a result, made mistakes that were costly to their organizations. Likewise, we heard of professionals who had developed the skills but lacked the confidence necessary to move into Stage II. Bryan Adams was typical of the latter:

> After graduating with an MBA, Adams landed a job as an internal consultant in a large electronics firm. Although he had done well in graduate school, he got off to a somewhat rocky start on the job. He was only 23 years old, and he looked even younger. Not surprisingly, he was sensitive about his age, which led to a lack of confidence. People would ask him how old he was and how his age affected his ability to work with older managers. He, of course, assumed that they were thinking, "You're too young for the job you're

doing—particularly too young to consult with older managers." It took more than 2 years for Adams to gain confidence in his ability to do the job. He finally realized that he was as competent as anyone in his department—a realization that led to excellent performance, promotion opportunities, and significant salary increases.

Adams was competent the moment he was hired, but until he gained confidence in his own skills, he was not able to perform satisfactorily nor move into Stage II.

LACK OF INITIATIVE

As pointed out in the previous chapter, the selective exercise of initiative is expected of high-performing Stage I apprentices. In Stage II, a person is expected to display much greater initiative in fulfilling assigned projects. Some are not prepared to accommodate such expectations and, as a result, perform poorly in Stage II:

> Don Hadley was a 30-year-old loan officer in a large New York bank. Having been with the bank for 3 years, he was responsible for 16 accounts. Yet in spite of Hadley's training and experience, his supervisor was not at all pleased with his work. "Hadley hasn't taken over his accounts," he explained. "He doesn't manage them—he *reacts* to them. He has no plans or goals of any sort. When I point this out to him he will say, 'I didn't know I was supposed to,' or 'I don't know what you want.' He'll go through the whole damned department—from trainees to vice presidents—to get help on a problem that he's perfectly capable of solving himself. That would be acceptable, within reason, if he made any real effort to understand the problem on his own, but he doesn't." The next year, Hadley was assigned to a new supervisor to see if additional training would help. It was evidently not enough: he was terminated at the end of his fourth year at the bank.

Although the supervisor seemed willing to tolerate Hadley's apparent lack of confidence, his failure to take initiative on his accounts was the most disturbing aspect of his behavior. Hadley's shortcoming in this area is typical of many professionals who seem unable to move into Stage II or who are not doing well in that stage.

LACK OF FOCUS

We encountered some people who appeared to be competent, confident, and willing to take initiative, but they were also having great difficulty adjusting to Stage II. Their problem was one of too much initiative: their interests extended in too many directions, and they were unable to focus their attention on any one project long enough to complete it. The personnel manager in a research laboratory made this comment about a bright but "naive" physicist:

> Gary Fowler has a good knowledge of physics, and he's one of the most creative people that I know. His problem is that his interests are too wide— he gets involved in too many projects. Everyone likes Fowler, and they ask him for his ideas. So he spends 2 or 3 days working with each of them, but he doesn't get any credit for that work. In the meantime, he neglects the project he's been assigned to. It's not hard to see why his work is judged as being mediocre. Fowler's just too naive about what the system will reward. He dabbles in every project under the sun, and his peers thank him for his help, so he thinks everything's hunky-dory. No wonder it hit him so hard when his manager told him his performance was bordering on unsatisfactory. Management can't see specifically what he's contributed, so right now he's in danger of getting the axe.

Fowler found that a lack of focus could be a serious problem when he learned that he was in danger of losing his job. Yet a broad range of professional interests is one of the important characteristics of those who move into Stage III. Hence the question: why was Fowler given such a low rating for enthusiastically pursuing his wide professional interests? The answer can be captured in one word: timing. Once Fowler and others at his level have established themselves as first-rate professionals capable of high-quality Stage II performance, then the pursuit of varied interests becomes appropriate, even encouraged. When that exploration comes too soon, it is perceived by management as a lack of focus.

To this point, we have identified the salient characteristics of Stage II professionals. In addition, we have discussed a few of the obstacles to successful entry and performance in Stage II. In each of these five areas, perception is a vital issue. Not only must professionals in Stage II *be* competent, confident, independent, etc., they must be *perceived* as such by their peers and superiors. In other words, the establishment of a professional identity and image is vitally important during Stage II.

Establishing a Professional Identity

Regardless of the industry they were in, nearly all of the professionals we talked to had wrestled with their original career choice. The process of deciding what to study—whether law, accounting, business, or engineering—is a difficult one for most individuals. Once past this decision, however, students are temporarily insulated from major career decisions; the required academic curriculum, in effect, programs their lives for the next few years.

A similar phenomenon occurs at the time young professionals take their first job. Throughout these apprenticeship years, of course, they face the decision of whether to stay with the organization or find a job in another. But the range and content of their professional activities are to a large extent determined for them.

Often, it is not until professionals reach the relative independence of Stage II that they again face pivotal career decisions—decisions that will shape their professional identity. These choices differ, of course, by profession. But for the sake of illustration, let's consider some of the alternatives open to a young accountant within his or her first 10 years of employment at a large CPA firm:

1. Stay with the CPA firm or go to work for one of the clients in the controller's organization.
2. Stay with the large CPA firm or go with a small local firm—or work alone.
3. Remain in auditing, or go into tax accounting or management advisory services.
4. Remain a generalist or specialize (if the latter, select a specialty).
5. Continue as primarily an accountant or prepare to move into general management.

Bankers, engineers, scientists, and other professionals face comparable sets of alternatives, and statistics indicate that many of them do, in fact, change employers during these years. Less than 50 percent of the accountants in CPA firms, for example, stay with their first employer more than 4 years (2). Studies of turnover among MBA graduates yield similar results (3).

Somewhat surprising, however, is the number of young professionals that change occupations altogether. One study on occupational mobility showed that over a 5-year period, nearly one-third (32.2 percent) of the workforce actually switched to a different occupation (4). Admittedly, those most likely to change occupations were hourly laborers, assembly-line workers, and other such non-professionals. But the percentage for whitecollar workers was not particularly low: within most professions, the rate of occupation-hopping was between 20 and 30 percent.

Furthermore, when these data were analyzed by age, it was found that most of the occupation-switching professionals fell in the 20- to 30-year-old range (5). Many of these people no doubt moved into areas related to their background and training. Even so, the fact that a significant number changed fields suggests that their identification with a specific profession was not yet set in concrete. If dissatisfied with their early choices, they were apparently willing to change.

Thus, the person in Stage II is at a critical decision point in his or her career. Although we cannot map in detail the myriad alternatives and choices associated with this career stage, we will focus on two broad areas of particular relevance to the establishment of a professional identity:

1. The individual's level of involvement.
2. The internal perspective versus the external perspective.

LEVEL OF INVOLVEMENT

Most professional jobs require long hours. In public accounting, for example, not only are the days long—often 12 to 14 hours—but it is not uncommon to work 7 days a week during the busy season. Some accountants suggest that in order to become a partner, one has to be "married to the firm." While public accountants are unquestionably engaged in a demanding profession, we heard bankers, engineers, and scientists all discuss the prominent role of overtime in their work. Some defined a "low performer" as one who left work at 5:30 P.M.

Rather than "marry the firm," some professionals change jobs (i.e., the accountant who leaves public accounting to work in the controller's division of an industrial firm). Others simply work shorter hours, resigning themselves to lower salaries and less challenging work assignments. Those whose *professional* identity is a vital part of their *total* identity, however, may find it hard to accept that low level of involvement translates into low performance. Indeed, this issue often influences an individual's career choice:

> During the last semester of his MBA program, Ivan Stewart was trying to decide whether to apply to Ph.D. programs or take a job offer. "I'd love to go on for my doctorate," he mused. "I think I'd really enjoy being a professor in a business school. But it has its downside, too. First off, if I were on the faculty somewhere, I'd want to be an outstanding teacher. In addition, I'm a real competitor—I'd want to publish, to get tenure. On top of that, I'd want to do some consulting, to apply my ideas in 'real world' settings. So where does that leave my family? My hobbies?
>
> My brother, on the other hand, has a 9 A.M. to 5 P.M., peon-level government job. The pay's not too hot, but it's secure. And he's got a 5-acre farm a few miles outside of town. He spends all kinds of time with his family. As near as I can tell, he's happy. Sometimes that really seems like the way to go."

Most professionals can empathize with Stewart and his dilemma. Much of what they do is interesting and challenging—hence the decision to enter a professional field. Hard work and long hours, however, are the norm among top-rated professionals. Alice Broadbent, a chemist with a large research and development firm, is one such professional:

> I've published quite a few articles, and several books, but it takes a lot of extra effort. I had to do that work in my spare time—lunch hours, weekends, even vacations. I have a laboratory at home, and my last two papers I had to work on there. It has its payoffs, of course. I've built a solid reputation in my field, and that becomes very important at salary review time.

Keenly interested in her field, Alice Broadbent has garnered national recognition and salary increases for her "extra effort"—effort that many others are unwilling to duplicate. Herb Sanchez, for example, an electrical engineer at the laboratory in which Alice works, has adopted a different strategy. We asked him how he keeps up with changes in his field:

> I'd have the energy to stay on top of electronics if I chose to invest it that way, but I've chosen not to. I want to have time to spend with my wife and kids. I want time to race motorcycles and cars. I'm not sure I could even keep up if I tried, but I haven't put a hell of a lot of energy into trying.

We asked Sanchez about continuing education as a means of keeping up. His reply:

> It isn't valuable to me, so I haven't used it. The agreement I have with [the research and development firm] doesn't include taking courses. It isn't a recognized part of my job or anyone else's here.

In many ways, Sanchez' career strategy is diametrically opposed to Alice Broadbent's. He clearly places greater value on activities outside of work. While this sort of philosophy may have its costs in terms of national reputation or salary increases, it would be ridiculous to assert that Sanchez is any less happy or less fulfilled than Alice Broadbent. The two have merely made different choices concerning the depth of their professional involvement—a reflection of differing levels of identification with their professions.

INTERNAL PERSPECTIVE VERSUS EXTERNAL PERSPECTIVE

Much of the career development literature focuses on the issue of specialization. In one sense, every professional must specialize to a degree. Each of the professions we studied is so broad and rapidly changing that no one individual can master all of its aspects. Young professionals moving out on their own in Stage II may therefore choose to pursue one facet of their area of expertise in depth, becoming specialists. Or, conversely, they may consider it wiser to apply the skills they have acquired to a variety of different problems, becoming generalists. Their choice on this issue is probably influenced more by the profession and the type of company they work for than by any other factor. Among research scientists, for example, developing a specialty for a period was described as almost always a successful strategy. Bankers, on the other hand, advised against specializing. Opinions of accountants and engineers were almost equally divided.

Within every profession, then, we found strong advocates of both the specialist and generalist point of view. A mechanical engineer, for example, characterized his career strategy as follows:

> I found an area I knew better than anyone else in the company so I worked at it and became an expert. Eventually the customers began calling the company and asking for me to work on their problems.

Another engineer described his philosophy in contrasting terms:

> The most successful people in engineering are those with breadth. A person who goes home at night and reads a novel is better off than one who reads technical journals. You are in trouble if you overspecialize because then you are of little use when the project is over. You become a commodity to buy and sell. They can get rid of one specialist and hire another one. It's not nearly as easy to find a person who has a broad approach and can see the total picture. The people who make money for the company are those who can look at a black box and see how it fits into the total system.

Both engineers were highly rated by their managers. This led us to the view that neither approach is inherently superior; each has its advantages and its risks. In fact, the rigid specialist-versus-generalist debate is itself an oversimplification. We have found it more useful to frame the dichotomy in terms of two distinct but complimentary perspectives:

1. An *internal* perspective: What is the professional's occupational self-concept? What are his or her self-perceived abilities, motives, and values?
2. An *external* perspective: How are the professional's skills and experience perceived by significant others such as superiors, peers, and customers or clients?

INTERNAL PERSPECTIVE

Our interviews suggest that a person's self-concept can be a major factor in controlling his or her career decisions and performance on the job. Involved in intensive research on this issue, Edgar Schein has developed the concept of "career anchors." The concept emerged from a 15-year study of 44 graduates of the Sloan School of Management. Schein closely followed the careers of these graduates, using a series of questionnaires, psychological tests, and interviews to monitor their professional development. Among other things, he concluded that their career histories "could be understood best in terms of the concept of 'career anchors.'" His definition of the term is instructive:

> The career anchor—the pattern of self-perceived talents, motives, and values—serves to guide, constrain, stabilize, and integrate the person's career. . . . The five career anchors are (1) security, (2) technical/functional competence, (3) managerial competence, (4) creativity, and (5) autonomy. They are expressed as the dominant need or motive, in the sense of that area which the person is least willing to give up. Most people want some of what each of the anchors imply. By definition, *the* career anchor is that area which the person would *not give up* if he were forced to make a choice (6).

Because of his emphasis on work experience, Schein indicates that, "It is not possible to predict career anchors from tests. The concept emphasizes evolution, development, and *discovery* through actual experience. . . . Career anchors, then, are clearly the *result* of the early interaction between the individual and his work environment " (7). This suggests that a professional begins to be aware of his or her career anchor during Stages I and II. A brief description of each of the five career anchors will clarify the concept:

TECHNICAL/FUNCTIONAL COMPETENCE

Many of the "specialists" we interviewed were primarily concerned with the technical or functional *content* of their work. Their self-image was closely tied to feelings of competence in a specialty. Consequently, such professionals were generally not interested in advancing to positions of management (though they would accept management responsibility within their area of expertise). Professionals with a technical or functional anchor would be willing to leave their company rather than be promoted out of their specialty.

Jules Schwartz is a person who would describe himself as having a technical anchor. He had been in technical management for several years, but he eventually changed employers to return to his work as a neutron physicist. As he explained:

> I was hired here not for my management abilities, but as a technical specialist. My training was in neutron physics—that's what I like, what I'm best at. I've developed a very narrow specialty and a reputation in that specialty. I'm not managing people and I don't sell programs. That is by choice. I enjoy research a lot more than management. That's the reason I came here in the first place.

While Schwartz is convinced that he wants to do research, he feels a certain conflict because the traditional career path calls for a move up the management ladder. When asked what the organization could do to help the careers of its employees, Jules answered:

> They should encourage professional development for people like me. A person who develops a national reputation should be recognized and rewarded. But the feeling here is that when you do that, you're not a company man.

The feeling that technical accomplishment is under-rewarded was common in all the organizations we studied. Most people said that the real rewards were contingent upon advancement to management—a dilemma for those with a technical/functional career anchor.

MANAGERIAL COMPETENCE

The ultimate goal of some professionals is management; for these people, work in a technical area is seen as a necessary means to an end. Many of the professionals in our study who described themselves as "generalists" clearly had managerial competence as their anchor. One ambitious young engineer frankly stated that he intended to climb the management ladder. When asked to outline the career paths open to engineers in his company, he said:

> There is a management route and a technical route, but the technical route is a dead end. You just don't get the range of problems in engineering that you'd get in management. It could easily take 20 years for an engineer to reach the salary of the first level of management. With a little bit of breadth, you can get into management in 4 to 5 years. I've been a supervisor for 2 years. If I'm on a project more than 6 months, I've been on it too long—it's

dead. Nothing more is happening and there is nothing more to learn. From the first day on a project, I start planning my departure to a better situation 6 months later.

This engineer is obviously more interested in a management career than in engineering and has developed a strategy that he believes will enable him to move into general management.

SECURITY

A person who is anchored in security will tend to do what is required by his or her employer in order to maintain job security, a decent income, and a stable future. The underlying concern of such a person is to make his or her career stable and secure, even if that means subordinating some personal talents and ambitions.

There are two sources of security orientation. Some people derive their security from stable membership in an organization. They are willing to move every few years as long as they stay with the same organization. Certain military or government employees would belong in this category. For others, security is more geographically based and involves a feeling of settling down in a community. In one engineering firm, a number of the people we talked to belonged in this category. They started work with the company because it was located "near the family and the mountains." Several turned down promotions that would have involved moving back to company headquarters. Others had changed employers three or four times in order to remain in the same city.

Many of the managers in our study intimated that companies take advantage of employees whose career anchor is security. It is not uncommon for companies to pay lower salaries to such personnel or to assign them to routine jobs, knowing that they will not quit to find employment elsewhere.

CREATIVITY

Professionals with a creativity anchor are driven by a compelling need to build or create something entirely their own. Schein noted that these people are often "entrepreneurs," constantly going into new ventures and trying their hand at new projects. This explains why in our research we encountered few professionals with a creativity anchor: a person with an entrepreneurial bent is likely to become frustrated in a large firm. A bank manager described his experience with such an individual:

I recently had problems with one of my account managers. He was sharp—a

> bachelor's in engineering and an MBA—but he just wasn't suited for the
> bank. A bank is a structured institution. He didn't understand the con-
> straints. He was an entrepreneur, interested in doing what he wanted to do.
> He just didn't worry about the bank's interests. Almost every day he was in
> my office pounding on my desk and arguing with me, always wanting to do
> his own thing. Eventually he left to become president of a start-up research
> company. I think he's finally found his niche, and he's doing a hell of a job.

Having so little information about this account manager turned entrepreneur, it
would be hard to decide whether his anchor was creativity or autonomy. Schein
acknowledges that this is often a difficult distinction to make.

AUTONOMY AND INDEPENDENCE

Those with this anchor have in common the need to be free of organizational
constraints. They find organizational life too restrictive, and therefore tend to leave
business or government organizations in search of careers that will permit more
independence and autonomy. Examples of the kinds of occupations these people
enjoy include freelance writing, small retail business management, teaching on a
college level, and management or technical consulting. Here again, we were not
likely to encounter many people in this category because of the type of organizations we studied.

Having described in some detail the career anchors concept, we wish to
encourage realistic expectations of its practical value. It is not a panacea.
Professionals who have identified their career anchor may yet face difficult
decisions. They will, however, be able to evaluate these decisions in terms of a core
professional identity. The experience of Joe Medeiros, a computer specialist in a
large research lab, illustrates the benefits of finding a solid career anchor:

> I went to Harvard as an undergraduate, but I didn't do well enough to get into
> a graduate program there. Next I went to Chicago for a year, but it looked
> like their Ph.D. would take me at least 6 years. I ended up at [a lesser known
> Midwestern university] simply because their program was easier—I could
> get my Ph.D. in 3 years. After school, I worked 4 years at [a private defense
> contracting firm], and then I came here. But I really wasn't going anywhere
> professionally until I went to Paris on a Fulbright scholarship. While I was
> over there, I was introduced to the computer. It really fascinated me. I
> started formulating complex math problems and then solving them on the
> computer. The next thing you know, I was deep into computational physics.
> Since then, my whole career has been built around computer problem-
> solving applications in a variety of technical fields.

Medeiros' supervisors informed us that he had been unusually productive: he had over 40 publications in major journals, and had also been instrumental in bringing in several lucrative contracts. Although he had been promoted to group leader, Medeiros was still deeply involved in his technical work with the computer. It would appear that he was just dabbling in science at school and work—and not doing particularly well—until he discovered the computer. He then found direction, and has since been productive and satisfied in his career.

Robert White provides further insight that may be helpful to professionals approaching their careers from an internal perspective. He identifies one of the aspects of natural growth in a personality as "the deepening of interests":

> The absorption of a scientist in his experiments, an artist in his painting, a musician in his composition, a craftsman in his work, all serve to illustrate advanced points in this development. It is a common experience with creative people that they lose themselves in their work. . . . It is toward a state in which the sense of reward comes from doing something for its own sake (8).

White has described a highly desirable state in professional careers. In the foregoing example, Joe Medeiros seemed to experience that "deepening of interests" when he began to work with the computer. As a result, he enjoyed his work and didn't seem to worry about other aspects of his career, such as performance evaluations and salary increases. He was satisfied with them, but they seemed unimportant compared with his work.

We interviewed many professionals who shared the same attitude, who were deeply involved in their work—from which they received great satisfaction. Consciously or unconsciously, professionals in this enviable category had analyzed—from an internal perspective—their own unique skills and natural inclinations. A successful manager in a research lab observed: "The high performers here are people who are at peace with themselves. They recognize their real strengths. They know what they like to do and what they do well."

EXTERNAL PERSPECTIVE

Most young professionals soon learn that successful career development requires more than an individual, or internal, perspective. Managers, peers, customers or clients, family, even neighbors—all of these groups observe with interest the unfolding of a career. Many professionals perform their public duties well, fully aware that they have an "audience." Others, however, seem less concerned with their image, claiming that they are professionals and not salesmen; their work should speak for itself. They refuse to worry about marketing their skills.

We concluded from our studies that the latter approach is risky. Personal image can be a determining factor in obtaining challenging work assignments, salary increases, and promotions. Sue Takemori, a first-level supervisor at a large bank, told us about a difficult decision relating to her professional image:

> I've had five different jobs in my 6 years at the bank. My longest assignment was 18 months and my shortest was 9 months. A couple of months ago, I sat down with the vice president of personnel to talk about my career plans. What he said was, in effect, "You've moved too fast. When people look at your resume, they'll question your credit skills. You haven't been in assignments that are credit intensive." It all boiled down to a perception problem—the way the division heads would see me. So he advised me to take that into account when I took my next assignment. I talked to several managers about various openings and was offered three positions. One was a lateral move to a supervisory position in another department, but I was assured that if I did good work, in less than a year I'd be promoted to department head. It paid a lot of money and being a department head would be fairly prestigious—but only in that department. It wasn't on the front line making credit decisions. It was more of a peripheral activity to the main business of the bank: lending money. The second position was also a lateral move, into a lending department. The third position was as a loan officer in a very credit-intensive area. I chose it for several reasons. First, the supervisor is one of the most respected people in the bank, a specialist in high-risk lending. Second, the job will be a real challenge. I wanted a sink-or-swim situation. I was a little worried about not being a supervisor anymore—some of my peers might wonder if I'd been demoted, that sort of thing. But you have to look at the long-term prospects. They've given me several accounts that are in deep trouble. If I succeed, it will do a lot for my reputation.

Sue Takemori's experience illustrates at least three aspects of professional life as seen from an external perspective. First, *the perceptions of superiors are important.* As the vice president of personnel told her, the senior officers in the bank—those who make decisions concerning job assignments, salary increases, and promotions—needed to see her as capable, experienced, and tough. If these managers perceived her as lacking credit skills, she would have trouble obtaining challenging job assignments in the future. Understanding the role of management's perceptions was thus of great value to her.

Second, *titles and pay levels are not always the best measure of career progress.* Unlike many young professionals, Sue recognized that most organizations allocate their largest rewards to those who are involved in core, or central, activities. For example, in an accounting firm, the core activity is accounting (auditing, tax, and M.A.S.). In an engineering organization, on the other hand, accounting may be a peripheral department.

We do not wish to imply that "peripheral" activities are of minimal value to the organization; organizational effectiveness depends on competent performers in *all* areas. Many professionals enjoy their work in peripheral areas and are able to make significant contributions to the organization through their efforts. We have observed, however, that professionals too often fail to direct their careers toward specific goals other than ever-increasing salaries and impressive job titles.

We interviewed a number of people who, attracted by such titles and pay increases early in their careers, moved into peripheral activities that diverted them from their basic professional interests. Many of these, after finding themselves in reasonably high-level, dead-end positions, later accepted reduced salaries in order to return to more central activities in the organization.

This last point leads us to our third observation concerning the external perspective: as Sue maintained, *a career decision's long-term impact must be considered.* Early in their career, young professionals are inclined to forget or ignore that advice. They are impatient to move from junior to senior in an accounting firm, to be promoted to assistant vice president in a bank, or to have the title of project engineer in an engineering firm. They fail to realize that obtaining needed skills can do more to build their image than simply acquiring a bigger title.

Thus far, in considering the external perspective, we have focused on the ways professionals are perceived by management. There is another group of people, however, whose perceptions of professional performance can make a difference: the clients or customers of the organization. Some professionals—loan officers and CPAs, for example—are likely to have more contact with customers than others—such as engineers and scientists. Almost all of the professionals whom we interviewed, however, had had some opportunity to interact with others outside of their organization. And for some, this interaction was the key to their professional identity:

> As a loan officer, Tim Dougal had specialized in lending to utilities. Learning all he could about financing utilities, he had become recognized as an expert on the subject. He was asked to testify at rate hearings held by public utility commissions of various state governments. As his customers came to him more and more to help solve their problems, Dougal became known as "Mr. Utility." In the early 1970s, the editors of a national magazine decided to write an article on the difficulties that utilities faced in financing their expansion. In the process, they interviewed Tim Dougal. This increased his visibility significantly in the industry at large. Soon thereafter, he was hired as executive vice president of a medium-sized utility company.

Managers who take their subordinates' talents for granted may show new respect when customers begin to make requests for a specific engineer, accountant, loan officer, or scientist. As a professional's image continues to grow, management will likely try to retain this individual—and his or her loyal clientele—by offering a higher salary, better job assignments, a larger office, etc. While some would argue that this implies a strategy of specialization, we prefer to think in terms of "focus."

Crucial to establishing a favorable reputation is the focus of that professional's energies upon one topic or process for at least 2 or 3 years. Two approaches may be taken in selecting a focus. One emphasizes *content* and is akin to the notion of specialization. The other stresses *process* or developing a set of skills that can be applied to many different problems. Of the cases we've presented in this chapter, Tim Dougal's is perhaps the best example of a focus on content. His specific expertise in the area of utility lending gained him extensive recognition. An example that we discussed earlier—Joe Medeiros' application of computer problem-solving to a number of technical fields—illustrates a focus on process.

The concept of focus on process presents a wide range of alternatives for developing a professional image and identity. The Stage II professional does not have to be a specialist to have a focus; a generalist can focus upon any process important to the organization. One CPA, for instance, had earned a reputation in his firm for his ability to deal with sensitive accounts and difficult clients:

> I've been assigned to several clients specifically because I can handle the "pain-in-the-ass" types. One client in particular has moved out of the area, but both our firm and the client have left me in charge of that account because I have been able to work well with their people. The costs are of course greater, due to the travel, but they must feel that my "special ability" is worth the cost!

Thus, the generalist may develop a reputation for effectively working with clients, aggressively starting new projects, or successfully handling recurring problems, all of which are vital, needed skills in any organization.

In this chapter, we have tried to illustrate the importance of successful—and timely—progression through Stage II. Since many professionals remain in Stage II throughout most of their careers, they must acquire the basic skills needed for continued productivity. Those who decide to advance to the next stage (and have the opportunity to do so) may have an even greater need to develop the skills of this stage. Trying to build on a faulty or inadequate foundation presents serious problems, unwelcome additions to the built-in dilemmas that can make successful Stage II performance such a challenge. During Stage II, professionals must develop an identity. They must decide, for example, how involved they will be in their careers, and whether they will become specialists or generalists. We have suggested that professionals need to look at their careers from both an internal and an external perspective. They must learn through careful introspection how they feel about their careers, and must know, in addition, how their skills and experiences are perceived by others—namely, managers and clients. We cannot guarantee success to those who use the concepts we have presented in this chapter, but we feel that our insights can be of value to those who make the effort to carefully consider and plan their careers.

Stage III

3

Barriers to Stage III

I've started to look around again, said Brent Foreman as we met him in a large west coast laboratory where we were interviewing. I thought that this was a place where a scientist could feel valued, but I've decided this lab is no different. I've looked around the lab, and I can't see any future for someone who wants to do scientific work. It was the same way at Gentex Labs. But this place had such a strong reputation for good science, I somehow thought it would be different here.

It's the 'salesmen' and papershufflers who get the high ratings around here, not the scientists. I'm not saying a lot of them aren't good scientists, but you have to leave science if you want to have a future around here. In fact, a career in science doesn't seem much like I thought it would be. I know my field; I publish; I'm a better scientist than a lot of those guys who seem to be 'fairhaired boys,' but I don't see anything to look forward to. I didn't go into science for the money; that isn't it. I just can't see any future, and that's no way to live.

Brent Foreman received his Ph.D. at one of the best graduate schools in the country. He was a hard worker and was contributing to his field. But he was very frustrated. Up to that point his career had gone well enough, but he couldn't see any real prospects for the future—and he didn't know what to do about it. He described his vision of a good laboratory as being a community of scientists. Perhaps the best senior scientist would be the lab director, but the "paperwork" would be handled mostly by others; the prestige, respect, and rewards would go to those who proved to be the best scientists. But it wasn't working that way. The influence, high ratings, and big offices went to those doing what he termed "nonscience" work—contract negotiations, project coordination, and administration of the laboratory. He had thought of doing such tasks himself; but whenever he did, he became angry, saying to himself, "This isn't what I spent all those years in graduate school training myself to do."

We encountered many like Brent Foreman in our interviews. Not all were as bright or as well trained as Foreman. Not all were scientists; some were accountants, engineers, or loan officers. But they were all frustrated. Something was wrong. Their careers were not "pointing anywhere." All they could see ahead of them was "more of the same," and they didn't know what to do about it.

Their frustration, however, was no greater than that of another group represented by John B. Cox III. John Cox worked for one of the largest banks in the country. He had joined the bank 6 years earlier after graduating from an Ivy League school. He had progressed rapidly through the loan-officer training program and had been quickly identified as an intelligent, hard-working, and personable employee with "high potential." For 5 years, he was assigned to a specialized lending group focusing on the energy industry. He had established excellent credentials and was especially commended by his superior for his attention to detail and meticulous preparation of loan proposals. Next, he was transferred to the Houston office as a team leader with 6 account officers reporting to him. It was clearly a promotion, and he was made an assistant vice president. His enthusiasm was evident to his new boss, and he plunged into the new job with the same ardor that he had evidenced in earlier assignments at headquarters. However, 3 months later, Cox' superior at the Houston office made the following comments:

> I was looking forward to having Cox join our team, but frankly, he's not living up to my expectations. He's working hard; in fact, I have seen him at the office on weekends with sleeves rolled up, working diligently on some detailed job that I thought one of his junior officers should be doing. I recall another instance when there appeared to be a mistake in a presentation, and he immediately took over the whole presentation from his junior officer.

Cox was equally dissatisfied with the way things were going:

> My boss is a nice enough guy to work with, but this pressure to get our loan volume up and clean up all the documentation is really sand-bagging me. I'm having trouble meeting deadlines. The only reason we are getting by is that I carry most of the workload. I try to get more work out of my people; but this inevitably means they ask me a lot of questions that waste my time, and I end up reworking a presentation from scratch.

Like Brent Foreman, John Cox was frustrated and bewildered. Others were expecting something from him that seemed to be both "unclear and unfair." Like Foreman, he was working hard, using all the skills that had worked so well for him to this point, but suddenly they weren't being appreciated.

Before we try to understand what was frustrating these two men, let's look at one more seemingly strange bedfellow, Henry Peterson.

> Peterson had just been promoted to associate professor at one of the nation's best-known universities. He had recently published a prize-winning book and had been asked to provide the formal leadership for the staff teaching a large, required, undergraduate course. He had also obtained his first major research grant and was chairman of the doctoral committee for a bright young doctoral candidate who would be doing most of the field work for him on a research project. Everything Peterson had been working toward was falling into place. The world seemed to be his oyster. Suddenly and mysteriously, his own teaching began to go poorly. Classes he had taught successfully many times before began to go flat, and his relationship with his students began to deteriorate. He found it difficult to make decisions the teaching staff needed. He began to worry that he had led the doctoral candidate into a blind alley for his research topic. He found himself unable to concentrate or rest. The feelings of success and confidence he had been feeling only a few months earlier were suddenly turned to an almost unbearable sense of depression.

What do the experiences of these three men have in common? In our view, all three had encountered the same problem, although in different ways. They had all proved themselves competent as independent contributors in Stage II but were facing the problems of understanding the issues, mastering the skills, or making the psychological adjustments necessary to move into the third stage. We have sometimes called this third stage the "mentor stage" because of its central tasks of training, guiding, and supervising younger professionals. The new activities a person must begin to perform in this stage, however, as well as the new relationships to be developed and adjustments to be made, cannot be captured in a single word. We have found it easier, therefore, to refer to this level simply as Stage III.

ACTIVITIES OF STAGE III PROFESSIONALS

What do we know about Stage III? First, we know that it is very real. In every professional organization that we entered—research laboratories, CPA firms, engineering firms, banks and universities—we found complete agreement that there is a very definite stage beyond the solo performance of professional tasks. As we listened to people talk about this stage, we heard such descriptive phrases as:

- Motivates and communicates with people
- Trains and develops others
- Has project responsibility
- Sets and monitors priorities
- Plans and administers budgets
- Sells programs and administers them
- Deals with the customer and/or top management

Many of the foregoing suggest that the difference between Stages II and III is simply supervising versus not supervising or management versus nonmanagement. In our studies, however, it quickly became apparent that such distinctions in professional organizations are much more complex. Certain nonsupervisors, for example, performed many Stage III functions and wielded greater influence than some supervisors. When we asked others in the organization about these non-supervisors, we learned that the latter, in fact, were clearly playing roles different from those of the independent contributor. We finally concluded, after analyzing hundreds of interviews, that there were three central characteristics that described the activities of those who were fully in Stage III, and that it was these traits—and not the title—that made the difference. So, what do Stage III professionals actually *do*?

DEVELOPMENT OF BROAD INTERESTS AND COMPETENCIES

Typically, individuals in Stage III have sufficiently penetrated one or more subparts of their professional field to acquire and demonstrate professional competence; but they have used their skills and competence in one area as a base to make informed contributions, judgments, and evaluations in a broader area of work. They have not remained "narrow specialists," a term we often hear to describe individuals who are not moving into Stage III. These widened interests and capabilities enable people in Stage III to help others formulate and solve problems in a broad area of the organization's activities.

DEALING WITH THE "OUTSIDE"

Stage III professionals help manage the interface with customers, upper management, professionals in other organizations, and with other parts of the organization. They begin to represent the organization, or at least their part of this organization, to important outsiders; and most significantly, this representation is seldom for their interests alone. They use their contacts and reputation with outside individuals and groups to obtain information and resources for others. They do so, however, in a variety of ways. They may obtain contracts, assignments, or new business, which provide work and opportunities for others. They may develop and maintain relations with important client groups in or out of the organization. In addition, they may negotiate with upper management for salary increases or new assignments. Finally, they may publish and develop a reputation and a network of professional contacts, which bring important information into the organization.

DEVELOPING OTHER PEOPLE

Probably the most important change that occurs as professionals move into Stage III is the nature of their relationships. In Stage II they had to learn to take care of themselves; in Stage III they have to learn to take care of others, to assume some form of responsibility for their work. When Stage III professionals receive an assignment that requires the collaboration of others, they soon learn the importance of tapping additional skills. To coordinate the efforts of even a small group of professionals requires more than just technical skills and presents an interesting problem.

This particular challenge helps those in Stage III to see the need to teach, guide, encourage, critique, supervise, and evaluate the work of other professionals. There are many different ways to carry out this responsibility but one cannot avoid it and expect to be successful in Stage III.

Each of these activities manifests itself somewhat differently in the various professions and organizations, but the remarkable thing to us was the consistency with which each one appeared again and again in each of the settings that we studied. These were also the same activities or functions that were missing in descriptions of individuals whose progress in the organization was "blocked," whose "potential was limited," or whose career was in danger of becoming "obsolete."

STAGE III ROLES

In recent years a great deal has been written about the role of a mentor in career development. In some ways it appears that too much emphasis has been placed on that one role. We found that organizations provided opportunities for Stage III professionals to play a variety of different roles. We were able to distinguish at least three different functions performed by those who were described by others as clearly having moved beyond Stage II: informal mentor, idea leader, and manager. These are not mutually exclusive; and individuals may play all three roles.

INFORMAL MENTOR

Often professionals begin to play the role of informal mentor as an outgrowth of their success in Stage II. The work they are asked to do because of their broadening capabilities and contacts increases their need for other people. They begin to find others who can help do some of the detail work and develop their initial ideas. In doing so they often become mentors for those people who assist them. They share ideas, knowledge, status, and time, in exchange for help and support.

One informal technical mentor described himself in the following manner:

> Right now I find the sponsors for our work. I do the conceptual thinking, develop the project, and then get someone to support it. After I get the job, then I mostly oversee and collaborate with others who, in turn, do most of the actual work.

He remained the force behind the project and also worked very closely with those doing the work.

IDEA LEADER

Some professionals are exceptionally innovative. Often it's this type of individual who becomes an idea leader—or consultant for a small group. Others come to them for help solving problems. Sometimes they originate an idea, discuss it with others, and the latter pursue it independently. Either way, they are involved with and influence more than their own work. A 59-year-old scientist described his work in this way:

> I would describe myself as an innovative scientist. When I work on a problem, it starts to bug me. At some time, I will read something and apply it back to solve the original problem. Others often come to me with problems they can't solve.

MANAGERS

The most common role in Stage III, and the one most easily understood and recognized, is the formal role of manager or supervisor. Usually, the management role for a Stage III person is not more than one or two levels away from the work itself.

Professional competence usually continues to be important in the performance of work. Frequently, the formal management role is given to an informal mentor who is performing managerial functions already. Hence, transition to the formal title of "manager" is not particularly dramatic. Bob Smith, a 37-year-old manager, described a fairly typical pattern of professional advancement to a Stage III management role.

> I gained knowledge of other programs and began to develop outside contacts. Finally, I discovered I could sell programs. With more programs coming in, I managed several long-term projects under time and money constraints. The business was expanding, and I was directing more and more technical people. Soon I became acting section manager and, after 3 months, the section manager.

In our interviews it became very clear that these roles fulfilled by individuals in Stage III were critical for organizational success. An organization that did not have a substantial group of its professionals (at least 26 percent) in Stage III would be in serious trouble. We also found that many professionals *wanted* to be carrying out the activities of Stage III. Most people felt their careers would be unproductive and unsatisfying without the opportunity to move into the mentor stage. Since Stage III is so desirable, from both an individual and an organizational point of view, we were surprised to find that a substantial number of professionals were unable to make that move. It would be worthwhile at this point to look at the problems that people encounter when attempting to make that novation.

Blocks to Movement into Stage III

Moving from Stage II to Stage III may seem natural enough to some, but it requires a fundamental—though often subtle shift in one's activities and relationships. Critical emotional shifts and adjustments must be made as well. The fact that these changes are difficult for many to understand and make is demonstrated by the scores of frustrated Brents, Johns, and Henrys whom we interviewed. These difficulties can probably best be understood if we consider specific problems that blocked the movement of various individuals into Stage III.

THE NARROW SPECIALIST

In the previous chapter, we pointed out that some people fail to move into Stage II because of an inability to focus on their own project. The novation into Stage III is sometimes hindered by the opposite problem—they have too narrowly focused on their own project and do not understand the broader needs of the organization. This issue highlights the importance of "timing" in career management. An ability to focus on one project is valuable in Stage II, but can become a liability in striving to move on to Stage III.

Many professionals never completely understand the needs of the organization that employs them. Not only does the organization need individuals who can perform required tasks—the "business" of the firm—it also critically needs professionals who can inspire the confidence of others outside the unit, and who are able to develop new contracts, or assignments. It needs people whose reputations outside the organizational unit are strong enough to benefit the organization as a whole and to enhance and stimulate the work of others. It needs skilled managers—those who can plan, organize, and direct projects that require the efforts of several people to complete. These needs are so critical to organizational survival and growth that those who evaluate contributions to the organization and allocate rewards almost inevitably give higher ratings to individuals who perform these functions, than to those who make only individual contributions.

Although the independent specialist may contribute significantly to his or her field, unless that work also significantly benefits the organization and the efforts of others in the organization, such efforts will not be as highly valued or rewarded as those of another whose work benefits the organization more broadly. Brent Foreman, the scientist to whom we referred at the beginning of the chapter, failed to recognize that the "paperwork," "sales," and "public relations" tasks that he felt reluctant to perform *were* of real value to his laboratory and, in their own way, were as important as the skilled scientific research for which he had been trained.

Interestingly, the stereotype of the "lone professional" often comes from the universities where the Brent Foremans receive their training. But even at the university, the stereotype is more myth than reality. Harriet Zuckerman, in a study of highly productive scientists, reported that while people who become Nobel prize winners started by publishing early, sometimes alone, they soon gathered associates and graduate students around them in a team, working on the ideas they were generating (1). A person who develops a solid competence in an area but who also broadens his or her interests and tries to find ways to involve others in the effort is developing a critical ability.

> They have the ability to conceptualize the project as a whole and then break it down into parts. They can keep the overall objective in mind but, at the same time, develop integrating steps to bring the project together (1).

Some professionals seem unable to take the broader view of their project. They seem to get locked into their narrow specialty and fail to see how their project relates to the success of the organization:

Several years ago we made a presentation to a group of second-level managers in a computer company. As a part of the discussion, we asked each manager to identify one person in the company who seemed to be blocked in Stage II and was frustrated by an inability to make the move into Stage III. In small group meetings, the managers discussed each individual in an effort to understand what was preventing them from moving into the next stage. When the managers reported back to the total group, they discovered that all 20 people who were identified as blocked in Stage II were described as so narrowly focused on their own specialty that they were not able to meet the broader needs of the organization.

While a narrow specialization is an important block to movement, it is certainly not the only one. Some of the people we interviewed suggested that there are certain professional groups that, because of the training of their members or due to the kinds of people who are attracted to the fields represented, were less inclined to encourage breadth. For instance, a manager of a computations department in a large research laboratory made these comments about his programmers:

> I'm frustrated in the computations department. I don't see the people developing. They really become competent specialists, but they don't seem to move beyond. As a group, they tend to be introverted. A good programmer can be content to sit at his desk and lay out his program. But it's like pulling teeth to get him into a brainstorming session—to shake him out of his narrow thinking. A few people make that transition, but not many. They get bogged down in academic logic and sometimes lose sight of what we're trying to accomplish.

If then, a failure to broaden one's perspective can retard or prevent career advancement, one may well ask how professional broadening occurs in instances where it does. We found that it happens in a number of ways. For those who are imaginative and intellectually curious, working with a narrow focus initially leads naturally to other ideas in tangential areas. In a contract research organization, for example, one researcher who had been very specialized described how he found himself being stretched by the work itself.

> When you are very close to the data, you are able to see the small differences. If you are observant and in a fruitful area, you soon have more ideas than you can possibly pursue by yourself. You run the risk of eliminating some potentially good ideas unless you get others to help you.

This researcher gradually found himself leading several individuals, then several groups, into a pursuit of the ideas he kept finding in his work.

Another type of broadening occurs by moving with trends in the environment into new, productive areas. This type of move generally entails a skills transfer from the old specialty, in addition to the learning of new skills and technology. One individual who was moving from a specialized area of chemistry into the application of lasers described the process.

> Now I am trying to expand my area of interest and broaden the application. We accomplished some very significant work in my old specialty, but now it is time for a change. The lasers are not a radical departure from my specialty, just a new logical extension, and I've got a group helping me explore it.

We found in our study of internal accountants that those who had shown an interest and aptitude as they interfaced with other departments in the controllership found themselves being placed in positions where they were given the responsibility for managing more than one functional area.

Other individuals adopt breadth as a deliberate strategy, partly because it fits their interests, and partly because they see how it allows them to play a critical role in organizations where so many individual functions must join to produce a single outcome. A mechanical engineer who has made rapid career progress in a research laboratory told us of his deliberate strategy to gain breadth:

> There are two ways of gaining independence. One is to take a job, and go off and do it by yourself. The second is to take a broader view than is normally taken. This is the approach I've taken. I find I can communicate with a lot more people and get input into the solution of the overall problem that way. I saw that people who do well are people who have had a wide range of experiences.

Recently, an historian wrote a fascinating account of his own broadening experiences. After he completed his course work on a doctorate at the University of North Carolina, Leonard Arrington began to study the regional history of the territory orginally settled by Mormon pioneers. He worked for 11 years on the project—6 years on the dissertation, and 5 years revising it for publication. All of this time he had worked essentially alone, without the aid of research assistants. The resulting book, published by Harvard University Press, was well received. But the work on the book had opened to him the vast amount of work that needed to be done on the economic, cultural, political, and religious history of the region. Accordingly, he began to enlist the assistance of others.

> I applied in 1959 for a grant from Utah State University to fund summer work on Utah and western economic history. Each summer, according to terms of the grant, I was able to employ a senior or graduate student to collaborate in researching and writing articles and monographs. This began the broadening of my career. Henceforth, I would not only be an individual scholar, but an 'historical entrepreneur,' organizing large projects and team efforts and often working in collaboration with graduates and colleagues.

Soon, a whole series of articles, monographs, and books began to appear. In describing three of the books that were published, Arrington makes the following interesting comment:

> While I am listed as the author of each of these publications, they really represent the research and writing skills of a large number of undergraduates, graduate students, and colleagues who contributed their time and expertise in return for compensation out of project grant funds. . . . These books represent an attempt to demonstrate that bright students can get good experience and training in research and writing by working under an historian director (2).

He had started as an economist, but had steadily made himself a competent economic historian. Now he was moving sure-footedly into intellectual and institutional history.

Dr. Arrington had also built a strong network of relationships outside his own department and university. As his own interests kept expanding, he "became acquainted with other scholars at other universities and in a variety of disciplines" who were interested in his expanded field of interest. He helped form a new historical association. He went to other universities as a visiting scholar. His publication record and his strong contacts with other scholars and publishers made it possible for him to help form *The Western Historical Journal.* He persuaded university officials to pay for overhead and editorial work and to have the Western Historical Association, of which he was vice president, pay for printing and distribution. Arrington makes a noteworthy model for those who may fear that they are beginning to be labeled as narrow specialists—and don't know what to do about it.

LOCKING ONESELF INSIDE

When William Foote Whyte went into the Boston slums in the 1930s to study the street corner gangs of those depression years, he found a number of very interesting things. First, he discovered that in the slums (which everyone else was describing as "socially disorganized"), there was a very carefully structured informal social structure with its own norms, roles, and rewards. But another of Whyte's clearest findings was that influence, or authority, inside a group tended to go to the member or members of the group who negotiated and dealt with persons outside that group—other gangs and social workers, for example(3). Whyte's findings were clearly replicated in our study of career stages in formal organizations. One of the clearest characteristics of those who moved out of Stage II was an ability to deal with key people outside of a particular sub-unit for the benefit of those inside the unit. They obtained contracts, got budgets approved and located resources. They often secured project funds and salary increases for others. The reputation that they had developed for solid achievement in Stage II became the keystone to similar activities in Stage III work.

In scientific laboratories and universities, external interaction often took the form of publishing or presenting papers at conferences. Those who advanced to Stage III didn't work or publish alone; they involved others in their efforts.

They became members of formal committees or informal networks that brought critical information or reputation to their organization, allowing them to benefit others in the ways mentioned above. Conversely, those professionals who had buried themselves inside their organizational sub-units and failed to take advantage of or create opportunities to deal with important "others" outside their units were often the ones who complained that they felt they weren't "going anywhere."

The importance of external participation often comes as a shock to individuals trained in a profession—scientists, accountants, and engineers. As one accounting manager in a large aerospace company put it:

> A lot of people have this stereotype of the accountant as an introverted guy who wears a green visor and spends endless hours poring over the firm's books. It's really too bad that that image still exists. It misleads others, but more importantly, it prevents our own people from seeing what their real job is. Because of that stereotype, many of us around here would prefer to be called "analysts." Our work here in the controller's shop requires a great deal of interaction with a wide range of people both inside and outside the firm. If a guy is going to be successful in internal accounting, he isn't going to fit the stereotype.

This accounting manager cited a long list of critical interfacing activities that had to be performed, including:

- Coordinating work and methods with changes in operations.
- Selling managers on the adoption of new accounting procedures.
- Developing and working out budgets with others.
- Working with clients and government agencies.
- Facilitating the work of public accountants to minimize the disruption of normal work flow.

> If someone is going to become highly valuable to us, he said, he or she has got to become interested in doing these things well. If someone just sits at his or her desk and won't or can't get out to deal with the rest of the company, that person's career here is going to be limited.

Public accounting firms placed even greater emphasis on what they termed "client relations." Skill at this activity was cited as critical in the early stages of a public accountant's career. We were told repeatedly that a certain level of technical proficiency was essential in public accounting; beyond that, however, interpersonal relations was the key variable in competent performance. If someone were performing an audit, for example, one of the key variables in keeping costs within limits would be to work with the people in the client firm in such a way that they would "not only cooperate with you but do as much of the detailed work for you as possible." Effective client relations skills become even more critical in the move from senior accountant level to manager level. It is at this stage in a public accountant's career that they are expected to develop a segment of an industry or business in which they can acquire special experience or abilities enabling them to represent the firm in this area of work. One senior partner told us:

> As our people become managers we look hard to see if they have the capacity to deal with high-level managers in client organizations. We want to see if they can represent us to business groups and professional societies. If they can show that they can develop outside visibility, they'll advance. But if they don't show that they can represent us to the people who count to the firm, we can't consider them as candidates for partnership.

The groups that must be dealt with are certainly not limited to clients or customers. Professionals need to be skillful in dealing with other subgroups inside their own organization. In a research organization, we heard about a scientist who had problems in this area:

Dan Rosenberg has been in our chemistry department for about 12 years. Recently he expressed an interest in becoming a supervisor. I decided to give him an opportunity to represent the group outside the department. We have been having some problems between the chemistry department and the chemical engineers. Each group has been complaining that the other one is infringing on their territory. In an effort to deal with this problem, I appointed a small task-force to study the situation. In the beginning 10 minutes of the first meeting, Dan blasted the chemical engineering group, accusing them of doing low-quality research and of trying to build an empire. The meeting ended in an uproar. Both groups are so upset that I have had to disband the task-force. It will be a long time before I give Dan another sensitive assignment outside the department.

The problems that Rosenberg created in this situation reduced his chances of moving into Stage III in the near future. One needs to be *both willing and able* in dealing with outside groups to help the organization.

But, from a positive aspect, how do people in Stage III describe this activity?

In my present role I have program management responsibility—defining the research. Then I try to formulate a program that meets the customers' needs. A lot of my role is communicating, acting as a liaison, and trying to convince the people in Washington that this research program is needed. Also, I go to France every year to do joint-publishing and work with people there. It's exciting to know that there are many people outside my organization who are working on my ideas.

We met other highly rated Stage III scientists, such as Henry Fowler, a Stage III professional in a research laboratory, who made it very clear that he "let other people do the selling." However, we noticed that Fowler had carefully published his innovative work and associated closely with others in the laboratory to ensure that his work could solve some of *their* problems. His manager told us that scientists from other departments—and other laboratories—telephoned or wrote to Fowler frequently requesting his help.

Demonstrated technical and interpersonal competence in Stage II is a prerequisite for both the opportunity to represent one's organization to the world and the background to do it well. Professionals who wish to move to Stage III, would do well to seek opportunities to represent the organization or the group at its interfaces. Having made the decision to do so, they can usually create such interactions by seeking contracts or tasks that will require the efforts of others all working together for the benefit of all concerned. They should develop outside contacts as well and offer to attend meetings that can be critical to the organization or the department.

FAILING TO HELP OTHERS

Probably the most fundamental shift that must take place if professionals are to progress into Stage III is a change in their relationships with others. To advance to Stage III, they must get involved in the development of others. For many, this is a difficult and sometimes impossible transition. Just because people are promoted to supervisory positions where they are expected to train and develop others, this is no guarantee that the change will take place. Intelligence and independent hard work in Stage II will often catapult an individual into management without his or her having realized that the new position requires different relations and activities than those which previously brought success. This was clearly the case with John B. Cox III, the young banking executive we encountered at the beginning of this chapter. Cox was still trying to rely on his old skills and behaviors—individual hard work and close attention to detail—to perform a job in which these skills were no longer adequate or appropriate.

This shift from exclusive concern with one's own performance and productivity, to involvement in the output and development of others, is critical for several reasons. First, as Cox began to discover, there is a finite amount of work one person can do alone. He or she must learn to delegate responsibility to others. It was this realization on the part of Leonard Arrington, the historian we met earlier, that so multiplied his output. Secondly, even if Cox were able to do all the work himself, he would still be failing to fulfill his new responsibilities, because a central part of his job was to train and develop others to perform the complex tasks of the organization. Delegation, then, is not just a means of getting work done; it is essential to the development of the professionals in the organization.

While the foregoing is less a revelation than a reminder, translating the obvious into action can be a challenge. As we interviewed the hundreds of professionals in the organizations we studied, we identified several different factors that can prevent individuals from becoming involved in the development of others, even when the job so requires.

FOCUSED ON THE TECHNICAL TASK

We found a number of instances in which managers focused so narrowly on the technical work that they were never able to see the need to help others develop. They often found supervision to be a frustrating activity and were eager to return to their own work as individual contributors. Such people have inspired the cliché, "We lost a good scientist (or engineer, accountant, teacher, etc.) and got a poor manager." The following comments were typical of what we heard about such individuals:

> Ted Browning is probably the brightest and most knowledgeable analyst in the firm. He always did the most innovative and comprehensive work of anyone around when he was working on his own. However, this is a problem now that Browning is no longer working independently. You see, since he has always been the best, he wants to make sure that the work his people do is also the best. But since he knows more than anyone else around here, his subordinates become overly dependent on him and he gets deeply involved in every minute detail. Consequently, his subordinates never learn to operate without his direction and consent, or without him hovering over them.

FOCUSED ON ONE'S OWN CAREER

We also heard of managers who were unable to advance completely to Stage III because they were so engrossed in their own personal career advancement; they were unable to see the need for development of those whom they supervised.

> In a group interview that we held with the first level managers of a small research and development group we were struck by the contrast between two managers. We asked them to talk about careers of professionals in that organization. The first manager, who had only been in his job for 2 years, spent nearly all his time talking about his concern that there was no place for first-line supervisors to go in that organization and how he felt locked in. The second supervisor, who had also been in the job for less than 2 years, talked almost exclusively about his concern for making a life of dignity and pride for his design engineers. He looked for ways to give them recognition, influence, and a chance to direct their own lives. After our interview, the director of the laboratory told us that the first manager was "not working out" and that the second was "one of their high-potential people with a great future."

Some people are unable to look beyond their own careers because they do not seem to find satisfaction or professional challenge in the development of others. An engineering manager observed:

> Some engineers are just solitary workers. They may have excellent technical abilities, but they just want to unload their knowledge and work,

rather than nurture it and teach others how to do it. Their satisfaction comes in working with "things" not "people."

Other professionals are able to look beyond their own career and their own technical challenge. They learn to derive genuine satisfaction from seeing others develop and grow in their abilities. As one supervisor expressed it:

> I just enjoy seeing other people do things they didn't think they could do. It's very satisfying to see both young and old achieve. I like to see people generate ideas and achieve them.

Our studies have indicated that unless one can begin to find satisfaction in observing the development of others, his or her efforts will be perfunctory and less than successful. Full advancement to Stage III will be more difficult as well.

FEAR OF OTHERS' PROGRESS

One of the characteristics most frequently used to describe those who were interested and successful in developing others was personal security. A secure feeling of one's own competence is, of course, likely to make one feel that he or she has something to teach another. More important, however, a lack of personal security is almost guaranteed to prevent a professional from becoming involved in the development of others. One accountant, in describing a supervisor from whom he had gotten almost no help, cited insecurity as a root cause:

> That supervisor never gave me nor any of my colleagues a chance for exposure. He insisted on doing all assignments that involved travel to the division or corporate headquarters himself. He never took anyone with him and generally kept all opportunities to himself. He also had a habit of trying to keep all important information to himself and avoid sharing it with the rest of us. He seemed to be afraid to give those of us under him any knowledge because if we improved or did something outstanding, he would look bad or incompetent by comparison. In fact, when I was promoted to a supervisory position, which made me his peer, he accused me of trying to take his job away from him.

LACK OF TECHNICAL ROOTS

Few supervisors or mentors can understand all the technology required of those with whom they work. The effort to do so would be counter-productive, and is not the job of the mentor. His or her task is to take a broader perspective, to deal with the outside and to help people develop. Every profession, on the other hand, involves one or more core activities, around which the mentor must have established a sufficient amount of technical depth and expertise to make a knowledgeable judgment about what should or should not be done. Mentors must be able to evaluate the judgments of others in the critical areas. If they have not established sufficient technical roots in these critical areas, they will find it difficult or impossible to gain the necessary respect and confidence from others to perform Stage III activities. One researcher for a large electronics firm told us he had been made a manager immediately after his postdoctoral year. "But," he said, "I found out my subordinates were so much more knowledgeable than I that I gave up management after a year-and-a-half." To illustrate how a lack of depth in critical areas appears to those who are dependent for direction or help, let's look at the comments of an accountant and an engineer who were working for supervisors who hadn't first acquired the knowledge and experience that come from working in the central activities of their field. The accountant described the problem as follows:

> You know, there are people who have come in here and moved into supervision without working long enough to know the system. Most of them have fallen on their faces. There was a program manager who came into that position right out of school. He never really learned the system and consequently never knew what the hell was going on. The problem is that he really didn't understand constraints and limitations and, therefore, made impossible demands on his subordinates and people in other departments. One day I heard him demand a report from one of his men that would have required 3 days of work; he wanted it in less than 3 hours.

The engineer described a similar experience:

> My supervisor is not very effective. In my opinion, he has moved too quickly and lacks an in-depth knowledge of the nitty-gritty technical details. As a consequence, he has very little to offer his subordinates. He can't seem to sit down and really listen to me long enough to be of any help.

TAKING RESPONSIBILITY FOR OTHERS

We have referred to those who were not able to develop an interest in the development of others or who, for various reasons, could not see the importance of doing so. For such, the major difficulty lay in adjusting to the requirements of new relationships. Now we focus upon professionals who may be keenly aware of the need to become involved in the development of others, but for whom the psychological reality of such responsibility is overwhelming. Henry Peterson, described at the beginning of this chapter, is a case in point. Peterson was intellectually well aware of the needs of the teaching staff, his doctoral assistant, and the students. The frightening thing to him was that he might not be able to fulfill those needs, a fear that others' trust in him might be misplaced.

The psychological adjustments required to become a mentor cannot be taken lightly. To assume the role of mentor, professionals take responsibility not only for their own output but for that of others as well. They must set objectives, allocate tasks, and become a driving force behind the efforts of subordinates. In so doing they explicitly assume an obligation to customers, to superiors, and to those whose efforts they direct, that they will be responsible for the outcomes. Implicitly, they promise all parties that the outcome will be satisfactory, thus guaranteeing results of which they can never be completely sure.

What makes it possible for some individuals to assume this responsibility when it is so difficult for others? For most, a part of the necessary psychological base comes from confidence in one's ability to produce and accomplish. Individual technical achievements, however, are often not enough. The ability to cope with the psychological demands of taking responsibility for others frequently stems more from prior life experiences than professional experiences. If one grew up in a family in which he was an older brother, for instance, he may find it more comfortable to take responsibility for others than if he had always played the role of younger brother. Or if he had a father with whom he identified, who was clearly head of the family, it may be easier still for him to assume the role of mentor. Charles McArthur, who helped conduct and analyze the famous Grant Study at Harvard, which followed the careers of certain Harvard graduates for several decades, reported that if the father of the family was the most influential force in family decisions, the son was mostly likely to pursue a management career. If, on the other hand, the mother was the dominant influence, the son was more likely to choose a "culture carrier" career such as law or teaching. But lawyers and teachers also work in organizations, and often find themselves expected to mentor others. The lack of a strong male role model may make this difficult.

> In one organization we studied, a researcher whose father had died when he was a very young boy entered the organization during a very trying period of his life. He had done brilliant work at some of the finest schools in the country, but because he could never find a field or a profession that could capture his interests for a sufficiently long period of time, he left graduate school in despair. An extremely innovative older team leader took him under his wing, and they worked together for over a decade. During this time, their work was so original that they succeeded in establishing a new field of study, which achieved international acclaim. Much of the work was published by the younger researcher independently. But when the older

man retired and the leadership of the research effort fell entirely on the younger man, he became anxious and depressed for over a year. Fortunately, those at the head of the organization and the members of the department maintained their high confidence in him. He took a leave of absence for 6 months and upon his return, he found a way to lead the group with less personal inner stress. Soon the group regained its position as one of the leading departments in the organization.

Even when taking responsibility is emotionally difficult, it need not be impossible. If one has not had earlier experiences or important role models that make mentoring more natural and less formidable, the role may be emotionally stressful for a period, and understanding from others is essential.

One woman section manager in a physics laboratory shared with us some of the stresses she had felt upon assuming responsibility for a section.

> The biggest problem I had was with myself. I just didn't realize how much healthy aggressiveness is necessary to do a job like this. I had had to overcome a lot of built-in inertia to move from being an assistant to becoming a good independent physicist on my own, but it took even more determination to begin to lead others. It's hard for a woman to break through the stereotype she has of herself that she cannot lead men. Friends are no help. Your so-called 'best friends' also stereotype you. It's just a shift you have to make, and it's harder for some than for others.

ORGANIZATIONAL STRUCTURES

To this point, the factors we have discussed that prevent advancement to Stage III have involved the individual—his or her attitudes, abilities, and preferences. Another major consideration, however, is organizational structure and climate. We found people who had the apparent ability and inclination to play the roles of informal mentor and idea leader in most of the professional organizations we studied. We noted remarkable differences, though, in the extent to which individuals in nonmanagement positions could find recognition for displaying such skills in the organizations to which they belonged.

In two research laboratories we studied, 65 percent of Stage III professionals held no supervisory positions. In another research laboratory, virtually all who had moved beyond Stage II held formal supervisory roles. In one large bank that hired a large number of people with graduate degrees, there was almost no way that an individual could extend his or her influence or obtain increased rewards without being promoted through management ranks; a competitive bank offered a number of nonsupervisory roles in which special talents or abilities could result in considerable informal influence, as well as substantial organizational rewards and status. Two of the universities we studied functioned in a hierarchical manner and movement through Stage II into Stage III was very closely linked to promotion into formal positions. In two other universities, on the other hand, influence, ability to obtain resources, and various rewards were more likely to be linked to informal roles, activities, and reputations.

In a few of the engineering organizations we examined, we discovered that some had found ways to perform Stage III functions without moving into management positions. In most engineering firms, however, the possibility of engaging in genuine Stage III activities and relationships was remote for those in nonsupervisory positions. Repeatedly, we heard comments such as these:

> You gain recognition and reward around here by being promoted into management. There is really no other way to get them.

> In this company, a person either moves into management or, using your terms, he or she stays in Stage II. There aren't any real alternatives.

These statements illustrate the level of frustration that can be felt when career expectations have been violated.

In the last 30 years, managers in many technical organizations have responded to these kinds of frustrations by creating "dual ladders."(4) A dual ladder is made up of an "administrative ladder" on the one hand and a "technical ladder" on the other. Technical ladders were usually established to provide a means of rewarding and recognizing those who made significant contributions to the company by remaining technically oriented. The clearest effect of technical ladders was higher than average salaries for qualifying personnel. We heard the frequent and often valid complaint, however, that the technical ladder seemed to promise that which was never achieved—an alternative career route in which the possibilities for respected contributions, influence, and organizational legitimacy would be equivalent to those offered professionals who chose the management route. The violation of that expectation brought a number of comments like the following: "The technical ladder is often a dumping ground for incompetent ex-managers"; or "Technical ladder positions are slowly declining in worth to the organization. Staff people cannot maintain their worth in this company. They have to go into management."

We heard numerous stories of the way small, symbolic events gave constant reminders that the value the organization placed on those in the technical ladder was not equal or even close to that placed on those chosen for management positions. One such account was given by a young technical man:

> Recently one of our scientists, who had a position near the top of the technical ladder, had a frustrating experience. He requested a table for his

work area and was given a wooden one. A few weeks later the facilities manager replaced it with a metal table, explaining that only managers were issued wooden ones. The scientist became so upset that he left the company within the week.

In our view, the "dual ladder" is not working in most organizations because it raises a false hope. It suggests that a person on the technical ladder can be highly valued by the organization by being a competent, solo, technical contributor. The descriptions conjure up the image of the lonely scientist or engineer working on a specialized project at his or her own desk. We heard complaints that the dual ladder wasn't being used properly because professionals on the technical side were being asked to perform inappropriate tasks, i.e., coordinate projects, manage small groups, represent the department outside the organization, etc. These were described as inappropriate because they are "management tasks." It is our hypothesis that they are legitimate Stage III functions and should be performed by both managers and nonmanagers.

To more fully understand this issue, we need to move beyond dual ladders, to see if organizations allow nonmanagers to perform Stage III functions.

MANAGERS ONLY?

We found some organizations where a climate had been created in which nonmanagers could legitimately play Stage III roles. In those organizations, a larger proportion of the professionals enjoyed the status that came from performing valued functions and the organization found ways to reward them. In some cases they had titles such as "assistant manager," although they had few, if any, subordinates. In other situations no titles were given. The key issue was finding opportunities for nonmanagers to play Stage III functions. We found people fulfilling those roles in two different ways:

1. As an idea person.
2. As an informal mentor.

In some organizations, we found a number of people who had a high amount of influence, latitude, and recognition because they were "idea leaders." They were described by others as clearly in Stage III "because their ideas have such an impact on the work of others" in the organization.

Although idea leaders had a significant impact on others, their influence was generally not a result of close personal relationships. They tended, in fact, to be more aloof than others at this stage. They held no special title, but there was general agreement on the impact they exerted. John Jensen, a chemical engineer, was one of these. In his early career, he had focused on developing new chemical separation processes that led to a number of personal patents and papers. He spent 2 years in the marketing area, returning later to the laboratory. After his return, he was credited with having brought in more and larger contracts than anyone else and was described by others as being very patient and original. He described himself as "an innovative scientist." When we asked him what he did, he replied:

> I sell ideas, and I'm successful at it. I am not a specialist. If you are an innovator, you don't have to specialize; you can hire a specialist. Others often come to me with problems. Generally, I can pull some information from my experiences or reading and give them a direction to follow in solving the problem. It doesn't always work out, but I'm able to help a large percentage of the time.

Another individual who played this role was David Jamison, a professor in a graduate school of business. Although Jamison worked closely with very few people, he probably had the most influence on the faculty and students in the department. His approach was clearly distinct, yet carefully thought out and very effective. Few worked in his department without feeling his influence directly or indirectly. The breadth of his approach and knowledge made it easy for him to explore different subjects and generate new insights. He was well known and highly respected throughout the university and was often invited to visit other departments, colleges, and universities.

If one were to spend any time in the organizations to which either of the men described above belonged, he or she would soon observe a number of nonmanagers who had a broad impact on the work, who were heavily involved in the development of others, and who interacted effectively with the external environment.

It was not as common to find idea leaders playing nonmanager, Stage III roles as it was to find informal mentors performing these functions. Our interviews included many mentors, and it was clear that they were making very important contributions. At a contract research organization, we interviewed a highly rated Stage III scientist. He pointed out that although he had never held a supervisory position, he had taught a high percentage of key people at the laboratory. Included among his "students" were the current director and associate director of the laboratory. He spent some time telling us what he tried to do:

> It's brutal to just let someone sink or swim in an outfit like this. I've seen too many new people turn bitter or dishonest because they don't know how to work in this business. Someone has to help them learn how to write in our kind of business and how to set up cooperative relationships. Until they

come here, no one has shown them how to do good science in the framework of contract research, how to butt-weld one project against another. I can teach them that because I had a good teacher.

It is evident that Stage III professionals perform vital activities for an organization, and that no organization could function effectively without a cadre of strong people at this level. It is also true that many professionals find it very difficult to move into that stage. A narrow specialty, an internal focus, or a failure to become involved in developing others, all may block professionals from Stage III. Organizational structures often make it difficult or impossible for nonmanagers to play Stage III roles. In this chapter, we have focused on the negative side as we looked at those situations that block movement. We also need to consider the positive aspects. We found many nonmanagers in Stage III.

In some companies as many as 65 percent of the people who were described as Stage III professionals were individual contributors. This large group of people did the work of Stage III without the benefit of management titles, private offices, or large budgets. In some ways, professionals can promote themselves into Stage III just by broadening out, dealing with those beyond their immediate unit, and helping people develop. The idea that one can actually create his or her own novation into the following stage is one of the most important concepts contained in this book.

And while such a novation into Stage III is vital and desirable, it is far from easy. Developing effective relationships is a crucial part of that transition, and we turn to that challenge in the next chapter.

4

Reciprocity

In the previous chapter, we discussed certain factors that block movement into Stage III or effective performance of Stage III functions. It is time to examine the other side of the coin. What does it take to be effective in Stage III? The key to this stage is reciprocity. An individual moves into Stage III by establishing and maintaining a complex set of exchanges with others. One side of the exchange is that of a mentor with one or more apprentices. The mentor provides resources, information, coaching, confidence, etc., to the apprentice in return for dependable assistance, information, and support. In addition, a mentor is usually involved with a person in Stage IV to whom critical support, information, and loyalty are offered in exchange for resources, visibility, and opportunity. In an effort to understand this complex network thus created, we will first consider the mentor/apprentice relationship. In Chapter 10 we will turn to the mentor/sponsor exchange.

MENTOR RELATIONSHIP

In Chapter 1, we briefly described the role of the mentor, pointing out that the mentor can assist the apprentice by providing training, knowledge of the informal system, challenging job assignments, and visibility. We return to that topic in this chapter because the relationship is central to high performance in this stage. While some of the same topics will be discussed again, this time we will approach them from the point of view of the mentor rather than from the perspective of the apprentice.

CHARACTERISTICS OF THE RELATIONSHIP

In recent years, there has been a great deal written about mentors and their importance in career development. Many managers have expressed an interest in setting up a formal mentor program so that all of their new employees get off to a good start in their careers. We are quite skeptical about formal programs, which involve assigning specific persons to become mentors, with others assigned to them. Our reservations come from an understanding of the complexity of the relationship. In our research, five characteristics of the mentor/apprentice relationship were identified that are helpful in understanding the nature of the exchange.

COMMON INTERESTS

During our interviews, we began to notice that common interests and shared nonwork activities were a definite part of the mentor/apprentice relationship. One pair, for example, enjoyed amateur carpentry and helped each other work on home additions. Another twosome shared a common interest in sports cars and went out driving together. Two accountants we observed never saw each other except at work, and all their conversations focused upon accounting; they shared a fascination with accounting theory and spent considerable time discussing it. The commonalities we observed covered a wide spectrum, ranging from basketball to computer technology to religion.

Why were common values and outside interests so prevalent in mentor/apprentice relationships? Some individuals, especially those who had never established a relationship with a mentor, were very critical of such associations. They suggested that it was a manipulation of company politics. From their point of view, such relationships were unfair, dishonest, and used by junior and senior members alike in a way that was illegitimate in an organization where they felt everything was supposed to be based on job performance alone. In one organization we studied, many of the engineers joked about the fact that under the old manager, a boating enthusiast, all those who were ambitious for promotion took up sailing. Later, when a new manager came in who liked golf, there was a sudden shift of interest from sailing to golf.

Undoubtedly, much of the criticism had validity. But there were a number of mentors who helped us understand why this phenomenon occurred so frequently. David Thomson, now a manager, made the following observation after a long conversation on the subject:

> It seems to me that to be able to talk casually with someone about things other than business—and maybe even associate with him off the job—opens the way to a more open business relationship. I've always found it easier to talk about business, and give advice and criticism to subordinates with whom I could also relate on some other level. Those are also the people whom I find it easier to trust and confide in. People think it shouldn't be that way, but it is.

Several supervisors and informal mentors made the point that professional criticism is a narrow area; a negative comment about someone's work is less likely to be taken as a "crushing blow" if the relationship between "critic" and recipient is multi-dimensional. Some things are easier to convey after a good golf game or tennis match than in an office. Mentoring relationships become more resilient, they said, when there are a number of dimensions and interests around which the exchange is built. Stage I and Stage III people who avoid such activities may do so to their own detriment.

At higher levels in the organization, we observed more reserve. Stage III professionals were more likely to explore common extra-work interests and engage in outside activities with those they mentored than with their Stage IV sponsors. One reason for this, of course, is that power becomes more of an issue in Stage IV; Stage IV directors must anticipate the day that they may have to withdraw their support from, or demote (or even fire) a subordinate.

EMOTIONAL BOND

Many of the people who described their mentor made statements like: "He was almost like a father," or "He was more like an older brother." The language of mother/daughter or older sister was less common because there were fewer women in our study. For many, the mentor/apprentice relationship was more like a family tie than a formal work relationship. As a result, there were often strong emotions involved that could prove to be helpful as the two people worked long hours together on major projects. The positive emotions caused the two people to look forward to being together and a commitment to one another was often established.

The negative aspect of such a bond occurred when the strong emotional relationship had outgrown its usefulness on a business level and needed to be severed or changed. We will return to that issue later in the chapter.

MUTUAL IDENTIFICATION

For many people, identification was a strong part of the relationship, and it often went both ways: The apprentice often identified with the mentor as someone whom he or she could look up to—use as a role model. We heard stories of the apprentice beginning to dress like the mentor or adopting some of the same mannerisms. On the other hand, mentors often selected apprentices that reminded them of themselves at an earlier age; or, it was not uncommon to hear statements like, "Doug is like the son I never had." The identification tended to intensify the relationship, and in some cases, make it more productive. In some instances, however, it got in the way of the team's work effort.

Voluntary Selection

In light of the three characteristics just discussed, it is not surprising to hear that mentors and apprentices are "selected" not "assigned." Many times it was natural for a boss to turn into a mentor, but that developed over time and didn't happen automatically.

In one of the companies that we studied, 65 percent of those interviewed indicated that they had had a mentor at some point in their career; other studies have reported similar percentages. The voluntary aspect of the selection process suggests that the formal assignment of mentors is not likely to be very successful.

Reciprocity

A dominant theme in the discussion of relationships was the idea of exchange. Both parties need to receive substantial benefits from the relationship if it is to endure. Because this exchange is so important, we will explore it in some detail in this chapter.

In listing these characteristics, we do not mean to imply that every mentor/apprentice relationship included all five of them. Obviously, some relationships are much stronger than others. Furthermore, the stronger relationships were not necessarily the most productive over the length of the relationship; sometimes the emotions or the identification got in the way of the productivity of the two people involved. Our point is that we found many people who had experienced the relationship, and it had impacted their careers. Next we want to look at the nature of the exchange between mentor and apprentice.

WHAT THE MENTOR BRINGS TO THE EXCHANGE

Provides Resources

Resources provided by the mentor are a basic part of the exchange between the mentor and the apprentice. In one sense, physical, financial, and human resources are provided by the organization as a whole. They are allocated or budgeted, however, only to those whom upper levels of management have come to trust. On the basis of this trust, persons in Stage III accept assignments or tasks for which they will be responsible, but that are larger, more complex, and time-consuming than they could perform alone. In some organizations, they may obtain contracts or new business single-handedly and, in cooperation with subordinates, bring in resources from the outside directly. Salary increases, equipment, assignments, and operating expenses, however, are usually obtained by negotiating with people inside the organization. Often this is done on the basis of the professional's reputation and past record, but it also requires that he or she engage skillfully in the budgeting process and in disdained "paperwork."

This, of course, raises the question of how anyone other than a person with outside contracts or direct budget responsibility (informal mentors or idea leaders usually have neither) could perform a Stage III role. The answer is that, in certain organizations, there are those who informally share in the obtaining and distribution of resources. Although they may not have formal budget responsibility, assignments and resources come to the organizational units to which they belong in large part because of their reputation for performance. Due to the intangible nature of this process, the informal system must be sufficiently powerful and well understood for their part of the exchange to be known and acknowledged.

We found wide differences in the way individuals performed the function of obtaining resources. In a meeting we held with six first-line supervisors, for example, all six agreed that their subordinates could be more productive in the long run and less vulnerable to obsolescence, if they could give them new or enlarged assignments. Five of the supervisors, however, spent most of the meeting discussing how difficult it would be to justify to top management any form of job rotation or enlargement because of short-term inefficiencies. However, Martin Lowe, the sixth supervisor, had found ways to rotate work among his subordinates and had already received authorization for a technician under one of his experienced engineers so that the latter could be training another while enlarging his own responsibilities. When we interviewed the subordinates of these supervisors, we were told that Lowe had greater influence over his people than any supervisor in the division, in large part because he was determined to obtain for his people the things they really needed. Repeatedly, we found highly rated Stage III people described as those who "knew how to squeeze the system" for logistical support and other resources.

INFORMATION

In addition to physical and financial resources, an individual in Stage III has access to information that others do not. Information on current happenings and future opportunities, and about how to get things done constitutes a valuable commodity that he or she brings to the exchange. A project leader in a research laboratory told us that this was one of the first things he learned when he began to be responsible for more than just his own efforts:

> Collecting and encouraging the sharing of information rapidly became an
> important part of my job. It took real time and effort. I found that a good

portion of my work was spent just keeping my people informed on the latest decisions made by top management and the latest opportunities in the company that might benefit them.

SHOWS INTEREST

Even with resources and information, it is difficult for one attempting to move into Stage III to establish a viable exchange with others unless they perceive that those other persons are genuinely concerned about their progress. This interest may be manifested in many ways, ranging from friendly, patient teaching to a gruff insistence that high standards of performance be maintained. The apprentice must be assured that the relationship is one in which both parties are to benefit, and that the association is reciprocal and not exploitive. We heard some interesting comments on the importance of this reciprocity in CPA firms, where teaching and training are assigned and more formalized than in most other professional organizations that we studied. Although the help was assigned, it never seemed to develop into productive interaction for both unless accompanied by genuine concern for the other's progress. One junior auditor told us earnestly:

> I would go to any length for someone who would come up to me 3 to 6 months after I had begun working for them on a job, and honestly and sincerely ask me how I was doing. If a guy has concern for me, I would stick my neck out to really help him.

We interviewed another young CPA whom we were told had excellent prospects in the firm and asked him what had been particularly important to his success to that point. He replied:

> The person who really helped me was a senior on a summer intern job. They needed someone to do ticking and tracing on a job 15 to 16 hours per day. I didn't like it and was about ready to quit when the senior recognized it. He got me off that activity and helped me see the entire picture. He took me out to dinner, sports, etc. and really helped me decide to stay. He was someone I could go to. I have never worked harder for anyone or learned more.

ROLE MODEL

A Stage III professional teaches, influences, and manages in large part by example, at least initially. What he or she has to communicate to others—how to operate effectively as a professional in an organization—is far too complex to put down in writing. Words cannot convey such subtleties. To teach effectively, a competent professional must share time and space with another, working through problems together. The learner gains much of what he or she will ever learn from the exchange by observation. In the early stages of one's career, a professional needs to model another; the areas of uncharted behavior are too vast to operate without some idea of how to proceed. Learning to play tennis, for example, is extremely difficult without seeing someone hit a backhand shot. Having watched someone hit the ball, however, a new player is forever influenced by what he or she has observed.

A division leader in a large, well-known research laboratory told us how he had become conscious of this need relatively late in his career. When we asked him how he tried to develop people, he replied:

> I found that a good way to help others develop was by setting an example. Before I came here, I had had no real guidance in my career. No one told me how important it was to write and give papers. But I was a finisher, and I like research. So on the basis of that, I was made assistant division leader after a number of years. I was 41 years old, and that year I first began to plan my own career. I saw that if we were going to compete for basic research funding, we were going to have to publish. I couldn't ask others to start publishing if I hadn't. So there I was, over 40 years old, giving my first paper. I was so nervous that I had to take tranquilizers. Soon we were all writing papers. Now we have a strategy of picking a big meeting and really hitting it. Several of us submit abstracts, then work like blazes to finish. We go in and dominate a meeting. The morale is high, and we are respected around here.

The mentor also plays a major role in establishing attitudes. One CPA in a large national accounting firm gave us the following reply when we asked who had played an important role in his development:

> The guy who has shaped my development most was the manager I worked under when I was first made a senior. He shaped my whole outlook toward clients and my job. In every area, the client came first over personal interest. If it meant working long hours, we worked long hours.

HIGH STANDARDS

When we asked people to identify those who had played a key role in their development, many replied that it was a formal or informal mentor who had set high but realistic standards for them. Meeting these standards had not only given them a sense of pride but had shaped their approach to work. For example:

I worked under one manager for 3 or 4 years. He had very high expectations; he just expected superior work. If I did sloppy work, he let me know. He surrounded himself with the best people in the place. We tried to keep up with him, and we have all done well since.

One man was critical in my development. He used to tell me, "You know you're good, I know it—but the world doesn't." He set objectives for me to publish, and then he'd read everything I'd write and raise hell in a helpful way. I became a fellow in the American Nuclear Society because he showed me what I needed to do.

CONFIDENCE

One of the critical commodities the Stage III professional brings to the exchange is confidence that the work will be accomplished successfully. The assurance that he or she "knows how" and can teach others what they need to know to assure a positive outcome, constitutes a part of the exchange with apprentice, clients, and sponsors. A young researcher told us:

One of the biggest things that Jim Francom (the project manager) does is to maintain our confidence that we are moving in a useful direction. Sometimes it's easy to feel like we are going down a blind alley and won't ever come up with anything. But when we have a meeting with him, I always come away feeling differently. Even when he can't suggest something right away to get us over the hump we are on, he has a steady confidence in the outcome that pumps us all up. We just have a lot of confidence in him so if he thinks we'll get there, I'm sure we will.

The importance of this function was demonstrated in an experiment undertaken in 1961 by Alfred Oberlander of the Metropolitan Life Insurance Company. Having noted that outstanding insurance agencies grew faster than others, Oberlander assigned his six best agents to the best assistant manager, an equal number of average producers with an average manager, and the remaining low producers with the least able manager. As Oberlander predicted, the top group increased dramatically in sales production and the bottom group actually declined. The "average" group, however, proved to be an anomaly. The manager assigned to that group refused to believe that either he or his subordinates were less capable than any other group, and challenged his people to outperform the top group. As a result, the middle group increased its productivity by a higher percentage than the top group (although it didn't attain as high a dollar volume). Sterling Livingston reported this experiment at some length, along with a series of studies that indicated that certain managers were consistently able to obtain high performance from subordinates while other managers were not (1). When Livingston was asked what accounted for these differences, he came to the following conclusion:

> The answer, in part, seems to be that superior managers have greater confidence than other managers in their own ability to develop the talents of their subordinates. Contrary to what might be assumed, the high expectations of superior managers are based primarily on what they think about themselves—about their own ability to select, train, and motivate their subordinates. What the manager believes about himself subtly influences what he believes about his subordinates, what he expects of them, and how he treats them.

COACHING

At the core of the exchange is the willingness of the mentor to teach the other party how to work effectively in the organization. This includes sharing information not only about the work but about the organization, and how to get things done through the system.

A good mentor must initially invest a substantial amount of time and energy, and willingness to accept a burden beyond the requirements of the normal work setting. One apprentice described what his mentor did:

> He spent a lot of time with me at first, trying to help me understand the work and the organization. In the beginning he would give me work and would explain in depth the nature of the task and specify what he wanted me to do, because everything was so new to me. At that time I was really quite helpless. I realized it, and so did he, and he took it upon himself to help me learn to work on my own by at first helping me get started and then monitoring my work as I proceeded.

To make sure an investment is worthwhile, the mentor anticipates that eventually he or she will gain time to explore new areas in greater depth. In that sense, the initial investment is a real risk. For some mentors, however, the satisfaction of teaching and the social exchange of information make the investment fairly satisfying immediately.

There are probably as many ways of coaching as there are coaches, and we haven't the space to discuss the coaching process here. But a number of characteristics surfaced repeatedly as professionals young and old described in various ways some critical person who had coached them. The effective coach:

- Takes time with you and explains things.
- Understands the system and knows the people.
- Shows you how to become a part of the system.
- Listens and thinks about your needs.
- Knows what you are doing and gives regular feedback.
- Emphasizes *why* you are doing something, as well as how to do it.

When we asked one highly rated accountant what had been the most important thing that had happened to him in his career to that point, he replied:

> Working under Jim Essig! He spent a lot of time with me. He gave me a lot of work and let me stumble along, but helped when I needed it. His critique was a learning experience; he never criticized my personality. Most of the staff felt he was a great trainer and not just a supervisor. He would let you do it and then come back with notes on things you had missed. He made you think it out first, try it, and then we would go over things I had missed. It was real luck that I got with him. He was the primary reason I was promoted so fast.

PROTECTION

This may well be the most controversial of the items listed as part of the mentor's exchange. It may seem paradoxical that a mentor may be working to make an apprentice highly visible, as described in Chapter 1, while protecting him or her at the same time. There are types of protection, however, that a mentor can legitimately be expected to provide and that only he or she can provide.

First, mentors must be willing to take public accountability for errors. Explicitly or tacitly, they have been a part of most decisions. When they turn out to be wrong (e.g., giving someone an assignment he or she can't handle), the mentor's position is strengthened if they publicly accept the responsibility. If they fail to do so, their ability to establish future relationships will be seriously impaired. A young engineer told us of such an instance and described the consequences:

> I had a supervisor last year who seemed to be interested only in his own career. He had the habit of suggesting that you do something, then if it turned out to be a mistake he'd avoid assuming responsibility for the error. In fact, this occurred once and I was nearly fired for what was really his mistake. I transferred as fast as I could, and those that are still there have grown very cautious. I personally question how long he'll last.

Innumerable decisions are made behind closed doors; and while a mentor cannot control them all, Stage I or II professionals are often completely dependent upon their mentors to speak in their behalf and protect their interests when decisions are made that affect them.

Another type of protection—against over-identification—is critical in an organization, but is seldom mentioned. Anyone who has remained in an organization long enough to reach Stage III realizes that conditions change, and that if another is too openly and publicly identified with someone, it may work to that person's detriment at some point. Therefore, he or she works to ensure that each apprentice begins to develop relationships with other key people as well.

CREATING EXPECTATIONS

In Chapter 1 we explored the contributions a Stage I professional must make to a relationship to make the exchange worthwhile for his or her mentor, including dependable help on detailed work, accessibility, availability, predictability, and loyalty. Therefore, we will not repeat that discussion here. What we did not discuss was the role of the mentor in signalling to the other party what he or she must supply to the exchange. Because of their social sensitivity and prior experience with mentors (in schools and at home, for example), some anticipate the needs of the mentor remarkably well. But there is almost always a need for training by the mentor at this point in the career. By word and deed, mentors must communicate what they expect and need. If they fail to do so, offering approval and resources before they are earned, and without receiving full reciprocity, they will do both parties a serious disservice. If mentors do not insist on competent performance and dedicated effort, they will have failed to teach their apprentices how to cope with the fundamental realities of organizational life. Apprentices will not feel that they must fully earn approval, attention, and rewards, thus losing respect for the mentor. Each of us has an innate sense of equity, and if either party feels that they have failed to contribute their full share to the exchange, a sense of guilt will alienate them from the other party.

BECOME A MENTOR, LEAVE A MENTOR

One of the natural but often painful things about moving into Stage III and becoming a mentor is that the process of doing so often radically transforms the relationship with one's own mentor. To be sure, the advancement to Stage II with its greater independence has already changed the relationship. Often, however, the rich association remains; the mentor still needs help. And the help of a Stage II professional can be more valuable since he or she may no longer need the instruction or the same kind of emotional support required earlier. The resources, information, and job assignments a mentor provides remain invaluable too, so a modified but tenable relationship often remains.

But moving into Stage III is a different matter. Part of the pressure to break the old mold completely comes from the fact that professionals in Stage III have competing demands from those whom they are beginning to mentor; and part of the pressure arises from feelings within. They feel strong needs to broaden themselves personally, to interact with the outside, and to take responsibility for others. They begin to feel irritated with others who give credit to the mentor solely, for work done jointly. They feel the need for a budget account to be able to provide resources for others. Growth begins to take new direction and a professional may be heard to make statements like, "It's just begun to dawn on me that Frank has been taking us in the wrong direction for the last few years."

Vaillant, in his analysis of the longitudinal data from the Grant Study of men's lives over a 30-year period, reported that by age 35, mentor relationships ceased to be important among their subjects (2). But usually there is more than just a loss of the old tie; there is a drift into indifference. Levinson and his colleagues at Yale report a period in the lives of their subjects, usually in the late thirties, when there is a strong inner thrust to "become one's own man."

During this time a person feels overly dependent on and constrained by persons who have authority over him or her. When this thrust begins, the mentor relationship ends. Levinson et al. report that:

> Sometimes it comes to a natural end, and, after a cooling-off period, the pair form a warm but modest friendship. It may end totally, with a gradual loss of involvement. Most often, however, an intense mentor relationship ends with strong conflict and bad feelings on both sides. The young man may have powerful feelings of bitterness, rancor, grief, abandonment, liberation, and rejuvenation. The sense of resonance is lost. The mentor he formerly loved and admired is now experienced as destructively critical and demanding, or as seeking to make one over in his own image rather than fostering one's individuality and independence (3).

In our study of people moving into Stage III in professional organizations, we found many of the same feelings reported by the subjects in Levinson's study. However, the process was often as painful for the mentor as for the person breaking away and starting into Stage III.

> In one research unit, the mentor, a famous researcher, wrote a report of the research that had been done under his direction. The young man whom he had been mentoring for a number of years and now had carried on much of

the field work with the help of two new people, suddenly objected vehemently to the interpretation placed on the data. He wrote a major section of the report with his own interpretation, and insisted that both versions be submitted to another senior researcher, without identification of authorship, asking him to judge between the two interpretations. The mentor was shocked, but he agreed. When the other senior researcher chose the challenger's interpretation, the younger man felt triumphant and vindicated. The relationship with his mentor, however, had been inalterably changed, and the study was completed with great strain. The research unit disintegrated, and no further collaboration was ever attempted between the former mentor and the young man whom he had considered "his most promising young colleague."

In smaller organizations, when the junior member of a mentor relationship is ready to move into Stage III and become his or her own person, one of the parties usually has to leave:

In a small tax firm that we studied, the proprietor of the firm had established a brilliant reputation and a lucrative practice. He had a number of accountants working for him, but he had never found anyone whose judgment he could trust to handle critical cases or major client relations. Finally, he found a young man trained in both law and accounting who had graduated first in his law class, and who seemed to be able to understand everything he taught him. For several years they worked together and as the young lawyer learned more and more, the "mentor" found himself free to travel and ski as he had always dreamed. The lawyer took over in his boss's absence and assumed the training of new people. Then the magic spell broke. The owner of the firm returned from one trip with a new idea for doing advance work on tax returns to relieve the last-minute pressure. When such suggestions had been made in the past, they were developed and implemented. Suddenly, the lawyer saw this idea as unworkable and impractical. When the owner insisted on trying it, the lawyer felt that his own position was being undermined, that the decisions were arbitrary and high-handed, and that the situation was intolerable. Within months, all plans for a gradual transfer of ownership were scrapped; the lawyer left, taking half the staff and clients with him.

Probably the most famous break-up of a mentor/apprentice relationship occurred between Carl Jung and his one-time mentor, Sigmund Freud.

As early as 1900, Jung had been heavily influenced by Freud's ideas, and over the years drew closer to learn what Freud had to teach him. In Jung's words, "Under the impress of Freud's personality I had, as far as possible, cast aside my own judgments and repressed my criticisms. . . . I had told myself, 'Freud is far wiser and more experienced than you. For the present you must simply listen to what he says and learn from him.'"

Freud meanwhile developed a strong attachment to Jung, indicating that he regarded Jung as his successor. He had told Jung in a letter that he had adopted him as an eldest son and crown prince. Jung, however, reached a stage in his career at which a continuation of this kind of relationship was no longer possible. Jung was in his late 30s and beginning to broaden his own interests in the direction of mythological history and collective historical archetypes, and their relationship to the individual psyche—a direction different from Freud's.

Jung was also dealing with the outside world himself; he was being invited to lecture in the United States, Britain, and elsewhere on his own. He was beginning to stimulate the development of others through his writing and lectures. Jung reports that he both anticipated and feared the break, months before it occurred. While working on a book, he began to write a chapter in which he found himself consciously taking issue with Freud: "For two months I was unable to bring myself to touch my pen, so tormented was I by the conflict."

Freud, likewise, was deeply troubled by the break. He had helped make Jung president of the International Psycho-Analytical Association and editor of its journal. During a psychoanalytic congress in Munich in 1912, when Jung took strong issue with Freud concerning a father complex, Freud slid off his chair in a faint. Jung picked him up and carried him to a sofa. Then, as Jung described it years later, "As I was carrying him, he half came to, and I shall never forget the look he cast at me. In his weakness, he looked at me as if I were his father." Whatever the truth of the event, the break between mentor and protégé was painful, perhaps inevitable, and certainly a powerful determinant of any future relations they may have had (4).

The example of Jung and Freud is useful to us as a public account of a phenomenon that occurs daily in dramatic or subtle ways among knowledge workers in organizations. The thrust toward becoming one's own person and the feelings of disappointment, betrayal, and ambivalent admiration for new-found confidence and independence are usually there in some form for both the old mentor and the advancing protégé. Thus, even when the transition to Stage III is fostered by the old mentor, the mentor relationship is gone. At best, the tie becomes that of sponsor and sponsoree; at worst, a relationship of bitter avoidance ensues. In any case, it is a time for moving on to new relationships and for conscious recognition of what has happened.

When the transition seems to have been smooth, one or both of the parties may fail to recognize that the shift has taken place. When this happens, the tension builds until both are forced to recognize it, or until an explosion occurs.

> In one organization we studied, Monte Black, a competent and aggressive department head, had hired and mentored Paul Schneider, an equally bright young researcher. Black accepted an attractive offer from a different organization, and Schneider took over the department and began hiring and training other new men. A few years later, Black was asked to come back as the director of the entire division. Schneider viewed his return with ambivalence. On one hand, he knew and was assured by Black that this would mean new and greater opportunities for him because of the confidence that Black had had in him. But Schneider knew that he had changed, and that his relations with others in the organization had likewise been altered in the meantime. When the return finally occurred, Black announced that Schneider, his old protégé, was to be the new associate division director. But meetings had unexpected moments of tension, and Schneider seriously considered leaving the organization because he could no longer play the old role. While he had been changing and establishing himself, they had not been together, and he found himself feeling resentment when he knew he was expected to feel gratitude. He questioned his own feelings and whether, in fact, Black was still treating him like one who needed mentoring or whether he was being oversensitive and counterdependent. Finally, Schneider decided that he must bring his feelings out into the open or resign. When he did discuss his concerns with Black, both were able to talk about the tension and the need to evaluate their relationship. They agreed to have a talk when feelings arose, and decided that Black would find an assistant to do some of the things he had been asking Schneider to do. Though the process of renegotiating took several months, the two men developed a new way of working together. They remained a strong and productive team, but a different kind of team. Schneider took a more independent hand in directing internal administration, and Black began to focus his energies on external relations.

In Chapter 2, we discussed the problems a professional experiences in moving from dependence to independence. That novation involves a significant change in the person's relationship with his or her mentor. The examples in this section have illustrated an even further separation from the mentor; in fact, in some cases, this transition marks a formal break, resulting in very little professional interaction thereafter. Some people, when reading about the pain involved in leaving a mentor, may be tempted to avoid even developing such a relationship. While this concern is understandable, it should be kept in mind that a relationship as intense as the ones we have described are likely to have some high peaks balanced by some equally low points as well. We are convinced that the potential for a very productive relationship is worth the effort involved in finding and working with a mentor as well as the risks of parting.

The mentor role has been our focus in this chapter because it is a complex and critical one. Some of those in managerial roles also play the role of mentor, and while the idea leader described in Chapter 3 is not likely to be a mentor, he or she may perform some of the functions thought to belong to a mentor (sharing information, role model, high standards, etc.). Thus, most of the information in this chapter should be useful to all those who aspire to move into Stage III. Next we turn to the rewards and dilemmas of Stage III.

5
Rewards and Dilemmas

In spite of the many difficulties of moving into Stage III and the complex relationships involved if one is going to be effective, most of the professionals that we interviewed were eager to make this move. What is it that attracts them? Although there are costs to be paid, there are clearly a number of benefits to be received from operating at the Stage III level, and we want to look at those next.

REWARDS OF STAGE III

We have already discussed the importance of the role to the organization. What does the Stage III professional receive for performing well?

INFLUENCE AND STATUS

Stage III brings an opportunity to expand one's influence in an organization and to try new ideas. Edgar Schein has suggested that the freedom to innovate does not move on a linear scale as one moves higher in the organization. Rather, shortly after one has moved from one stage or level to another, and before he or she begins to "bid" for advancement to the next, he or she enjoys a period of increased freedom and opportunity to try his or her wings, to change old ways, and to bring new life to the organization (1).

With increased influence comes the status and respect afforded those who have been entrusted with responsibility and to whom others come for direction and help.

ORGANIZATIONAL REWARDS

In the introductory chapter, we presented data pointing out that those who move into Stage III are likely to receive higher performance ratings. In fact, the difference is dramatic. The average performance rating in Stage II was the 37 percentile, but in

Stage III it was in the 67 percentile. Those higher ratings are also reflected in higher salaries and more challenging job assignments. Senior managers want the most capable professionals working on the most important assignments, which are usually also the most interesting. Higher performance ratings and challenging assignments are more likely to lead to opportunities for promotion. Overall, it is clear that more organizational rewards are available to the people in Stage III than to those who remain in Stage II.

GENERATIVITY

Erik Erikson, who has been more influential than any other single person in prodding us to think seriously about changing tasks and needs as we move through the human life cycle, points out that the central task of an adult is that of generativity—bringing along the next generation. The alternative, of course, is increased self-absorption. For many, this task can be met through the rearing of one's own family. But the genuine satisfactions that come from fostering the development of others can be easily extended into the 8 hours of a workday as one moves into Stage III (2).

JOB SECURITY

Although advancement into Stage III by no means eliminates career risks, we observed that during periods of layoffs, those in Stage III were far less likely than their junior colleagues to leave. Generally, Stage III professionals are regarded as more competent, but, perhaps more significantly, the organization has made a greater psychological investment in them. They have become more a part of the company "family." Gaining this security may be offset by having to leave one's technical roots, a price that must often be paid for this novation.

DILEMMAS OF STAGE III

What are some of the other costs that must be balanced against rewards in Stage III?

OWNERSHIP OF TIME

One of the dilemmas of moving into Stage III is that the network of exchanges that we have described dramatically affects the control over one's own time. Those who assume responsibility for others and their output must be available when they need direction or support. If inaccessible, one plays the role of mentor less well. Moreover, when taking responsibility for dealing with the external environment, he or she must be responsive to the needs and demands of maintaining such contact.

When we interviewed people about what they noticed most when beginning to move into Stage III, one of their most frequent responses was that their time was no longer their own.

> If I want to write out a report that's due soon I have to sit down on Sunday night and finish it because I can't be sure that I will have time at work to do it. When I was working alone, I could schedule my time and stick to it. Now there are a lot of people who have rights to my time.

CAUGHT IN THE MIDDLE

Another way of describing the complex set of exchanges of Stage III professionals with sponsors and bosses on one hand and those they are mentoring and supervising on the other, is that they are subject to the tugs of the proverbial "man [or woman] in the middle." Mentors must learn to cope with divided loyalties. If they are seen as only "looking upward," they will find it hard to maintain the loyalties of those working for them. At the same time, research shows that unless they have strong upward influence, they are likewise unable to effectively influence those working under their direction. The tension of these often conflicting demands were first studied and described in studies of foremen on the factory floor. In 1945, Fritz J. Roethlisberger wrote "The Foreman: Master and Victim of Double Talk" (3). It soon became a classic article on the seemingly impossible demands imposed on foremen from management, workers, technical specialists, and union representatives. In 1964, Robert Kahn and his associates completed a study on conflicting expectations felt throughout an organization, and found that they reach their greatest level in those middle levels of management occupied by those who perform the Stage III functions that we have described (4).

Both Roethlisberger and Kahn point out that much of the conflict arises from the fact that logics of the formal organizations do not take into account the informal organization and the social exchanges that we have described. Coping with these conflicts is one of the great challenges of a person at this stage in a career. It is interesting to see how well those coping mechanisms were described by Roethlisberger 30 years ago:

> In business (and in unions too) there are not only 'men of goodwill' but also men with extraordinary skill in the direction of securing cooperative effort. These men, at all levels, perform an "administrative" function, the impor-

tance of which is too little recognized. Much of their time is spent in facilitating the process of communication and in gaining the wholehearted co-operation of men. Many of them are not too logically articulate, but they have appreciation for a point of view different from their own. Not only can they appreciate the fact that a person can be different from themselves but, more important still, they can accept his right to be different. They always seem to have the time to listen to the problems and difficulties of the others. They do not pose as 'experts'; they know when to secure the appropriate aid from others.

Such 'administrators,' selfless and sometimes acting in a way which appears to be lacking in ambition, understand the importance of achieving group solidarity—the importance of 'getting along,' rather than of 'getting ahead.' They take personal responsibility for the mixed situations, both technical and human, that they administer. They see to it that the newcomer has an effective and happy relationship with his fellow workers, as well as getting the work out. Accomplishing their results through leisurely social interaction rather than vigorous formal action, more interested in getting their human relationships straight than in getting their words and logics straight, more interested in being 'friendly' to their fellow men than in being abstractly 'fair,' and never allowing their 'paper work' to interfere with this process of friendliness, they offer a healthy antidote to the formal logics of the modern factory organization previously described (5).

LEAVING ONE'S TECHNICAL ROOTS

We have talked about the problems that technically trained people can have moving from Stage II into Stage III because they don't understand the importance of Stage III functions to the organization or how to perform them. But there is also a genuine reluctance to leave one's technical roots even when a person clearly understands the significance of Stage III. For some, this stems from the freedom of movement they feel that they lose by moving away from their technical specialty. As one manager put it:

> I've learned to run programs and meet deadlines. I have a multi-disciplined group and have become a generalist. In some ways that's helped me, and in some ways it hasn't. It would be hard to go back and compete with a guy who has become the world's expert in an area. If this laboratory closed up, it would be hard to move laterally. I've tied my career to this lab.

Fear of reduced mobility, in part, makes people hesitant to leave their technical roots, but it is usually deeper than that. Some kind of unexplainable tie holds them to the technical work in which they have been so deeply involved. We heard statements like the following:

> I planned to spend 10 to 12 years in engineering. Now I'm at the twelfth year, and I am not sure that I'm ready to move away from technical work.

> No one was qualified to be group leader so I applied for the job and got it. I've done that for 6 years. Now I find myself at a real decision point for some reason. Should I go on in management or go back to physics. I thought I had made the decision, but something keeps bringing me back to it.

As we tried to understand the ambivalence that these professionals felt, we kept encountering statements reflective of what Daniel Levinson and his colleagues at Yale have come to call "The Dream" (6). As we talked to these people who feel the conflict most, they told us of what they had imagined themselves to eventually become during their high school, college, and graduate school years. It was "The Dream" that drove them on through the difficult courses and long hours of study. "The Dream" contained not only the math, the science, the laboratory, and the dedication to the pursuit of truth rather than money and power, it also had hero figures who embodied those values. "The Dream" is hard to dismiss or change radically.

One of the authors of this book spent a number of years studying a group of 170 managers and scientists at a development laboratory of a large United States corporation. He studied the values of those who were planning to make their contribution from positions of management. About half of these men identified more strongly with economic and pragmatic values. He labeled these men "oriented" managers because of the congruence between their stated values and the tasks of a manager in an industrial development center in which the major task was developing large-scale and less costly production methods. The other half of the managers, however, identified with the pure values of science. The author called this group "conflicted" managers, because of the incongruence between their values and their chosen role. The differences in the two groups were interesting. Although the superiors of the "conflicted" managers saw more potential in these men than in the "oriented" managers, the "oriented" managers reached higher levels with regard to position and salary. More importantly, no matter how well they had done by objective measures, "conflicted" managers, especially the older ones, expressed significantly greater dissatisfaction with the way their careers had turned out and with what they had done with their lives, than did the older "oriented" managers. There was some evidence that their subordinates had been more innovative and received more patents than those of the "oriented" managers; but this had not translated into satisfaction for these "conflicted" managers themselves, for whom leaving their technical roots had exacted a severe cost (7).

For some people with professional training, moving away from one's technical roots presents no problem. Many have planned to enter management eventually, since early in their college careers. A survey among Ph.D. candidates in Chemical Engineering at Cornell University indicated that 77 percent were expecting to go into management jobs even at that time. For many people—the "oriented" managers, for example—technical training is regarded as an effective means of moving into business and management.

For others, however, technical and professional work has an emotional and intellectual appeal that is not easily dismissed. The further they move away from it, the more uncomfortable and unhappy they become. They move into certain management jobs and find them stressful and boring, often because they cannot see the intellectual challenge in that type of work. When this occurs, the question is whether they will have to return to Stage II, or whether they can find a role with a strong technical component in which they can still exert a broad influence without holding a supervisory position. The following example falls somewhere between these two alternatives:

> In one research laboratory we visited, a chemist had developed a product that was reported to have earned the company one hundred million dollars. In large part, because of this success, the chemist was made the manager of a department. He stayed in this position for several years, feeling increasingly less successful and less satisfied. Finally, he came to the director of the laboratory and tendered his resignation. He had decided, he said, to build a laboratory in his basement and work at home. If he came up with anything, he'd like to be able to come to them to sell a patent. Management countered with a proposal that he work at home but that he be paid a salary, that they help him equip the laboratory, and that any patents or discoveries become the property of the company with the usual bonus if something became a large commercial success. Under this arrangement, once a week he came into the lab and discussed ideas and problems with key people.

As a third alternative, professionals can find or create a supervisory role that allows them to keep themselves heavily involved in the professional work, which means so much to them without failing in the supervisory work. We found a number of Stage III people struggling to do just that. One of those, Bill Rivers, described both his feelings and efforts as follows:

> I assumed when I came here that being a good scientist was all that was necessary. I later found that science was more than just research. You have to conceive, sell, and direct a program. I began to do all those things and found myself in management mainly because I didn't want to work for the other guys they were considering. I want to stay close to technical work and

maybe move back into it. Because I know it is difficult to move out of management into technical work, I have stayed close to my field, written papers, and still consider myself a scientist.

Some supervisors actually make effective use of their position to remain involved and up-to-date in technical work, by developing mentor relationships with young, recently trained professionals:

> I have a young man working with me now. He has a knowledge of the latest technology, and I have the experience. We learn a lot from each other. It's an effective way for me to avoid obsolescence.

Some people can successfully keep one foot in each camp, but only with considerable effort. The truth that must be faced is that if professionals have strong technical roots and also a desire for management responsibilities, they must learn to accept and cope with conflicts—which may be stronger than even they suspect.

REMAINING IN STAGE III

For many persons, Stage III provides a satisfying combination of activities. Remaining in the stage indefinitely, however, presents new problems, as well as some genuine satisfaction if these challenges are handled successfully.

LEVELING OFF OF REWARDS

For those who remain in Stage III very long, increases in salary and other rewards begin to level off. Although they may have attained a salary that allows a comfortable lifestyle, the stabilization of rewards can be disquieting. They see former peers attending meetings to which they are not invited, being admitted to executive bonus programs, having larger offices, and being given country club memberships. Being passed over for these perks can symbolize failure to those who interpret it that way.

REDUCED FEEDBACK

Although they may continue to perform as well or better than before, as they remain in Stage III longer, the amount of feedback received from others diminishes. The longer they stay at the same level, the more uncomfortable it is for superiors to discuss their performance or future. If superiors are pleased with their work, they hesitate to say so because they fear raising the question of why they are not being promoted. If they are less than pleased, their reasons have probably been discussed many times before, without success. Superiors also gradually become younger relative to Stage III professionals' own age and experience and find it uncomfortable to discuss performance. They, in turn, must resist reading into a smile or a conversation more than it is supposed to mean.

DISPARITY CRISIS

While professionals may be pleased with their accomplishments and enjoy the work, at some point, those who remain in Stage III are confronted by the disparity between actual attainments and certain aspirations that have grown up, partially hidden from consciousness. Arriving at the day when professional horizons are no longer unlimited, and learning to live with that fact, often requires far more emotional energy than they ever anticipated. Usually this is even more difficult for the nonsupervisory Stage III people because their position has fewer visible symbols of attainment.

BLOCKING OTHERS

One of the dilemmas for Stage III professionals who remain at that level for long periods of time is that others see them (and they see themselves) as blocking the progress of younger people in the organization. Their own position is not opening up for those below; yet it's more than that. When they first move into Stage III, the prospect exists that they will be able to carry their subordinates upward in the organization. As this prospect diminishes, several things happen. Others, for example, may be less likely to look to them for mentoring. They may also be more reluctant to mentor, fearing that the apprentice's prospects for mobility might be better with another mentor. Finally, they must learn to see those they had mentored leave and attach their loyalties elsewhere.

None of these challenges, however, is insurmountable and, in fact, can be turned to their advantage. Those who have accepted the fact that they have reached the ultimate level from which they are going to exert influence in the organization can often invest more of their energies in fostering the careers of beginners. We met a young woman in a large bank who was looking for just such a person. She said she was looking for a "professor of credit," who could teach her the credit analysis skills that she knew she was going to need as she rose higher in the organization. Competent women were advancing rapidly to upper management positions, and she could anticipate the same thing happening to her. But she had seen that other women had arrived at those positions without the critical analytical skills that she wanted to obtain from a long-term Stage III banker.

Stage III long-termers often have the patience to spend time imparting what they have learned and the security to spend time doing so. They may well have reached the age at which they can take an unselfish and parental interest in the progress of others, as well as a genuine pride in what happens to those they have coached. Researchers at one large company we visited told us that someone had done a study to determine the career paths of the top executives of the company. To their surprise, a large portion of them had all worked for one particular man at some point in their careers.

SHIFTING SANDS

One of the most serious dilemmas involved those who had performed successfully in Stage III for a number of years, but because of poor planning or changing circumstances found themselves unable to continue in Stage III and ill-equipped to return to Stage II. For instance, we encountered professionals who had been made project heads on aerospace projects, obtaining commendable results from their work. They stayed with the project so long, however, that the technology and their own technological base became outdated. When the assignment ended, they were no longer considered candidates to head new projects, and found themselves at a serious disadvantage competing with junior engineers for positions as individual contributors on new projects.

The aerospace industry with its fast-moving technology, however, was not the only place we found the phenomenon:

> Darwin Nance, with a Master's Degree in Chemical Engineering, progressed in the Chemical Engineering Department to the level of assistant director. After a few years, he was transferred to head up a multi-disciplinary, long-term project that dealt with chemical engineering problems but later came to deal mainly with information dissemination. The project lasted for 5 years and as the funding declined, the project was transferred to the economics department and finally phased out. Nance found himself with nowhere to go. He could not return to the Chemistry Department—technology had passed him by. He was out of place in the Economics Department, since he had no formal training in the field and very little real experience along those lines. Partially as a result of this, he suffered an emotional breakdown and was off work for almost a year. Upon his return, he was again assigned to the Economics Department. He continued to receive psychiatric help but to little avail. Many people felt Nance had the capability of being an excellent researcher, but the experience of leading a major multi-disciplinary project and then being left in a 'no-man's' land had apparently convinced him never

116

again to take a leadership role. He is 50 years old and at a high salary level. The Economics Department had no spot for him and no longer wished to carry him on the payroll, as project leaders could not afford to use him. The technical departments could get little from him since he had come to consider himself an economist. No one knew what to do with him, and this knowledge put even greater emotional pressure on him.

Stage III professionals can lose their viability in a number of ways. We encountered a case in which an experienced engineer was assigned to act as project head of one of the largest contracts the company had ever received. The project was an early success, and the system being produced under the contract was so well received that offers of later generations of the system were received in annual contracts. The project head's major function was coordinating work from various departments to deliver the final product. "Familiarity," however, "bred contempt," and departments often delayed their obligations to this old reliable contract for new opportunities and more demanding customers. The project head found himself having to intervene personally to correct production problems, to reject the work of one or another of the divisions, or to go over the head of the division manager from time to time to meet deadlines. In the process, he became discouraged and his relationships with both the customer and the supplying divisions deteriorated. The customer demanded an improvement in the management of the project. Although the project head had devoted his entire professional attention to the project for 10 years, his engineering skills were rusty and his relationships with the staff had worsened to the point that he could find no other work in the organization. He was put on early retirement, disappointed and embittered.

STAYING PUT OR MOVING OUT

What do professionals do when a long-term Stage III career begins to deteriorate? As we mentioned earlier, such persons are relatively unlikely to be laid off unless there are broad layoffs throughout the organization. Usually their performance ratings over the years have been fairly high and now with age legislation placing persons over 40 in a protected class, they are even less likely to be fired than before. Nevertheless, they can find themselves feeling unwanted and unappreciated. Responsibilities may begin to be taken from them, and they may find themselves shifted from one poor assignment to another. How do they react?

We have seen some move away from all Stage III activities and go back to what they call "working in the trenches." They try to work out a renewed technical career for themselves, and, for some, this works reasonably well. One man, for example, after having had a heart attack, decided that what he really enjoyed was being creative. No matter what mundane assignment he was given, he tried to find a way to do something creative with it. If his new ideas found no use in his own division, he passed them on to people in other divisions. He very seldom received credit for his innovations, according to his supervisor, but found the personal gratification of such activity sufficient to continue.

Most others who returned to Stage II work adjusted less well and often reported, with a certain amount of resignation, that they were waiting out their years to retirement. Many felt trapped by their age, retirement benefits, and family constraints to stay where they were. A number were fulfilling Stage III or IV roles in civic, neighborhood, or church organizations, however, and this helped fill the void.

Others, often after painful reappraisal, decided that they would use the contacts they had built over the years and move forward into something else rather than remain in a structure in which they no longer fit. Several aggressively and successfully sought positions in other divisions where they could use the Stage III skills they had developed over the years.

One man had remained active in a professional association and knew a great many people in his field. Even though he was not completely up-to-date on the latest developments, he decided to try consulting in areas he knew well. He examined his financial situation, and concluded that he could live reasonably well on an early but reduced pension even if his consulting didn't do well. When he made the break, however, his many contacts helped him greatly, and he was soon making more money than he had in his old job. Once again, he felt needed and respected.

An engineering supervisor whose group had merged into another, leaving him feeling stranded, went into building contracting with a neighbor. In another case, a former Stage III idea leader who found himself with a new supervisor who didn't respect him or know how to use his abilities, decided to buy an apple farm in New England where he had been reared. In both instances, the decision to change was made only after long nights of soul searching, but each man reported that he felt at last he was moving forward, after months of being "in limbo" in his old organization.

Because the rewards in Stage III are greater than those in previous stages, most people are eager to make such a move. However, this stage also presents a number of dilemmas, including the ownership of time, pressures from above and below, and moving away from one's technical roots. Many people reach Stage III at a fairly young age and are faced with some difficult choices. To remain in Stage III indefinitely, one must recognize the dilemmas of doing so and find ways of coping with them. Those who return to Stage II, for the most part, find that a difficult transition. A small group move on to Stage IV, and we will describe their activities and challenges in the next five chapters. Finally, a few decide to leave their current profession and pursue a variety of other activities. The challenges that these latter people face will be pursued in a later chapter entitled, "A Different Drummer."

Stage IV

6

The Director Stage

Right after World War II, a moderate-sized consulting firm was getting back into full operation. At that time it was about the size of one of its competitors—Booz, Allen and Hamilton. The three partners who headed the firm had strong reputations and good lists of clients. Several principals were hired to supervise, on a day-to-day basis, the consulting projects that the partners managed. After a year of renewed operations, two of the principals asked to meet with the partners to make some recommendations. They pointed out that several competitor firms were beginning to expand and become national in scope. Their own firm already had several competent principals who could manage consulting jobs. There was also a good supply of professionals readily available to hire and train. These principals pleaded with the partners to be allowed, along with the other principals, to manage the projects so the partners would have time to formulate a national strategy, seek more clients, and broaden the firm's base of operation. The partners assured the principals that they were aware of these options, and that they would give serious consideration to these recommendations when several big projects were completed. Yet each of the partners persisted in the details of current and subsequent projects. The firm didn't grow, and eventually broke up.

In one sense, the above is a story of individual choices or failures, but it is also a story of an organizational failure. It illustrates a lack of understanding and appreciation for a set of individual roles and functions that are vital to the vitality and growth of an organization. The roles or functions we refer to are not performed by people in the three career stages we have examined so far.

These functions are performed by people who had moved into what we have come to call Stage IV. Those who had moved into this stage were the ones who had demonstrated the capacity and had been entrusted by others to act for the organization. When we entered an organization or a large subdivision of an organization, it was not immediately apparent to us who had moved into Stage IV. It was rarely one person. An examination of the organizational structure was sometimes helpful, but never sufficient. Some individuals in Stage IV did not hold traditional management titles, while some managers with high-level titles had clearly not moved into Stage IV. However, there was usually rapid and general agreement among people we interviewed concerning who the Stage IV individuals were in their organization.

But gaining agreement on who the Stage IV people were and understanding in any depth what it was these people did that distinguished them from others were two different things. When we asked managers and professionals to help us understand what sets Stage IV individuals apart from those in other stages, they usually began by mentioning unique abilities, personality characteristics or character attributes. As we looked into each situation more deeply, however, we found that personality and character traits did, indeed, play a part in either blocking or facilitating an individual's novation into Stage IV. But what fundamentally separated Stage IV individuals from others was the fact that they performed a set of functions that were vital to the organization's maintenance and growth.

We pursued several different strategies to gain an understanding of these functions. Professionals and managers in over two dozen organizations whose major functions were performed by professionals were interviewed. We asked groups of high-level managers and professionals in some of the country's largest banks, research laboratories, and manufacturing organizations to describe the most important functions performed by individuals in their organization who had moved beyond Stage III(1). The document on staff advancement of one of the largest management-consulting firms in the world was studied(2). We were given a document written by the academic vice president of a large university describing the functions that deans of the major colleges in the university were expected to perform(3).

In our examination of these interviews, group discussions, and documents, it became apparent that Stage IV individuals basically perform four interconnected but conceptually distinct functions for the organization: providing direction, exercising power, representing, and sponsoring key individuals.

STAGE IV FUNCTIONS

PROVIDING DIRECTION

Individuals in Stage IV play major roles in providing direction for the whole, or at least a significant part, of the organization to which they belong. This does not mean that they originate all the ideas or make decisions single-handedly. On the contrary, much of the critical information and many of the ideas that guide the organization come from those who are dealing more intimately with clients and operations. But those in Stage IV draw together and distill critical information. They integrate the data and ideas of others with their own to form maps of the organization's environment, highlighting the opportunities and dangers that their maps reveal. They envision for themselves and for others the unique capabilities, and the "distinctive competencies," of their organization. Finally, they articulate and demonstrate through their actions a sense of direction that guides the actions of other members of the organization.

EXERCISING POWER

By nature, organizations involve the joint efforts of various individuals and groups. These individuals and groups often have independent plans and different priorities. Each individual in the organization has some potential to influence these outcomes differently. One of the unique characteristics of individuals who have moved into Stage IV is their skill in the exercise of power. In order to be in Stage IV, they have had to demonstrate that they are willing and capable of using the power at their disposal to take action responsibly and to influence others' decisions toward satisfactory ends for the organization. They initiate, request, review, set agendas, persuade, assign, and design their own and others' time in order to get decisions made and work done that will benefit the whole organization. They have informal access to other significant decision-makers and to formal meetings where decisions are finalized. They use this access to obtain resources, assignments, and approval for those who are dependent on them to do so.

REPRESENTING INTERNALLY AND EXTERNALLY

Stage IV people build and maintain complex networks inside and outside the organization in order to gather and share information, contacts, and resources. Formally and informally they represent the organization to its essential publics. They usually work at the interface with critical organizations, whether they are key clients, government agencies, regulatory bodies, scientific communities, or financial sources. They have also developed relationships with a broad cross-section of employees inside the organization with whom they maintain contact as they have moved up in the organizational structure.

SELECTING, SPONSORING AND DEVELOPING KEY PEOPLE

Those in Stage IV consciously select and sponsor key individuals who, in their opinion, have the capacity to make significant current and future contributions to the organization. This sponsor relationship is different in both focus and depth from the mentor relationship of Stage III. The sponsor provides opportunities and experiences of greater responsibility for those individuals who have already proven themselves in the basics. Though the direct one-on-one teaching process of the mentor is not characteristic of sponsors, they still build reciprocal relationships to support and "groom" people for key positions in the organization.

A SEAMLESS GARMENT

Of course, these four functions are not independent of one another. In practice, the four functions that we have described are often inseparably linked, overlapping and interconnected. If someone is going to have an impact on the direction of the organization, that person cannot be far removed from the exercise of power. Ideas need to be advocated and defended, individuals need to be persuaded, support needs to be sought and given. Anyone who is able to give useful direction to the organization needs access to the kind of information and knowledge that can only be obtained through a wide range of contacts outside as well as inside the organization. Usually that kind of familiarity with the organization's capabilities comes only through staying in contact with a network of individuals in various parts of the organization. In addition, most of one's power and influence are gained through the support of people whom one is sponsoring, and, to be an effective sponsor, one must have power.

Frequently we had individuals tell us that they had had to learn to perform one of these functions more effectively in order to improve their performance of another function:

> One chief accountant explained to us that he constantly felt that he lacked influence in the division because he had little to offer in planning discussions. In several evaluations, the division director had said that he was disappointed because this man had had so little to contribute in these particular discussions. The chief accountant told us that he finally concluded: "I had to develop my staff more so I could concentrate on where we are going instead of where we had been. Ever since I realized that, things have improved. It has given me more time to myself to think about our contribution to the overall effort." While the director couldn't pinpoint where

his chief accountant's problem lay, he could tell him that he was not making enough of a contribution to planning. The chief accountant had to discover for himself that his problem lay first in his failure to develop his own people.

But interlinked or not, these four functions seem deceptively simple. Why shouldn't most intelligent individuals be able to perform them? Most highly trained professionals have spent much of their lives mastering every system that they have entered. They have been the best and the brightest in high school, college, and often graduate school. They are the ones who could handle the technical subjects that intimidated everyone else; they have been the systems experts. Many have also shown great promise in earlier stages, only to find themselves unable to move into Stage IV. Why should this part of the organizational career system prove to be any different? What's the truth behind the old saw that "there are plenty of people in their twenties that seem like they would be great presidents, directors, and managing partners, yet so few of them in their forties"? Why is this transition into Stage IV the most elusive and difficult to achieve?

As the reader may have guessed, making the novation into Stage IV is complex, frustrating, and often lonely. Reading, or writing, about these four functions is much simpler than performing them. Convincing other key people that you will be able to perform them ably can be even more difficult. We shall be exploring separately each of the functions and the obstacles to their performance. Some of the blocks to those who are attempting to move into Stage IV are the inaccurate stereotypes that we hold about those who direct and shape organizations. We feel that it is important to examine and challenge some of these stereotypes before we go further.

STEREOTYPES VERSUS REALITIES

As we began studying Stage IV individuals, there were some substantial differences between what we found in reality and the popular stereotypes.

MORE THAN ONE DIRECTOR

There may be organizations where the mythical, all-powerful chief drives the organization alone, according to the plan that he or she has devised, but they were not among the organizations that we studied. As we shall discuss later, there were differences among the organizations that we studied as to the proportion of employees who were playing Stage IV roles and the types of positions from which it is possible to play such roles. In all the organizations that we studied, when we described the career stages model and asked professionals and managers to tell us who has moved into what stages, there was always a group of people, mentioned by nearly everyone, as having moved into Stage IV. These individuals were not isolated but usually had contact with one another in formal and informal settings. Some met with one another on a more regular basis than did others, but they always composed a loose confederacy. Far from being a simple pyramidal structure directed entirely by one person at the apex, they reminded us of the "dominant coalitions" described so well by James Thompson (4).

NOT JUST AN INTERNAL FOCUS

One stereotype about those who direct organizations is that they remain largely within the organization to manage others; that they send out the salesmen to see customers, geologists to find oil, and the purchasing agents to get new supplies. Our observations disabused us of this stereotype very quickly. If anything, people in Stage IV tend to be away from the premises of the organization more than those who are in other career stages.

In one research center for a large petroleum company, the director of research and his three division directors were gone well over half the time during the 3 months of our study there. They were negotiating for exchanges of technology for possible joint drilling operations in several foreign countries; they were visiting small firms that the company was thinking of acquiring and arranging to fund research at several universities. They went to dozens of meetings and made on-site visits at various locations in the operating divisions.

In the CPA firms and management-consulting organizations that we studied, the major part of "practice development," as the accounting firms call new business development, falls on the shoulders of the Stage IV people: the managing partner, or other partners. The stereotype of the stay-at-home executive seems to be more the exception than the rule.

It reminded us of the paradox of aerial combat in modern warfare. In former times the enlisted men have fought on the front lines, while the officers have often stayed out of range and directed operations from behind the lines. Now the officers are the pilots and the ones in combat, while the enlisted men stay out of range at the bases or carriers. In organizations composed of professionals, where information is the vital commodity of exchange, the critical boundaries and interfaces are overseen by individuals in Stage IV.

NO "ONE-MINUTE MANAGERS"

Another stereotype for which we found no counterpart among the Stage IV managers we studied was the image of managers who have raised delegation to such a "fine art" that there was little or nothing for them to do. In these wishful "one-minute" fantasies, there is nothing for managers to do but hear reports once a week on what their subordinates have done, give praise or reprimands when appropriate, and to work on their golf game. The simplicity of this pastoral model of the manager's world was not replicated in any of the lives of the Stage IV managers whom we studied. Many were excellent delegators who chose competent people and entrusted them to make decisions in their own areas of responsibility. But that still did not leave these Stage IV managers with "time on their hands."

As we pointed out earlier, they spent a large part of their time representing the organization to outside people, gathering and dispensing information, and updating their views of the environment in which they and their competitors operate. A great deal of time was spent with people other than their direct subordinates, exchanging ideas about the organization's opportunities and capabilities. They found resources for people with promising ideas, and worked with peers to find new opportunities and assignments for their people. Managing subordinates was seen as an important part, but only a part of their job; it was only one of the multiple relationships with people they had to manage. Their relationships with parties outside the organization, as well as with networks of people inside the organization, also needed careful management.

FEW "MOBILE MANAGERS"

Neither did our Stage IV professionals match the stereotype of the mobile managers who had job-hopped from one company to the next in order to get into positions of influence. Instead, most of them had worked for one or two organizations, spending most of their career in one industry or profession. They knew the industry well and had performed well in Stage III, most often in the same company in which they were currently employed. Our findings, in this regard, paralleled those of John Kotter (5).

In the early years of our investigation, we did a study to see what effect high or low performance ratings had on those engineers and engineering managers leaving their companies. It was the group whose performance ratings fell in the middle third, not the top third, who were most likely to leave the company, looking for better opportunities and greater appreciation. The top third were less mobile. (The least likely to move voluntarily were those in the bottom third.) The Stage IV individuals whom we interviewed usually said that they had found a great deal of challenge and many opportunities in the companies for which they currently worked.

NOT ALL "BUSINESSMEN"

Another stereotype about those who direct organizations is that they all had financial or marketing training, probably with an MBA from Harvard or Wharton. In some industries, such as banking and management consulting, this stereotype was more likely to fit our group of Stage IV people. But even in these industries, a surprising number of the individuals in Stage IV have legal, technical, or liberal arts degrees. Over half the managers in the United States are engineers, and we found many Stage IV engineers in our study. We also found many Stage IV lawyers, accountants, editors, and scientists. The dean of the Harvard Law School used to claim it had produced more company presidents than had the Harvard Business School. The president of M.I.T. would usually join in the public debate and claim that a higher proportion of M.I.T. graduates were presidents or vice presidents of the organizations to which they belonged, than was true of Harvard (or any other university for that matter). Though we do not have data to support these claims, our sample of people who had reached Stage IV could certainly not be used to deny them.

NOT ALL MANAGERS

The view that those who direct organizations are all managers is another common stereotype. While in some organizations and industries it is difficult to perform Stage IV functions without at least having the title of manager, in the organizations that we studied, we found that there were a variety of roles played and titles held by those who performed these functions. While titles vary widely, we were able to categorize the roles played by people in Stage IV into a fairly small set: managers, program directors, internal entrepreneurs, and idea innovators. These four roles were not mutually exclusive. Some individuals simultaneously played all four roles. But we can understand these different roles better if we first look at Stage IV people who have played only one of them.

Manager

In the organizations that we studied, about 75 percent of the people in Stage IV were managers. This is not surprising, since many organizations consider activities such as allocating resources, identifying key people, and dealing with persons outside the organization to be exclusively management functions. Conversely, we found that not all managers described to us were in Stage IV. In our study, over 40 percent of the people with the title of manager were actually in Stage III. Some managers lacked the opportunity to move into Stage IV. Other managers had the opportunity but found it hard to pull back from detail work long enough to undertake Stage IV activities.

In public accounting firms, for instance, certainly not all partners were in Stage IV. Many accountants view partnership status as the ultimate achievement during the early part of their career. But as one partner noted:

> Entrance into the partnership is just like reaching the foothills, compared with the real mountain. It's a new world in some ways, and I am just beginning to see what I'm going to have to learn in order to have any influence around here.

In nearly every public accounting office, the "managing partner," or the "partner-in-charge (P.I.C.)," was described to us as being in Stage IV, as were the divisional and national managers. In the larger offices, most of the line partners who managed a specialization were also described to us as having moved into Stage IV and performing Stage IV functions.

PROGRAM MANAGER

In some organizations, especially where the organization is based on a matrix structure, we found that some program directors had moved into Stage IV. This usually occurred when some program was of such importance and urgency to the organization or a client that large amounts of money were involved and the program had high priority. Someone of stature and skill was needed to deal with the client group, to assure them that their ends were being met, as well as to coordinate with the division, laboratory, or plant heads, from whom the program had to obtain on a nonpermanent basis both people and facilities.

When we went into a world-famous research organization, we were told:

> In my view, the senior project guys are clearly in Stage IV. Their projects are usually high visibility, high cost, high risk, or technically very difficult. When they screw up, the whole organization suffers. There is national interest, either positive or negative, in their projects. These people have a very strong influence on the internal and external system of this place. You might not think they have a lot to do with developing people, but they do. They find and develop people to work with them, and a successful or unsuccessful stint with one of them can make or break someone's career around here.

INTERNAL ENTREPRENEUR

There were a few people in several organizations who were sometimes admiringly, sometimes begrudgingly, described as being in Stage IV, whose roles could never be made more explicit than "entrepreneur," "super salesperson," or "maverick." As the need for innovation has increased in the last few years, the most positive term used to describe these people is product champion or product sponsor. They had titles ranging from manager to individual contributor, but the role they played brought together resources, money, and people to pursue an idea that may or may not have been theirs initially, but which they sponsored and kept alive. They often exerted an important influence on the direction of the organization, but frequently they did so at some risk to their own careers. One such professional, who was described by many as being in Stage IV, sums up his position:

> I had an idea for a new product area but was getting very little support through formal channels. So I talked to a couple of people on my own level and convinced them that it was a good idea. We went ahead and did it. Today it is bringing in a significant part of our sales. Luckily, it worked out all right for all of us.

In several universities, we had some of these internal entrepreneurs pointed out to us. They are able to attract large research grants and competent professionals. Several of them have established major institutes.

IDEA INNOVATOR

We found a fourth type of Stage IV individual in certain kinds of organizations who was clearly valued and rewarded accordingly by the organization. In their purest form, these idea innovators were neither managers nor entrepreneurs. Their influence was not brought to bear on the organization through persons they supervised. Their influence came from the force, the intellectual clarity, the disciplined and informed originality, and, above all, the utility of their ideas.

Their ideas, intellectual breakthroughs, discoveries, and new constructs had clearly helped to shape the future of their organizations. Much of their power came from the depth of their knowledge and insights, from their ability to penetrate a problem to its core, and find solutions that cut through the anomalies. They often worked in small teams to train and develop others who worked with them. Paradoxically, many of the people they had trained and influenced had gone on to become Stage IV managers in their own organizations. They often teamed up with a Stage IV manager to communicate and sell their ideas and obtain funding and resources for their research. They usually had a wide reputation for their intellectual contributions inside and often, but not always, outside the organization. Most of them did not serve as consultants but concentrated on problems at hand, carefully managing their time and efforts. They had many titles, ranging from that of deputy director to individual contributor, but even if they had a management title, they often managed no subordinates.

When we looked at nonmanagement professionals in many organizations and industries, we concluded, in general, that the likelihood of someone reaching Stage IV as a nonmanager varied directly in proportion to the organization's need for both high-technology research and original contribution. We found the greatest concentration of idea innovators in independent research organizations, research-oriented universities, and young high-tech firms. We shall discuss in subsequent chapters the way Stage IV nonmanagers in these kinds of organizations provided direction, exercised power, represented their organizations, and sponsored others.

As the need for a combination of high-technology research and original contribution decreased and the power of a management-oriented culture increased, we were less likely to see nonmanagement contributors play Stage IV roles. This was true in large, older manufacturing firms with big research and development centers. While specialized expertise was valued in these firms, the importance of high-technology and original contribution was not recognized as central in the cultures of these companies. Hence, the probability of playing a Stage IV nonmanagement role in one of these firms, while possible, was not as likely as in the types of organizations that we have already described. This was largely due to the strong tradition of the manager performing the Stage IV functions and even the very explicit efforts of management to reward key "individual contributors" seemed to underline the fact that providing direction, exercising power, representing the organization, and sponsoring key individuals were ultimately managerial responsibilities.

In our study at a large research center of one of the largest organizations in the country where high-technology products are designed and manufactured, no one could name a nonmanager who had moved into Stage IV! We were told:

> Even though we do very sophisticated technical work around here, the technical people themselves have very little influence. They have lots of freedom and are paid well, but technical people are not given much authority or power here unless they are in a management position. Even the geniuses who make the real breakthroughs are kept on narrow programs and are usually involved with one project. They can wear anything they want, they can come in to work anytime they want, which is very unusual in other parts of our company, but you couldn't call them Stage IV types. One of them decided that he wanted to move to San Francisco and do his work in

an apartment there. That was all right. They just mailed him his check and he sent in his work via telecommunications hook-up. You have to do pretty impressive work to have that kind of freedom, but freedom and money are what you get, not influence.

In the engineering divisions of the companies discussed above, or in the companies we studied that were primarily engineering based, we found it was even less likely that nonmanager idea innovators were able to make the novation into Stage IV. Of course companies differed, but we were told over and over in engineering organizations how unlikely it was for an idea innovator to move into Stage IV unless he or she was a manager:

> It's very unlikely. In an industrial situation, the technical aspects of the job are so well known that the chances of having expertise so great as to change the direction of the organization is very slim. We have Stage IV engineers, but they are mostly in management. There are no Stage IV, nonmanager, technical people here.

We did find nonmanagement idea innovators who had moved into Stage IV, in research and engineering-related departments in large industrial organizations, both on and off technical ladders. But their numbers were fewer and their ability to influence was always more circuitous than in the independent research laboratories, the research-focused universities, or in the young high-tech organizations.

The world is changing, however. The proportion of the work force and even the actual numbers of employees working for Fortune 500 companies are decreasing. The growth is often in smaller, high-tech firms where ideas and knowledge are more highly valued. Large manufacturing firms are trying to create a climate that fosters innovation. Most have not yet discovered how to do it. In the process, a few are trying to create conditions where idea innovator nonmanagers can genuinely play Stage IV roles. Those that do not find a way to make this possible will find it harder to hold and attract idea innovators.

We also studied two banks, one among the largest in the United States, the other a famous but moderate-sized regional bank. When we asked about nonmanagement people who played Stage IV roles, we were told that such individuals were very rare. Only two people could be named in the largest bank and one person in the other one. All three were individuals with unusual credit analysis skills. In the banks in which we studied the idea innovators, those valuable specialists who had genuine influence on the direction of the organization also had management positions.

In the national CPA firms we visited, we found a very similar pattern. Nonmanager Stage IV people were very unusual. In each of the national firms, we were told of some unusual individuals who had become industry experts in specialties such as mergers or bankruptcies, and succeeded in helping to build a reputation for their companies, bringing in considerable additional business in those areas. But the public accountants performing Stage IV functions were primarily managers, partners-in-charge, or major department heads.

In our study, we found there were a number of individuals in organizations who had successfully made the novation into Stage IV. They performed vital functions for those organizations: providing direction, exercising power, representing the organization, and sponsoring key individuals. Unless these functions are performed well, the organization itself suffers. These individuals in Stage IV did not fit the stereotypes often held in our society about the people who direct organizations. They did not just manage subordinates. They were not all presidents, not all "businessmen," and not all managers. The functions they performed, when stated abstractly, seem straightforward and not overly complex. Yet the novation into this stage is the most complex, most unstructured, most unforgiving of all the career stages we have examined..The demands, the blocks, the traps, the choices, and the rewards of making this novation into Stage IV form the subjects of the four following chapters.

7
Providing Direction

In the early 1970s, David Patterson was chosen to be chief executive officer (C.E.O.) of the Ajax Company. Ajax, a moderate-sized organization in the service sector, had enjoyed the reputation of being *the* high-price, high-quality leader in the industry. Ajax prided itself on hiring the best professionals in the field and training them well. People who left Ajax were usually sought after for leadership positions in competitive firms because Ajax was so respected for its achievements. Patterson had come to Ajax only a few years before, but he was widely respected in the firm. His appointment was well accepted.

In one of his first meetings with junior managers, Patterson explained that he saw the new decade as having very different challenges than that of the 1960s. Domestic and foreign markets could not be expected to expand as they had in the past. Patterson explained to them that the firm was going to hold the line on new hires and conserve resources. New ventures were to be carefully scrutinized. Promotions would be less rapid and would be based on new criteria, although these were not specified. Patterson chose a long-time Ajax man as his second in command, who also made it clear that growth, per se, would no longer be viewed as favorably as it had been in the past. He developed manning patterns to perform tasks with fewer professionals. Over the next few years, several former "young stars" who would have been almost sure to be promoted under previous conditions were not promoted and left the company. Profits held steady and the financial assets of the firm were strengthened.

During the same period, Beta, Ajax's nearest competitor, also with a new outside C.E.O., poured a great deal of resources into a product line in which Ajax competed, but did not emphasize. Beta brought several key senior managers with strong reputations into that division and commissioned them to recruit the strongest young professionals that they could find. Within 5 years, a trade publication published a survey that listed Beta ahead of Ajax as the strongest firm in the industry. Several senior managers at Ajax were vocal about the firm's "loss of focus." One member of the board reported that a young manager with an attractive offer from the outside had been advised by two senior people to leave a "sinking ship." The board of directors finally announced that it had accepted Patterson's resignation.

The second largest division of RTW had just lost its director. Jack Drake, with an excellent record in the Production Department, was an obvious candidate to replace the director. Drake brought the Production Department into an efficient operation where two predecessors had failed. He was the retiring director's choice. In a meeting to discuss the replacement, however, two serious concerns about Drake arose. One vice president reported attending a meeting in which Drake had taken an unduly possessive position about his department's having complete control over a proposed product area. Even though there were several possible related products that Drake's people could not handle technically, Drake insisted on having complete jurisdiction. The vice president said that he thought Drake was just trying to support a team leader in his department who had spent a lot of time on the product and wanted control. Still, the vice president said he was worried that Drake had allowed himself to be pushed into such a parochial position. The president added that Drake had never worked in the marketing area. He saw this as problematic because the whole company was moving toward a stronger marketing focus. Several people noted that Drake agreed with others that a stronger marketing focus was needed, but they wondered if Drake could lead others into a shift that he had not fully made himself. They also questioned if he could attract and evaluate a stronger marketing team. After some discussion, Drake was dropped from the list.

Patterson and Drake are typical of a number of people we met who were already in or were being considered for assignments requiring them to perform the most central Stage IV function: providing direction. Although many organizations have well-understood missions or strategies, conditions constantly shift, competition intensifies, and disagreements arise on needed direction. Organizations need people who are constantly surveying the environment, who understand the organization's capacity and character, who can manage the process by which the organization maintains or changes direction. The abilities, experience, and trust required to meet that need are critical for those moving into or performing adequately in Stage IV. Patterson was removed for a failure, and Drake was rejected for a suspected failure to perform this needed function.

Patterson had tried to read the hundreds of signals coming from the environment that might affect Ajax and had tried to form in his mind a map of the new, uncharted territory into which Ajax was sailing. He didn't do that alone, of course; he read, discussed, and analyzed the many new indicators and theories with others. Many things were clearly different than they had been in the preceding decade. But reading the environment is not a passive process. He chose an executive vice president (E.V.P.) who reinforced his first hunches. Patterson's speeches and actions also influenced the data that he received from others. Patterson heard some criticism, but it was not for misreading the environment; rather, some claimed that he did not understand Ajax with its strengths and vulnerabilities. They accused him of being so intent on adapting Ajax to external challenges, that he never took into account what Ajax already did well. They claimed that he was alienating and losing the very people whose strengths had carried Ajax to its impressive achievements. Others claimed that Patterson had primarily failed to manage Ajax. He had not helped members of Ajax learn from the new territory or gain confidence as they were proceeding in a useful direction.

While Patterson failed to convince the members of the board that he had provided the direction Ajax needed, Drake failed to prove to others that he *could* provide the direction needed. He had failed to convince them that he had the ability, particularly where marketing was involved, to read the environment adequately, or to evaluate the judgments of others. They feared that as they moved toward more sophisticated marketing, he would be even less competent at evaluating the organization's capabilities. They also worried about his ability to help manage the process of directing the company. His insistence on having complete control over a product revealed a parochialism that could prevent him from seeing issues from the perspective of the organization as a whole. They feared that he might go beyond the legitimate role of advocate for his division and only be able to see things from that myopic perspective.

Of all the functions of an executive or leader, there is none more universally agreed upon than the function of providing direction. Chester Barnard in his book, *The Functions of the Executive,* concluded that one of the three functions of a high-level executive was "to formulate and define the purposes, objectives, ends, of the organization." Barnard likens this function to "that of the nervous system, including the brain, in relation to the rest of the body. . . . It exists to maintain the bodily system by directing those actions which are necessary more effectively to adjust to the environment" (1). Philip Selznick claims that, "It is the function of the leader-statesman . . . to define the ends of group existence . . . " (2).

Recent studies have stressed the ambiguity and the complexity of directing and defining ends. McCaskey has made a telling case for the contradictory and ambiguous nature of the data with which a manager must work(3). Wrapp(4) and Quinn(5) have shown that, contrary to stereotypes, successful executives announce only a few goals. These announced goals are frequently broad and general, rarely quantitative or measurably precise, and are arrived at through highly incremental "muddling" processes.

Our own data confirmed the importance of the directive function, the swirling ambiguity within which it must be performed and the enormous complexity of managing it. Many individuals attempting the novation from Stage III to Stage IV were blocked because they were unable to cope with the quantum leap in ambiguity.

As we discuss the process of providing direction for an organization, it must be kept in mind that, except in the smallest organizations, this is seldom, if ever, the work of one person. While we may see the picture of Roger Smith, C.E.O. of General Motors, on the cover of *Business Week* accompanied by a feature article describing Roger Smith's bold new strategy, we may be assured that Smith's picture merely symbolizes the work of many Stage IV managers and professionals in General Motors. These Stage IV managers and professionals have worked long hours for 5 years to do the analysis, the conceptualizations, the negotiating, and coordinating necessary to bring the strategy to this point. And there will be hundreds of thousands of hours spent by those same people and others trying to implement the policies described only in sketchy outlines in *Business Week.* Nor is such strategic planning only done by those in large organizations like General Motors. Only 38 percent of the workforce in the United States work in organizations with 500 or more employees. In each of the thousands of smaller organizations, there are teams and networks of individuals working to direct and plan strategies for those organizations. So we are not discussing the work of a small handful of people when we talk about the task of providing direction for organizations. Moreover, while the full test of someone's ability to direct is highly visible for the C.E.O.s like David Patterson of Ajax or Roger Smith of General Motors, their capability to perform the complex tasks, which will be discussed here, will have been evaluated many times before they have reached such a visible position.

We have also talked about providing direction as if it were some singular activity. It is a complex, multifaceted process that could be broken into an infinite number of parts or explored from a variety of viewpoints. But as we have tried to understand this function and have seen so many people performing or failing to perform it, it seemed logical to us to break this task down into three subfunctions: mapping the environment, understanding the organization, and managing the process by which an organization comes to move in some direction.

MAPPING THE ENVIRONMENT

Most organizations exist in unstable environments. Markets shift; new needs arise; old needs become satiated and competition comes from unexpected sources. Organizations need individuals who can make some sense of the emerging, subtle, and often conflicting signals foretelling or disguising these changes. They need individuals who can see opportunities in these signals, which their organizations can seize. Perhaps most importantly, they need individuals who are not easily deluded by ephemeral trends, trapped into losing track of fundamentals, or made complacent by the seeming permanence of exclusive markets. Organizational members, and especially Stage IV members, are constantly on the lookout for individuals who can discern those parts of the environment that are relevant to their activities and create some kind of a map that defines a logical direction for the organization to take.

No one really knows the future. But because organizations need to make large investments based on projections about future events, they must be keenly aware of already existing trends that may foreshadow future events.

> We talked to the managers of a food processing firm who had moved from preparing 1-year operating plans to 3-year plans. They found that it forced them to ask questions and gather data about population and market shifts that they should have been monitoring all along. The exercise has been so helpful that they are starting to force themselves to make 8-year plans and update them yearly. They realize how far off the target these future scenarios may be, but the process forces them to examine assumptions that they are unconsciously making, which have direct effects on decisions they are making this year.

Some individuals have a strong impact in their organizations by individually and informally following a similar process. The recently appointed chief engineer of a large electronics firm was described to us as having a strong impact on the direction of the company in this way:

> Ralph generates enthusiasm and gets people thinking by his ideas about where things are going. I get a sense when I talk to him that he is full of ideas of how things are going to unfold. You have the feeling that if you will just listen to him, you can find out what is going to happen. Ralph has a strong impact on the organization just by building a vision of where the company is going, the impact it is having, and what things we need to be looking for on the horizon. He's always two steps ahead of most people's thinking. I guess

he isn't always right, but he's accomplished so much that people respect his judgment. Before he came to this position, he was connected with 6 of the company's 15 highly successful products.

In effect, such individuals create a verbal map of the future. McCaskey likens this process to the creation of early crude maps of the New World in the sixteenth century, which organized what was known, projected relationships, encouraged exploration, and gradually became more accurate(6). The co-founder of a rapidly growing computer firm told us that, as a professor of computer science, he would go repeatedly into companies and find them "10 years behind the state-of-the-art." While they expressed no needs for better technology than they had, the then-professor said that he found he could create a need in their minds when picturing what was technically possible. On the strength of this experience, he joined with another professor to begin creating "products no one knew they wanted until they were shown they existed."

The mapping of a new technical product and an innovative method of distributing it resulted in a successful national software firm:

> At age 26 after starting two unsuccessful ventures, Don Trent decided to create a new business software package for microcomputers. He worked on it for 18 months in his bedroom. After developing a careful business plan, Trent began marketing the software as other competitors in his part of the software industry were doing. But Trent quickly began to see the advantages gained by a salesman calling on computer stores. Within a few months, Trent had hired and trained a sales force that had captured 50 percent of the market in his own city. Soon Trent's new company had established profitable sales offices in 14 cities throughout the country.

Theodore White, in describing his 1944 visit with Mao Tse-tung in a cave in Yenan, northern China, reported a surprisingly similar pattern. From these caves, "the People's Republic of China was about to declare its sovereignty and at its head was Mao." White recalls:

> The reverence given him [Mao] had been earned over the years; earned in battle. . . . But, above all, the reverence arose from his authority as the teacher. He was the man who had been right when all others had been wrong. . . . It was as if Mao held before him the book of history, written in cabalistic symbols only he could decipher, and from this book he lectured the comrades and their leaders, telling them where China was going, how he would take them there, what they must do when they arrived(7).

While one person holds a new map, that map is still tenuous. Even the person holding it does not have a high probability of continuing to see the world from that framework. We know from the Asch experiments that one person alone in a group who sees the world differently is very likely to give up his or her map of the events encountered(8). But the map becomes more robust and influential as it is accepted by more people. The coherence of a group or organization is dependent on the development and maintenance of a relatively common map. Group members have a range of rewards and inducements for pressuring members into accepting a commonly held map(9). We have come to call this commonly held map in organizations the "dominant map." There are always other ways of viewing the world that are used by certain members of the organization. But in most organizations we found that there was usually fairly common underlying agreement, especially among those in Stage IV, about the assumptions underlying this dominant map.

Still, that map is always incomplete and changing. The commonly held map must be constantly accommodated to new events. In fact, an important factor that confirms the utility and reality-explaining quality of the commonly held map is that it can be made to accommodate new events. Organizations don't view environments in the abstract; they selectively perceive and enact them(10). Organizations and individuals must sort among millions of events they see, hear of, or encounter to define trends, uniformities and ascribe significance. Certain members of the organization who have demonstrated a high level of sophistication in understanding and interpreting the environment are looked to for selecting trends that must be given heed.

In one high-technology instrument company, a leader of a small development group was described by several members of the company as "the most powerful man in the company" because he was seen as having this sophistication. "Doc," as he was called, had made the original suggestion and led the company into the development of the two largest products that the organization produced. One of the vice presidents of the company said, "When Doc suggests something, you can't ignore him. He's been right too often."

At one of the most prestigious research laboratories in the country, we encountered a number of people who were considered to have the kind of sophistication necessary to sort out the significant trends in the field that ought to be followed. But one person was mentioned to us more often than any others. His division manager described him as follows:

> We have one scientist here by the name of Jack Westin who walks into the
> office every 6 or 7 years and says, "We ought to start working on such and

such if we are going to stay ahead in this field." So he starts working on it and within a few years, as many as one-third of our several thousand people at the lab might be working on some area related to what he has started.

ASKING THE RIGHT QUESTION

Another way that individuals provide direction for the organization is to pose the "right question." Obtaining and processing data are not nearly as complex as deriving meaning from those data. The ability to solve problems often isn't as important as putting one's finger on the right problem to solve.

In a Midwestern firm we visited, the management had been frustrated that despite continuous gains in manufacturing and sales volume, the company had not been able to increase profits. It was only when two of the vice presidents began to focus on the ratio of staff to operating volume that they were able to begin to raise profits. In anticipation of each new market area that they had entered, they had increased staff in the home office at a faster rate than the resultant increase in volume. Once attention was focused on this relationship, a variety of ways to improve profits without cutting into effectiveness were quickly found.

Tom Vanderslice, later to become president of GTE, while he was still with General Electric, reported how much trouble he had had trying to help the turbine group determine whether their forecast for the United States annual electrical load growth was correct. Because 4 or 5 years can elapse between an order for heavy electrical equipment and delivery of the finished product, manufacturers have trouble discerning long-term trends in their markets. It was only when Vanderslice hit upon what he considered to be the right question—What about pricing?—that the turbine group was able to determine whether the retreat from the 7 percent growth rate of the 1960s was permanent or temporary. Given that question, his analysts were able to find data that showed how consumers, and especially corporations, cut down their use of electricity as energy costs increased. When this elasticity was factored into the forecasts, they were able to drop their forecasts by 42 percent with some degree of confidence(11).

REPLACING THE DOMINANT MAP

One of the paradoxes of organizational life, indeed of life in general, is that although maps can be terribly helpful in highlighting certain things, they can be a serious stumbling block to seeing other things. The very cohesion that a dominant map of the environment can bring to an organization is the same force that makes resistance to a change in that map so powerful. Even more paradoxical is that the very persons who must demonstrate their sophisticated understanding of the current dominant map at the time they are making a novation into Stage IV will later be depended on to help change that map when a change is needed.

Jack Drake, who had done an excellent job of managing a production-oriented organization, was dropped from the promotion list because the organization saw itself as moving into an environment in which marketing sophistication would also be critical. Those making the decision were afraid Drake would not be a strong contributor to that transition.

Environments change. The recent success and the message of John Naisbitt's *Megatrends* attest to that. He argues that to understand and to move with—rather than to be bypassed by these changes—requires dramatic rethinking (12). And it is easier to give up an old map, if you have a new one with which to replace it. Leaving one safe position is less distressing if the next position is in sight (13). We saw the distress in Ajax Corporation when David Patterson began to undermine the old dominant map without providing anything to replace it other than the vague notion that the "world was growing smaller." Conversely, from Theodore White's description of Mao in the caves of Yenan, we get a powerful picture of a new map being provided, "He (Mao) was not campaigning against Chiang K'ai-shek; he was campaigning against Confucius and two thousand years of ideas he meant to root out and replace with his own" (14).

An intriguing example of someone who had moved into Stage IV in an organization with one map of the world and who helped supplant that map with a very different one is the story of Harry Cunningham and the transformation of Kresges into K-Marts.

> Harry Cunningham started as a trainee for the S. S. Kresge Co. in 1928 in the sub-basement stockroom. He became general vice president and heir-apparent in 1957. He had proven his competence and understanding in the variety store world in which Kresge's had operated in those years. During the 2 years before the president retired, Cunningham became interested in discounting. He spent days at a large new discount department store called E. J. Korvette, talking to salespeople, managers, buyers, anyone he could find. Cunningham wanted to take Kresge, whose earnings in the variety store field had been declining since World War II, the discount route. But he kept his own counsel. "Discounting at the time had a terrible odor," he explained. "If I had announced my intentions ahead of time I never would have been made president." Instead, Cunningham set about sharing his map of how the world had changed. A suburban population, which travelled to shopping locations in automobiles, could best be reached by free-standing department stores, located in the suburbs, with plenty of parking space. This conclusion had been amply demonstrated by Sears. Customers

could be profitably reached through a mass-merchandising approach: low prices and low gross margins, convenient open racks, and bargains promoted relentlessly through an advertising barrage. Cunningham suffused the company with his vision and enthusiasm for the new direction. Other key people became so committed to the direction that before the first K-Mart was open, they had made a commitment of $80 million in leases and merchandise for 33 stores. If they had failed, Kresge would have gone under. "It wasn't a gamble, really," says Cunningham, "because we were so certain. We couldn't miss" (15).

AMBIGUITY AND SENSE-MAKING

It is difficult to describe the ambiguous and piecemeal nature of the data that are available to those who are trying to read and map the environment. Experts argue strongly for contradictory positions. And while key data are being interpreted in conflicting ways, Stage IV managers and professionals have to take action. Often, the only way they can get more significant data is to commit themselves to certain steps. Two researchers who happen to have the same last names as the authors of this book, Melville Dalton and James D. Thompson, argue that it is the very quality of being able to deal constructively with major uncertainties and ambiguities that allows certain individuals to become essential and influential in organizations(16). Moreover, the cause–effect sequencing is also difficult to represent in words. William James noted that often we don't run because we are afraid, but are afraid because we run. In a similar manner, effective managers and professionals don't always act upon the basis of plans and goals; their plans and goals emerge from the actions they take. March argues that this is a legitimate and effective strategy(17). Much of this part of providing direction is post hoc sense-making. But post hoc sense-making is not an unimportant part of providing a sense of direction.

Perhaps the greatest challenge for someone trying to read the environment is to accept ambiguity as inevitable. To deal effectively in ambiguous situations, it is important to neither ignore nor avoid what is fundamentally unclear. But it is equally important to avoid the temptation to impose artificially clear meanings on ambiguous events(18). We often hear the cliché that managers have to take action on the basis of insufficient data. It may be more accurate to state that in many cases, the amount of data is great—almost overwhelming. The greater challenge is to take action in situations where the *meaning* of the data is unclear: to take active steps that protect the organization from undue risk, exploit what seems to be the most promising of available opportunities, and increase the probability that the meaning of the data available will become less obscure. A person must demonstrate the ability to realize that challenge if he or she is to make the novation into Stage IV.

Understanding One's Own Organization

As we mentioned at the beginning of this chapter, providing direction for an organization, or a major part of it, is a complex process. Reading the environment is only part of the function. An individual must be able to relate those events and opportunities to the capabilities and character of the organization. The people and the resources of an organization—and particularly the joint experiences those people have had together—make up what Selznick described as that organization's "distinctive competence" (19). This simply means that the members of an organization have developed a collective skill at performing certain tasks. Organizations also develop values, in the sense that the members of the organization prefer to perform certain tasks over other tasks and feel a sense of identity around the performance of those tasks. No one who attempts to provide direction for any significant part of that organization can ignore the collective competencies, values and identities that have become a part of that organization. The difference between this understanding and reading the environment is probably best illustrated by two hypothetical scenarios set up by Herbert Dreyfuss.

Imagine a group of Japanese executives observing a group of American executives deciding what new ventures to undertake. The Americans consider a wide range of ventures from waste disposal to manufacturing microchips for computers. These proposals are all soberly considered and compared in terms of the return on investment each is projected to bring. The one with the highest projected return is selected.

Imagine next a group of American executives observing a group of Japanese executives trying to make a similar decision. At the Japanese meeting, one executive stands and quotes a piece of poetry. Another quotes a saying from a book written by the founder of the company. Presently, they all nod in agreement, seemingly having settled that issue.

Each group of observers would go away mystified. To the Americans, what they have witnessed the Japanese doing seems to be no problem-solving session. No alternatives were considered, no criteria applied, no comparisons made, and no decision was announced. What the Americans fail to understand is that the Japanese were asking a different question: Who are we? When that question is answered, many questions about what to do are resolved. But the behavior of the Americans seems equally incomprehensible to the Japanese. How, they ask, can a group of executives consider going into such a polyglot of businesses without thinking about who they are and what they value? (20)

Dreyfuss' apocryphal story, although highlighting some important differences between management approaches, is overdrawn, of course. Most American business executives give serious heed to the questions about knowledge, experience, and developed capabilities. Richard Rumelt's important study demonstrated that companies concentrating their efforts in industries where their already developed capabilities could be brought to bear were more profitable than companies that seemed to ignore this issue(21).

Our observations corroborated Rumelt's in the sense that most of the Stage IV managers and professionals that we interviewed were extremely knowledgeable about their organizations, and gave serious thought to the distinctive capabilities and limitations of their organizations in making any decisions about direction. Moreover, they showed serious concern, before giving anyone heavy responsibilities in the organization, that the individual "understood" the organization and its possibilities and limitations. An academic vice president of a large university told us that when he was looking for a dean, he "usually found only one or two people in a college who had a grasp of what the college could realistically be."

When individuals demonstrated a fundamental understanding of the organization and its critical processes and character, their movement into Stage IV was accelerated. Let us examine two such examples:

> In 1981, when interest rates rose to historic highs, many savings-and-loan institutions found themselves in serious difficulty. The largest savings-and-loan institution in one state suddenly found itself facing an unprecedented operating loss of nearly 50 million dollars. Moreover, already existing long-term commitments had been made, which made it very difficult to see how the savings-and-loan institution could long survive in the face of high, short-term interest rates. Not only did the savings-and-loan institution have a portfolio of 30-year mortgages at 6 to 8 percent interest, which was being funded by 2- to 3-year certificates of deposit, which were costing the savings-and-loan institution 12 to 13 percent interest, but it had commitments 2 and 3 years down the road to make more loans of this type. The board of directors demanded that the management team bring to them a plan for meeting this crisis.

> The plan presented was rejected by the board. Several senior managers were forced to retire, one of the members of the board became the new C.E.O., and a new president was hired from the outside. The new president appointed a senior officer to come up with a formal survival plan to present to the board. Ron Colliard, a young manager of internal auditing who had the confidence of the board's auditing committee, was chosen to assist him technically. After meeting with all of the managers, Colliard and his boss could find no consensus. Several of the managers hoped to save the S&L

through diversifying into other financial services, but when Colliard did financial projections on their proposals, he reported that the projected earnings from those sources were not great enough to offset the huge losses that would bankrupt the S&L within 2 years if short-term interest rates stayed up.

An outside consulting firm was brought in. Colliard had already identified 15 areas where savings could be made or earnings increased; the consultants found 25 more. If all 40 of the painful cuts or difficult improvements could be implemented sufficiently, the hemorrhaging in losses could be stanched before the company went under. The plan was presented to the board and accepted. Colliard, who had come to play an increasingly stronger role in the planning, became the eyes and ears of the president, reporting progress or delays on each project each week, working with the managers over the improvement areas and with the outside consultants. The bank was moving toward the break-even point when the interest rates began to ease and the question of mere survival moved to one of future direction.

Colliard was put in charge of planning and initiated a depositor-analysis study, which determined that the heart of their clientele, young and old, shared certain common characteristics. These depositors were cautious and frugal, and wanted the very services, treatment, and image that the savings-and-loan institution was uniquely qualified to provide. This study formed a solid base for a new mission statement and provided the touchstone for settling the many questions about diversification and direction that had so plagued the savings-and-loan institution since the crisis had begun.

Colliard's movement into Stage IV was accelerated by his increasingly sure-footed understanding of the organization. As the manager of internal auditing, he was operating as a competent Stage III professional. The crisis in the savings-and-loan institution accelerated his movement into the next stage, but it certainly didn't have that effect on everyone's career. Of the 12 people chosen to be on the first team to make a presentation to the board, Colliard was 1 of only 3 people still left with the organization at our last contact. Colliard was chosen as the youngest member of that first team because he had already shown some of the understanding of the S&L to the board's audit committee that he was later to show others. It was Colliard who ascertained that diversification alone could not offset the losses coming from the central operations of the savings-and-loan institution in time to save it from bankruptcy if interest rates stayed as they were. Changes were going to have to take place in the heart of the operations in the savings-and-loan institution to have sufficient impact to do that. When the outside consultants arrived, Colliard had already identified 15 of the areas where changes could be made in those operations to cut the losses. By this time, the president had developed confidence enough in Colliard's ability to help managers make painful cuts and hard decisions while still maintaining their cooperation and respect, that he gave Colliard overall responsibility for the survival operation. But Colliard's greatest contribution to the bank may have come in finding a way to affirm the bank's distinctive competence. With the jarring changes in financial services and interest rates, there were many in the bank who were trying to move far away from the traditional business of the savings-and-loan institution, which had left it so vulnerable during the wrenching interest-rate escalation. Many were ready to believe that the cautious savers who had patiently put their savings in these institutions were products of the 1930s depression and were dying off; their children were a different breed. But Colliard's profile of the depositors reaffirmed the bank's distinctive competence. There were still a large number of depositors who were not interested in dealing with Merrill Lynch or Sears, but who wanted the steady safety for their earnings that the savings-and-loan institution symbolized for them. Adjustments had to be made to eliminate the institution's vulnerability to interest-rate mismatch, but that could be accomplished once the savings-and-loan institution had reaffirmed its primary strength and role.

Our second example of someone's using a thorough understanding of the basic functions of the organization to aid his novation into Stage IV happened even more rapidly:

> Jack Ames joined a large international real estate investment firm upon graduation from an MBA program and was assigned to work in a foreign office. An analysis that Ames undertook during his evenings and weekends allowed the firm to take action in time to save several million dollars. He was brought back to the home office to try to gain an understanding of the accounting process in the firm. Ames dug in and tried to learn from the accountants how they accounted for the "deals." He took an accounting class at night and immersed himself in the accounting problems of the firm. The accountants were impressed by his effort. Three years after joining the firm, Ames was appointed treasurer, partly on the basis of his grasp of the financial operations of the firm and his acceptance by the accountants.
>
> In the treasurer's role, Ames began an in-depth analysis of the finances of the organization and concluded that, in fact, the firm was in serious financial trouble. This had been masked by the accounting system that they had been using. He took his analysis to the managing partner of the firm, and together they determined that the large firm was near bankruptcy. Rapid action was taken to protect the solvency of the firm, and a new accounting system was designed to give the partners clearer data about the finances of each project. The partners, and particularly the managing partner, had developed

a great deal of confidence in Ames' analytical abilities and judgment, and
began to invite him to be a part of all important decisions. Within another
year, Ames was made the chief financial officer and was asked by the
managing partner to manage the internal aspects of the sprawling real
estate operations.

Again, an ability to understand the essential nature of the organization's
operations and the ability to communicate a picture of them made a major
contribution. The partners became convinced that Jack had developed a fundamental understanding of their operations and had used that understanding to
improve their decision-making processes. It was not Ames' accounting expertise or
his analytical tools that earned him such rapid credibility; it was his determined
effort to understand the core mission of the organization and to find ways to
measure and communicate how well the organization was performing that mission.

Philip Selznick claims that this understanding of the character and competence
of the organization is critical for leadership in that organization. "Leadership sets
goals," he asserts, "but in doing so takes account of the conditions that have already
determined what the organization can do and to some extent what it must do." For it
is the leaders, he claims, who "infuse with value" the organization and the tasks it
performs. This is the process by which "individuals become attached to an
organization or a way of doing things as persons rather than as technicians . . . "(22). The most effective way to influence someone is not to tell him
what to do, according to R. D. Laing, but to communicate who he is(23). If others in
an organization are to follow someone's lead, they must sense that that individual
has a deep understanding of what the organization can and, to some extent,
must do.

UNDERSTANDING PRECEDES CHANGE

We mentioned earlier the paradox that to earn the trust necessary to make the
novation into Stage IV, individuals must demonstrate a deep understanding of and a
commitment to the organization's character and distinctive competence. Yet,
paradoxically the organization depends on these same individuals to institute
necessary changes.

Fortunately, the same sensitivity and intelligence that enables someone to gain a
deep understanding of the organization's character at one point can help that
person to discern the need for change. Often, we see Stage IV individuals sponsor
individuals with viewpoints and approaches quite different from their own. An
interesting example occurred at Citibank, then called First National City Bank, in
the late 1960s:

Traditionally, Citibank had been chiefly a lending institution. Operations was a low status department and received little attention. But as the volume of paperwork increased, becoming not only a major expense but a source of irritation to clients, the management of operations received greater attention. John Reed, a man who had made a name for himself in the international banking group was recruited to assist in operations. Reed had quickly made a name for himself by applying systems concepts to the international banking field. Two years later Reed, at age 31 and with a nonbanking background, was selected to head the operations group. The bank had been in the forefront of the use of computer technology for a decade, but with productivity per worker going down, costs accelerating, errors alienating customers, and volume skyrocketing, Reed began to question the approach they had been taking:

> We've been running this operation as if it were a computer center. We've been hoping for some Great Mother of a software system to come along and pull the family together. Well, she's slow. None of us children has heard one word from her. Maybe she's not coming. What if it's *not* a computer center we have here? . . . What if it's a *factory*?(24)

Having recognized that the bank's operations unit could usefully be viewed as a factory, Reed began to organize the unit as a high-speed, continuous process production operation. He placed operations under someone from Ford Motor Company who had a firm conviction that the only way to run a production operation was with the production-tested tools of budgets, measurements, and controls. Managers were brought in who knew nothing about banking, but who had been trained in production management. Costs were contained, efficiencies improved, and errors eventually brought under control.

Reed had largely negotiated his transition into Stage IV before the events above took place, but he came to see the nature of the organization and its tasks in ways that were not being comprehended by others. The fact that he used the credibility and power already entrusted to him to help Citibank adapt to new demands and opportunities increased his credibility and power.

MANAGING THE PROCESS

We have discussed thus far the conceptual aspects of providing direction for an organization: mapping the environment, and understanding the character and competencies of the organization. Of the three aspects of providing direction, these two are easiest to write about, but they are by no means the most important. Nor were they manifested most frequently in the organizations that we visited. The most common and important element of direction was the management of the process of dealing with daily uncertainties and crises. They were unable to manage the process by which members and groups within an organization come to accept a new map of the environment or of the organization. The conceptual abilities outlined above are rare and indeed valuable, but they are less valuable if a person is not capable of translating them into actions. Strategic analyses and plans can be drawn up in classrooms or in staff offices; implementing them is another story. Moreover, most strategic plans are not fully formed beforehand, but emerge in part as action is taken and as the responses received shape further action. Therefore, the ability to manage the process by which an organization moves down a road where only the next few yards are fully visible is critical.

> Bob Johnson, after 17 years as a lending officer of one of the nation's largest banks, was given an assignment to study an industry that had been largely overlooked by the bank because its potential for profitable banking services had seemed limited. Johnson accepted the assignment with enthusiasm, determined to prove his capability. He identified the concentrated market areas with the greatest profit potential and prepared a strategic plan to solicit them with a carefully thought-out program of credit and noncredit services. Johnson's unit head and department manager were impressed with Johnson's work. Things moved faster than even Johnson had hoped, and within 6 months he was promoted to unit head over a group working on the program he had designed.
>
> After Johnson had been a unit head for only a year, his department head unexpectedly left the bank for a corporate position. The department head position was given to Johnson, the most experienced banker and only vice president unit head in that department.
>
> Within another year, however, Sam White, Johnson's division manager, concluded that the assignment had been a mistake. In White's opinion, Johnson showed some substantial shortcomings in the way he directed his much larger staff and also in his failure to execute a plan to increase the department's penetration in the markets it served. Several of the unit heads had come to White and expressed their concerns that when they went in to discuss their problems or plans with Johnson, they received almost no help. Johnson would listen and tell them that he would look into the subject and get back to them. By the time he got back to them, however, they usually had had to take action. They felt that they were having to make decisions without knowing how their decisions fit in with what other units were doing. Morale

had deteriorated; members of the department talked about losing momentum and confidence. White decided it would be unwise to wait longer and replaced Johnson.

Johnson's problem didn't seem to stem from an inability to map the environment nor from his understanding of the bank. It was an inability to provide direction as new and unexpected events unfolded. Sam White talked about Johnson's not having had enough managerial experience. But we observed and were told about so many instances that reminded us of the Bob Johnson story, that we began to ask what lay behind the easy "lack of experience" explanation. It is not the mere passage of time in a related position. We saw many instances where individuals with less "experience" than Johnson were given responsible Stage IV assignments and handled them well. We concluded that there is a capability required by someone providing direction for an organization that is separate from mapping the environment and understanding the organization. For want of a better term, we have called this the capacity to "manage the process." But since this term seems nothing more than a tautology, let us try to describe the uniformities that we uncovered, which seem to be central to this capability.

IDENTIFYING A CREDIBLE NEXT STEP

While it is comforting to have a vision of "where the organization is going," we all realize that the vision is bound to be general at best, probably imperfect, and often hard to discern. The collectivity of individuals in an organization can accept that. What they find critical, however, is the confidence that the next step or set of steps "make sense," or at least the confidence that the individuals calling for the action seem to know what they are doing. The rationale for the next step need not be elaborate—perhaps nothing more than the simple beliefs that "by taking the step, we'll learn something we need to know" or "we have exercised good judgment in the past; trust us." The individual managing the process need not have originated the idea, but he or she provides a rationale for taking the step or at least gives it credence. In some way those who successfully manage the process of providing direction communicate steps that allow the members of the organization to suspend their disbelief that the organization is moving in a useful direction.

In one high-tech firm, the top management had two terms that they used to describe individuals who could provide the credible next steps for the part of the organization in which they worked. One of the terms was "seeing reality." When we asked them what they meant by seeing reality, they defined it as: "You've got to grasp the situation enough to do something that can be done now that will help, even though it may not be possible to see everything perfectly." They talked about a relatively new marketing director who came to a 3-day meeting about a new computer model that was within months of being due to customers. At the meeting, he began to say that "they were going to have to back up and do more market research." The project was so far along and the commitments to clients so specific, that the rest of the managers said they couldn't believe their ears. One manager who had been at the meeting reported, "His comment was so inappropriate, given the realities of our situation, no one took him seriously after that." Seeing reality, in their terms, was the ability to see the essential things that must be accomplished to meet an objective, without getting lost in the forest of details.

The other term they used in connection with "seeing reality" was "burn-rate." Burn-rate was the use of resources in terms of time. If a manager had a given amount of resources to accomplish an objective, he or she had to be able to maintain a clear sense of what had to be accomplished before those resources were used up. A product had to be delivered; the terms of a contract had to be met. They talked about a director of engineering who had to get a product out within a specific amount of time, which required more engineers. Yet he spent almost 6 months of critical time, much of it alone, working on an inventory package without hiring new engineers. Those who didn't understand burn-rate let themselves and their people get distracted by unpressing details or side projects. They'd get involved in getting papers to give at conferences and fail to make sure the proposals for new contracts were written; or they would allow themselves to be concerned about seeing that everyone got word processors but fail to assure that key deadlines were being met on the way to meeting an objective. Those surprisingly rare individuals who appeared to understand "burn-rate" gained the confidence of significant others in the company; those who didn't, lost it.

These two terms came from one small company, but the concepts they represent were in force in every company we studied. In large firms and small, one of the critical tests for those making a novation into Stage IV was a demonstrated ability to see through the details to the core of the task, and to help the organization move toward its accomplishment.

When one C.E.O. was asked to describe what differentiated those whom he placed in positions to carry out Stage IV functions from those whom he rejected for these positions, he responded:

1. I don't have to worry about them; they grab an assignment and run on their own.
2. I don't hesitate to give them an assignment; they possess the judgment necessary to make the important decisions.
3. They are not afraid to take risks and usually their risks pay off.

As we talked to other senior executives, they talked about a sense of time. Those whom they felt comfortable entrusting with critical responsibilities:

- Didn't procrastinate.
- Met deadlines.
- Managed their own time judiciously.
- Faced up to difficulties rather than avoiding them.
- Understood that there are "tides in the affairs of men [and women]."

AMBIGUITY AND INCREMENTALISM

In using the term "burn-rate," there is the hint of someone operating with at least a generalized P.E.R.T.* Chart in the back of his or her mind, trying to assure that certain steps are taken or sub-objectives achieved on the road to a larger objective. In fact, most situations in organizations permit some of this. But in many instances, the problem is so poorly structured or even understood that the task at hand is to cope constructively with the ambiguity and contradictory nature of the data available while trying to get some grasp on the nature of the problem itself. McCaskey likens these problems to a poorly mapped jungle terrain and concludes that they respond best to a guerrilla style of coping. When working on a poorly structured problem, according to McCaskey, managers (and we would add nonmanagers) need to take an iterative, experimental, learn-as-you-go stance. Not only is it necessary because of the nature of the problem, but it is valuable because it can protect future options(25).

This is the point that James Brian Quinn has made in his excellent study of the process and politics of strategic goal-setting in organizations. Quinn found that while executives are constantly under pressure to define specific goals and objectives for their organizations and to state these goals clearly, explicitly, and preferably quantitatively, successful managers seldom respond to this pressure. They actually announce only a few goals, and the few that they do announce are frequently broad and general. Only rarely are they quantitative or measurably precise. According to Quinn, the determination and announcement of precise, integrated packages of strategic goals, the type that are advocated by theoretical strategists and expected by constituents, have serious negative effects. They evoke an undesired centralization, provide a focus for often insurmountable opposition, and lock the executive into a dangerously rigid position. Successful executives, Quinn found, carefully formed and announced strategic goals. They followed what Quinn described as a process of "logical incrementalism": a very complicated,

*Program Evaluation and Review Technique—a management technique used to assure that critical steps are taken promptly enough to avoid bottle necks in the completion of a project or product.

largely political, consensus-building process outside the structure of most formal management systems(26).

Quinn's study focused on the strategy formulation and implementation at the highest levels in very large companies. But we found that the phenomena that he observed among successful C.E.O.s was very similar to the behavior we saw among Stage IV managers and professionals in small organizations and in divisions of large organizations.

> We spent a great deal of time observing a research scientist named Alex who had been pointed out to us as someone who was acquiring a great deal of influence over the direction that the division was taking. Alex had been a successful group leader and deputy director of the division, but he had asked that someone replace him as deputy director so he could pursue a research interest, which he thought had high potential for the organization.
>
> What most impressed us about Alex was the role he played when any group he was in hit an impasse. When it became unclear what should be done, it was usually Alex who found some action that would move the work forward even in the face of the uncertainty. In one long meeting that we attended, the allocations committee found itself in a serious deadlock. Important and difficult political issues were at stake, and no one could see a way out. Alex proposed they take 2 days to gather more data and reconvene. At the next meeting, Alex presented some new information that he had uncovered, which changed his position and helped him to argue strongly and per-suasively for the new position. Even those whose position he had abandoned felt Alex had found good evidence for the shift, and all involved were grateful for a way out of the deadlock. A manager later told us, "No group or organization that Alex is a part of ever stands paralyzed for long." Six months after we attended the meetings, we heard Alex had been made director of the division.

Clearly, one part of managing the process by which organizations are given direction, particularly under conditions of ambiguity and uncertainty, is to help identify a credible next step. Often, to attempt more is to ignore Selznick's warning to "avoid premature self-definition" (27). But providing that step, when needed, is a genuine act of leadership.

COMMITMENT AND FOCUS

There are times, however, when more than a next step is needed. The electrifying effect of N.A.S.A.'s vision, announced by President Kennedy in 1960, of "putting a man on the moon by the end of the decade" was clear from the moment it was announced until it was accomplished. It provided structure, organization, and focus that would never have been provided by a statement such as, "We are going to be a leader in the exploration of space." There comes a time, and it is one of the critical capabilities of a Stage IV leader to determine that time, when the commitment to a specific objective is not only helpful but badly needed.

Even James Brian Quinn, whose work has done most to explode the myth that C.E.O.s should, on a regular basis, establish a strategy, then announce specific, quantitative goals, notes that there are appropriate times for managers to announce specific goals. Quinn notes that specific goals can be helpful in precipitating action in an organization, or helping it through major transitions. "By making selected goals explicit at the proper moment, managers can create a challenge . . . or crystallize defined thrusts." When trying to define the "proper moment," Quinn gave illustrations of times when executives knew that the goal was feasible, that key people understood and supported it, and that the horizon was sufficiently distant to allow for alternative approaches to ensure the goal's achievement. Quinn also noted that after a prolonged disaster or a major trauma, or when it is necessary to signal a major change from the past, the announcement of distinct and clear new goals can be very functional(28).

Of course, the announcement of specific goals is probably the least important part of the process of focusing attention. When we were talking to an executive of an electronics firm about Stage IV people whom he knew in the company, he suddenly realized that there was a uniformity running through all of his descriptions:

> There's a characteristic here that keeps recurring. It's commitment; it's a positive attitude, a can-do, never-say-die quality. There's a sense about all of them that they have a thrust, that they are going someplace, and that it will be fun to get on board.

In the two successful high-tech firms that we studied in which the founders were still managing the companies, we heard more about commitment than about any other quality. Both founders said that they had had to mortgage their own homes to obtain capital; one talked about having to limit his family's diet to "fried bread and beans" so that they could meet the payroll some months. One told about a brilliant co-founder who had pulled out because he couldn't sleep at nights knowing that he was personally liable to pay off the huge debts if the business failed. Both mentioned that had they not been so personally committed to making the enterprise succeed, others would have been willing to quit.

In a large contract research organization, we heard the president state repeatedly that he "wouldn't fund any project unless there was some person who really believed in it, and who was willing to bet a substantial part of his own career and reputation that he could make it work."

In a large oil-chemical company, we tried to trace the factors that contributed to the company's most successful product, which had grown from the company's research efforts. A serendipitous technical discovery led ultimately to a highly profitable polymer. Yet, as we delved into the various accounts of events that finally brought the profitable product into being, it became clear that the path from the discovery to the developed and marketed product was far from smooth or inevitable. There were many times when the eventual technical and economic success of the product was in serious question. Most of those closely associated with the project attributed the success of the product to the commitment and focus of its sponsor, the vice president of research. He believed in the product; he allocated large amounts of resources to its development. He argued persuasively to the board of directors that the money and time being spent on the project be accelerated rather than cut off as some persons had advocated. There was no question in the minds of those interviewed that the vice president's commitment and focus had been critical to the success of the project.

We talked to the people who worked under a manager whose sales division had ranked number one in the nation in a large office products firm for 3 years in a row. When he visited the offices of his subordinates, he spent a great deal of time asking questions. His subordinates seldom seemed surprised by the questions; they usually had the information necessary to answer the questions available in a loose-leaf binder similar to the one the manager carried. When we later asked the subordinates about these visits, they said:

> We know pretty much what Jake is going to ask before he comes. He certainly doesn't try to keep it a secret. We all know the key things you have to keep doing well in order to increase long-term sales: service, customer contact, recruiting and training good people, acknowledging good and poor performance, etc. We know he's going to ask us about those things and about the things we need to be doing now to see that those things will be in place 1 or 2 years from now. If we have any questions about what he's going to be asking, we can call his assistant. He'll gladly tell us. Jake is not hard to figure out. That's his strength. He is so committed to strong fundamentals that he keeps us all focused on what we know we ought to be doing. It's no wonder we are number one in the company; if any division focused on fundamentals the way we do under Jake, they could do as well as we do.

We asked a group of partners-in-charge of city offices for a national accounting firm what they thought was the most important thing for a partner-in-charge to do.

They agreed that it was to keep everyone's attention focused on doing the fundamentals well, even when everyone, including the partner-in-charge, was doing an incredible number of things.

There is also the issue of confidence. When we talked to the subordinates of the vice president of research in the oil-chemical company that we referred to earlier, several said that if the vice president hadn't been so confident that they could do it, they might have given up. A highly effective Stage IV plant manager told us, "I am the one that convinces people that they can do it." We heard almost the identical words from a Stage IV nonmanager whose ideas had been turned into major new products. This obviously overstates the case. Confidence for individuals comes from their own sense of capacity, from their own sense of the situation, and from peers as well as from Stage IV leaders. But a critical part of providing direction and moving into Stage IV is being able to act in a way that promotes confidence in the members of the organization, the feeling that they can accomplish what they are setting out to do.

As we observed effective Stage IV individuals and Stage IV candidates in action, many of those who seemed to be outwardly acting in "participative" ways to gain agreement and commitment from others were singularly unsuccessful. Yet, others who made less effort to gain participation in a decision attained deep commitment and identification with new goals and direction. The variable that seemed to be most closely associated with those who received a deep commitment from organizational members was trust. Miles and Ritchie's distinction between the quality and the quantity of participation(29) seemed to explain this apparent incongruity better than any formulation we have seen. The most successful Stage IV leaders that we observed were trusted to consult with others when the decision would affect them in any significant way or when they could be expected to contribute. In other decisions, they expected and trusted these leaders to go ahead without their participation. Trust and commitment were reserved more for those whose judgment had been confirmed by events in the past than for those who seemed to make a fetish of participation.

Still, we found that those who had successfully moved or were moving into Stage IV worked diligently and skillfully to obtain the commitment of those who had to carry out decisions.

A west coast division of a large electronics firm had moved simultaneously to a new casing material and a new production process. Both moves reduced the requirement for skilled and unskilled workers. At the same time, there were strong needs for reduced unit costs. A consulting firm was called in for analysis and recommendations. The consultants made a presentation to the new division manager, who had come in since the consultants had been engaged, suggesting that the unit costs could be significantly reduced through layoffs. The division manager listened carefully to the presentation and then said, "The analysis seems well done, but the process is wrong." He took the analysis and the problem to the departments that would be most deeply affected. He asked them to find ways to obtain the needed cost reductions. Within 2 weeks, they came back with a program that reduced unit costs even further, but avoided layoffs through a series of reassignments, subcontracting with other divisions and retraining.

When we asked the regional director of a national public accounting firm what differentiated those who successfully moved into Stage IV from those who failed, he said, "I can answer that in one word—communication." When we asked him what he meant when he said communication, he said:

> In our best offices, the partner-in-charge makes sure that he or she meets regularly with the key people in the office. They talk things over, make plans, and hash things out. From time to time, they go off somewhere for a day or so to strategize, agreeing on who is going to do what. When the partner-in-charge comes back from a regional or national meeting, he or she gets all the key people together to go over what came up at the meeting. Those key people learn to do the same with their subordinates. Conversely, the partners-in-charge who are floundering are almost invariably the ones who can never seem to find the time to meet with their people, work things out with them beforehand, and then keep them posted. I tell those partners-in-charge that their department heads and others may be busy, but probably not too busy to call me one of these days and ask *me* what is going on in their own office!

We were referred to a plant manager who had trimmed operating costs so quickly after he had taken over management of the plant that he was already being considered for greater responsibility. When we asked the young plant manager how he explained the rapid improvements in the plant's performance, he told us:

> I had found when supervising a small group of analysts that a lot of people have good ideas and will work hard to make them work if they get the support that they need to make those ideas work. When I was asked to take over the plant, I found that we needed to trim costs to be competitive. So I told the people who asked me to take the job that I'd have to have their support where I found a need to make changes and some capital budget for improvements. When I got to the plant, I found the assistant plant manager was savvy and knew the people. Together, he and I went to each department, told them that we needed to trim costs and asked for their ideas. We

discussed their proposals and decided together which ones were most feasible and promising. It often meant I'd have to go after changes or funds. But when we agreed on something and I came up with what they said they needed, they usually came up with the cost reductions, which they said they could get. When people believe in a feasible idea, they can make it work.

As the reader can see, providing direction in an organization is not simple. Those who perform this function must not only be able to read an often complex and ambiguous environment well, but must also formulate some kind of map out of the equivocal information and communicate it to others. They must understand the distinctive competences and the limitations of their organizations as well. Most importantly, they must be able to manage the process by which direction is provided and accepted. Much of the above, however, cannot be accomplished without the effective exercise of power, the function to which we turn next.

8
Exercising Power

Rex Matkin, a highly respected scientist and group leader in a contract research organization, was enthusiastic about his appointment as program director of the Waste Containment Program. Although the organization's several divisions had traditionally worked independently, the Waste Containment Program with the federal government called for a series of complex finished systems that would utilize the skills of many of the divisions. Matkin had headed up the proposal team, and his technical ideas and reputation had played a key role in winning the contract. The contract was worth well over $2 million in the first year.

At first the program ran smoothly, but within 2 years Matkin was experiencing difficulties. Over the following two years, his difficulties increased. Some of the divisions postponed obligations to Waste Containment in favor of new opportunities and demanding external customers. Matkin found himself in the role of an internal customer, too readily pushed aside for one reason or another. But Matkin was not one to accept the disinterest of his associates lightly. He frequently rejected the work of different divisions, and he did not hesitate to go over the heads of the department or even the division managers to demand effort. These actions, however, steadily made his coordination and management role more difficult.

Matkin changed as these experiences began to wear upon him. He became increasingly possessive of his program, even more introspective, and disappointed by the unresponsiveness on the part of others in the organization. His frustration and, in his terms, "powerlessness," led him to be openly critical of his associates in the company. The Waste Containment Program suffered to the point where the contracting government agency recommended an "improvement" in program management. Matkin was replaced and took early retirement, disappointed and embittered.

Why do so many managers or professionals who have been effective in small departments or work teams find themselves ineffectual and frustrated when they move to problems and responsibilities involving the larger organization? We repeatedly met or heard about managers and professionals whose experiences, frustrations and disappointments were similar to those of Rex Matkin. They weren't all program directors; some were partners-in-charge of large accounting offices, directors of research laboratories, senior scientists, company presidents, and university deans. Many more were individuals being considered for such assignments or positions. But one uniformity among all of these individuals was that they were taking on, or were being considered for, assignments where they had responsibility for seeing that effective work was accomplished throughout the organization. The other uniformity was that they were either removed from, passed over for, or were failing in these assignments because they "couldn't handle it." That was the phrase we kept hearing: "he [or she] couldn't handle it." In our efforts to understand what "it" meant in that phrase, we found that we had to add to our original formulation of the functions performed by someone in Stage IV. The "it" that these people were not handling well was power in organizations; the function that we had omitted was the exercise of power.

LEARNING ABOUT POWER IN ORGANIZATIONS

We didn't bring the notion of power to the study readily. We were more likely to use words such as influence or authority (1). But those whom we interviewed in the organizations began to point out to us that the effective exercise of power is a critical function in Stage IV roles. We were told by several successful program managers and division managers in Matkin's organization that his failure lay in his inability to understand and use the power he had available to him:

> The Waste Containment Program was and is a viable program. Matkin just didn't understand the very real power that he had or how to use it. He had the support of the divisions, the lab directors, and the president. He had a good program, technical respect, and long-term funding. But when things didn't go according to script, Matkin started zapping people until he had bankrupted all the power that he had. If you are a battleship escorting a convoy, you don't fire all your 16-inch cannons at the first tug that falls behind; you've used your ammunition and started the war. Of course, the divisions were going to get distracted looking for new customers and projects, but Matkin could have handled that. He had the time and knowledge to keep on top of each part of the program and remind others of

what he needed from them to keep clients happy. When someone was being irresponsible about obligations to the program, all he had to do was "belly up" and call them on it, explaining the consequences for the program and the labs. He had the resources to do things for every division and lab that they couldn't do without him. But he dissipated rather than added to his power, and he paid for it.

A vice president and director of development told us:

> I had never thought much about power or aspired to it. But when I got this job, I quickly found out that there were so many people depending on me to fight for their programs that I had to learn to line up support, build alliances, and take strong positions without feeling enmity with those with whom I differed.

THE CONCEPT OF POWER IN ORGANIZATIONAL LITERATURE

At the same time that we were learning the importance of power to someone who moved into Stage IV, other students of organizations were beginning to find it important in explaining the phenomena that they were observing. In political science, the concept of power has always been considered a central construct, and we readily found several thoughtful studies of the exercise of power in organizations. The most useful of these was Richard Neustadt's *Presidential Power,* where he pointed out that, like Rex Matkin, when presidents of the United States resorted to the use of formal sanctions, it was often a sign of weakness rather than strength and resulted in an erosion of their power rather than an enhancement of it (2).

The management and organizational studies in the private sector largely ignored the concept of power for many years. The focus on rational decision-making and individual motivation steered organization studies away from the concept of power. Kotter reports that, "Of the roughly two thousand articles that appeared in the *Harvard Business Review* between 1955 and 1975, only five, or about one quarter of 1 percent, had the word 'power' in their titles" (3). Increasingly, however, students of business and other nongovernment organizations have found the concept of power necessary to explain what they were seeing in the organizations that they studied. In almost every case, however, these writers have felt the necessity to acknowledge the negative connotations that the word carries in our society. Zaleznik, one of the leaders in pointing to the importance of power in organizational life, acknowledged, with Kets de Vries, that, "Power is an ugly word. It connotes dominance and submission, control and acquiescence, one man's will at the expense of another man's self-esteem. . . ." But they also go on to point out the central role that power plays in organizational life: "Yet it is power, the ability to control and influence others, that provides the basis for the direction of organizations and for the attainment of social goals. Leadership is the exercise of power" (4).

Kotter, as noted above, concluded that power was a neglected aspect of management, at least in management literature. Kotter noted that, as he has observed them, "Managers regularly acquire and use power. They do so deliberately and consciously, as well as intuitively and unconsciously"(5). Kotter was impressed by the managers' dependence on others—subordinates, superiors, peers, staff members, customers, and suppliers—to get his/her work done. In fact, it is this very dependence on others that makes power so important to managers, according to Kotter. He points out that, "successful managers cope with their dependence on others by being sensitive to it, by eliminating or avoiding *unnecessary* dependence, and by establishing countervailing power over others" (6).

Kanter noted that, "Power is America's last dirty word" (7). But she came away from her study of a large industrial corporation deeply impressed with the importance of power—and powerlessness. She observed that a manager's interpersonal style with subordinates usually had less to do with perceived effectiveness than that manager's power in the organization:

> What does make a difference is power—power outward and upward in the system: the ability to get for the group, for subordinates and followers, a favorable share of the resources, opportunities, and rewards possible through the organization(8).

Having declared how important power is in the lives of those working in an organization, as well as to the organization's functioning, Kanter makes some interesting observations about where this power is obtained. People were given formal titles of leadership (e.g., director, manager) and were expected to mobilize others to attain objectives. They had responsibility and accountability for results, "but as everyone knew, power did not necessarily come automatically. . . with the delegation of formal authority. People often had to get it not from the official structure, but from the more hidden political processes" (9).

Pfeffer takes a different position and examines organizations as almost exclusively political systems in which the greatest power goes to those sub-units and individuals viewed as controlling the "critical contingencies." (Critical contingencies are the boundaries or relationships through which the organization obtains its most critical or vital resources.) Viewing organizations as a setting in which there is a constant, but latent, contest for power over outcomes, Pfeffer concludes that, "power is most effectively used when it is employed as unobtrusively as possible." Pfeffer further notes that, "Most strategies for the exercise of power" (where the decision is to be determined on the basis of the relative power of the parties involved) ". . . attempt to legitimate and rationalize the decision" on grounds other than the power of the parties (10).

How do we account for the fact that power is considered an ugly, dirty, and, at best, a suspicious word, when the effective exercise of power seems so important to the Stage IV managers and professionals we studied, as well as to an increasing number of other researchers? Is the exercise of power, as Pfeffer suggests, an important but illegitimate function that is best carried out unobtrusively, and rationalized on other, more socially acceptable, grounds? William James once advised that when faced with a contradiction, one should make a distinction. David McClelland has made a distinction between different power orientations, which we think is an important contribution to the understanding of power in organizations.

McClelland, who has been studying and measuring individual power orientations for over two decades, distinguished some time ago between those with "personal power" concerns, who manifest the need to dominate or win out over someone else and those with "socialized power" concerns, who manifest a need for exercising power for the benefit of others (11). More recently, McClelland found that those with a high need for power divided themselves into four different groups on the basis of the actions that they typically took to meet the need for power. He classified these four groups as being in different stages of ego development by means of a simple table with two dimensions, identifying whether the source of power is outside or inside the self and whether the object of power is the self or someone or something outside the self (12). (See Table 8.1.)

McClelland's classification interests us for several reasons. First, it clarifies the distinction between power sought or accepted where an individual is the source (influencing others to accept *his* or *her* ideas, domination, and help, as in Stage III) versus power sought or accepted where the source of power is outside of an

Table 8.1. McClelland's Classification of Power Orientations (12)

OBJECT OF POWER	SOURCE OF POWER	
	OTHER	SELF
Self	Stage I	Stage II
Definition	"It" strengthens me.	I strengthen myself.
Manifested actions	Power-oriented reading.	Accumulating prestige and possessions.
Developmental stage	Being supported.	Autonomy, will.
Others	Stage IV	Stage III
Definition	It moves me to do my duty.	I have impact on others.
Manifested actions	Joining and leading organizations.	Competitive sports, arguing.
Developmental stage	Principled assertion, service.	Assertive action.

individual (influencing others to act or accept action on behalf of something—the organization or collectivity, as in Stage IV: "This may not be good for me, or for you as individuals, but it is good for the corporation"[13]). Many of the negative connotations about power come from personal—not organizational—power. Many of the horror stories of someone "wielding power" in organizations are really abuses of power.

But the second reason the classification interests us is far more important than the first. The importance of the Stage IV power orientation outlined in Table 8.1 is that it pictures what those of us in organizations think that we are entitled to expect from those who are empowered to act on behalf of the organization. Certainly, on a formal basis, we feel entitled to expect that the directors or presidents of organizations will use the power given to them by their organizations in the best interest of the organization. Similarly, we feel entitled to expect that others who are given different assignments and positions will use the power given them in the best interest of the organization. If they use the power entrusted to them for personal rather than organizational ends, we think that they have violated our trust. If they fail to use their power to prevent others from cheating, or stealing from the organization, we think that they have been derelict in their responsibility. If they subordinate the interests of the larger organization to benefit their sub-units, there is also the basic feeling that a trust has been violated. Moreover, if they do not use the power entrusted to them wisely, judiciously, and even courageously, we think that they have failed in their stewardship. Such is the nature of the explicit and implicit contracts into which organizational officers and members enter.

But what of the informal organization? A similar process of entrustment of power takes place, but it is given much more conditionally and monitored much more carefully. We live in a society where there is a pervasive perception that power *can* corrupt and that absolute power will corrupt absolutely. But we also live in complex organizations where it is necessary that someone represents the organization to which we belong while we are not present. Others must represent our interests in meetings where we are not present. Therefore, as subordinates, superiors, and peers, we informally grant power to those who demonstrate that they can and will use power responsibly and wisely on behalf of the organization, while taking our interests into account. If they are able to use that power well and comfortably, if they understand reciprocity and alliances, and can bring in greater resources and help the organization work more effectively, we will entrust them with greater informal power. If they are ineffectual or indecisive, if they ignore our interests or fail to treat us with human dignity, if they take personal advantage of our trust, we withdraw the informal power that we have given them. These are the "hidden political processes" to which Kanter referred. But the constraints are very real. We can see why Kotter found that managers are dependent on so many people; all those people from whom he or she must gain trust can also remove it, and much more quickly than can the formal system. Conversely, the informal empowerment need not coincide with, nor wait for, the formal system. Individuals without formal management positions can wield significant power. Other individuals are often given formal positions after they have already earned much of the informal power that would go with the position. If individuals are entrusted by those around them to use power responsibly, that trust can add to their power and effectiveness. An experienced and respected division head who was described to us by several people as one of the two or three most powerful people in the organization told us:

> If I don't have to reveal all my reasons for taking a given action, that gives me greater power to do things which will result in long-term benefit to more people. If people trust me to give them their fair share of resources over time, that gives me power to give people what they really need when they need it. So I have to work hard to earn that trust.

But if the position that we have taken makes the exercise of power seem a less odious undertaking, let us be clear that we see the task no less difficult or demanding. If we have not stated it before in this book, let us state here that organizations can be dangerous and unforgiving places. They are not benign. Good intentions, honesty, and selflessness do not make someone immune to failure and disappointment. Justice does not always nor automatically prevail. If individuals do not understand the nature and the limitations of power in organizations, they do harm to themselves, those who count on them, and the organizations in which they work.

As we observed those individuals who were attempting to make the novation into Stage IV, we found that, emotionally, the most difficult part of the transition was learning to exercise power. Some found it impossible to make the difficult decisions that might bring the displeasure of others or foreclose attractive possibilities. Some found themselves unable to deal with the moral dilemmas that the exercise of power raised for them. Some were unable to understand how their power was dependent on the trust and support of others. Some lost power by promising more than they could deliver or allowing themselves to take stands that ultimately they could not defend. Finally, there were a number of individuals who failed to understand the very real limitations in our society that are placed on the exercise of formal power. We shall be examining examples of each of these in the pages that follow. But first let us try to be more explicit about what we have come to mean by power in organizations.

DEFINING POWER

Power in organizations, as we are using the term, is the ability to get things done, to obtain, mobilize, and dispense resources in order to achieve organizationally desirable goals. It comes, in part, from the ability of individuals to *earn* and *continually* obtain the empowering responses of others. Power is loaned or entrusted to individuals who are expected to use it effectively and responsibly. It comes from a combination of formal and informal sources. To use an analogy that has been used by other writers, it is somewhat akin to electric current, which can be cut off at any time from its source of supply.

Definitions, however, have limited usefulness. Let us turn to the ways in which we saw individuals block themselves from moving into or performing adequately in Stage IV because they failed to understand the vital function of exercising power.

AVOIDING THE USE OF POWER

Ted Smith, a managing partner in a large national C.P.A. firm, had only been in charge of the city office for a year, but already he was experiencing difficulties. Everyone liked Ted personally. But he was a constant procrastinator when it came to making decisions that might bring the displeasure of others. And even if he was forced to make a tough decision, he would not follow through and implement it. He avoided getting involved in the difficult internal conflict problems in his division. He found it difficult to confront people about irresponsibility or poor performance. If a client objected to a bill, he wouldn't send someone to talk to the client or go himself; instead, he put off sending out those bills again. Other partners and members of the staff lost confidence in him. Finally, Smith was relieved as partner-in-charge and placed in a position where he did not have to make major decisions involving others.

We saw a number of managers like Smith who were respected and liked as individual performers and as heads of small departments, but who were ineffective when given larger responsibilities. Quite often the problem lay in their inability to make the difficult decisions and to use the power available to them to help solve the organization's problems and to help it move forward. Those in responsible positions are expected not only to use the formal power given them, but to use themselves and their relationships to move the organization's efforts forward. When they fail to exercise the power given them when it is appropriate and necessary to do so, they lose it. If they don't appear to have the energy, capability, or willingness to make difficult choices and then to explain to others the validity of their decision, they are unlikely to be entrusted with either formal or informal power. An academic vice president and former dean told us, "A dean has to be tough. Deans must convince their faculties that they must decide what is important and to decide to stop doing what is not important." A division chief explained to us, "Power comes to you by not exporting your problems. If you don't solve your own problems, if you are constantly taking your problems upward and asking for more resources to do your job, you lose credibility."

Those entrusted with power in organizations are also expected to hold themselves and others to high standards of effort and performance. Athletic coaches are popular speakers for executive groups partly because managers want to hear from someone who successfully does something that they find difficult but important, namely, challenging those who give less than full effort. An engineering executive who admired Vince Lombardi gave one of us an article where a player described Lombardi's coaching:

> You knew in advance to accept his discipline, you *wanted* his discipline. . . .
> A player needs discipline so he doesn't cheat. . . . I've cheated, every player
> has, and you hate yourself for doing it, for dogging it on a pass pattern when
> you know you're not going to get the ball, or sloughing off a block. You won't
> cheat with Mr. Lombardi because you know you'll be out and you know he'll
> be right (14).

Because the use of power places demands on those who exercise it, executives are reluctant to place individuals in a position where they will have to exercise power unless they feel that the individual both wants it and can "handle it." Said one executive, "I like to give a job to someone who really wants responsibility." Another replied, "I like to choose people who are willing and able to make the tough decisions, to say 'no' when it is needed."

An individual's willingness and capability to take on such responsibilities is communicated in many ways. One division manager in a large research laboratory, with whom we were discussing career stages, told us, "In order to move from [Stage] III to IV, you have got to be willing to take a chance—make some recommendations." A research manager in a large electronics firm, who wanted to have the technically capable people in the organization take more active leadership in moving the company into new technical areas, gave a speech on power to the research fellows on the company's technical ladder. He warned them, "Overendowing others with power, particularly your managers, happens frequently with technically trained people. You assume, 'They'd never let me do that' and don't ever find out."

Using Organizational Power for Personal Ends

> A division manager of a large international corporation had just been promoted to the office of area vice president and made a member of the executive committee of the corporation. During the many years that he had been a division manager, he had been engaged in a series of conflicts and rivalries with another division manager who was still in the area now headed by the vice president. The vice president was discussing these conflicts and rivalries in a conversation with the executive vice president of the corporation. The vice president made the comment, "Now I have the power!" The executive vice president responded, "Yes, but now that you have it, you can't use it."

The executive vice president was merely citing one of the unwritten rules surrounding the exercise of power in organizations. The power given the vice president was given him to advance the work of the corporation. If he used it for personal ends, to take vengeance on his former rival, he would not only be abusing the power given to him, but he would lose power in the process. If others in the area he now headed, or on the executive committee, suspected that he was using the power given to him by his new appointment in a personal vendetta with his old rival, they would withdraw some of the support that they had offered him. We are suspicious of undisciplined power, and we give it to others for defined purposes. If they are not able to discern the limitations placed on that power, we will work to withdraw that power.

Probably the most dramatic instance in our time of organizational power being taken from someone who abused that power for personal ends involved the televised deliberations concerning the impeachment of Richard Nixon. Theodore H. White's anger at this abuse led him to write the book, *Breach of Faith*. His thesis is distilled in the following paragraph:

> The true crime of Richard Nixon was simple: he destroyed the myth that binds America together, and for this he was driven from power. The myth he broke was critical—that somewhere in American life there is at least one man who stands for law, the President. That faith surmounts all daily cynicism, all evidence or suspicion of wrongdoing by lesser leaders, all corruptions, all vulgarities, all the ugly compromises of daily striving and ambition. That faith holds that all men are equal before the law and protected by it; and that no matter how the faith may be betrayed elsewhere, at one particular point—the Presidency—justice will be done beyond prejudice, beyond rancor, beyond the possibility of a fix. It was that faith that Richard Nixon broke, betraying those who voted for him even more than those who voted against him (15).

The same reaction that resulted in the resignation of President Nixon for using the power entrusted to him for personal rather than institutional ends works in less dramatic but similar ways in most organizations.

A recent study by McCall and Lombardo at the Center of Creative Leadership looked at why managers are "derailed." The study showed that many managers failed because they were seen as individuals who would use power for personal agendas. Two of the top four reasons given for managerial failure were:

- Betrayal of trust.
- Excessive ambition—thinking of the next job, playing politics (16).

Similarly, some managers fail because they become so short-sighted in their own interests, their own territory, their own careers and success. They devote little attention to the concerns of others and/or the needs of the organization. In one small organization that we studied, a president was having difficulty with subordinates and board members alike because they thought that he was taking unfair advantage of a flexible schedule. Said one senior officer, "People are suspicious that George is doing personal work when he's not here during work hours. It undermines his authority and destroys the motivation of others."

Finally, those who are entrusted with power are expected to act to see that others do not use their power, position or assignment in the organization for inappropriate personal ends. To the extent that those empowered to act for the organization wink at abuses, they lose power. To the extent that they act to stop or prevent abuses to the point where others feel that they can trust the integrity of the system, these individuals *gain* power.

> Kerry Jensen, a sales executive of an electronics firm, was transferred to take over management of the company's southern sales division. Not long after he came into the division, he heard rumors that the supervisors in two of the leading sales districts were "neglecting" to report returned machines, thus inflating their sales figures and entitling them to win special bonuses and rewards. Jensen spent a year establishing himself in his new position, getting to know the people, and gathering data about what was being done in these two districts. When he had fully determined that the practice was deliberate, ongoing, and dishonest, he took action. He went to each of the two supervisors and told them what he knew. He also told them that he realized how difficult it was to get someone fired in their company. But he vowed that he would spend every effort for as long as it took to have them fired if they didn't resign. Both resigned within a month.
>
> The story of what Jensen had done quickly spread throughout the division. Other supervisors and salespeople came to Jensen and told him that they

had known of the practice and were relieved to know that something had been done about it. Jensen's credibility increased. The southern sales division, which had been among the sales leaders in the country, rose to the number one position in sales and service.

For organizational systems to work effectively, the members of the organization must trust the system to treat all members fairly. They must believe that effort and performance will be recognized and fairly rewarded. If some parties in the organization are allowed to take advantage of their positions to gain what is perceived as an unfair advantage, trust in the system breaks down. Those who are granted power in the organization must not only discipline their own exercise of power, but use it to see that others do not abuse power for inappropriate personal ends. Ultimately, this responsibility may seen to rest on the shoulders of the C.E.O. But everyone who has been entrusted with power in the organization shares that responsibility.

MISMANAGING CRITICAL DEPENDENCIES

As a new director of the research and development center of a large industrial company, Lynn Mathie introduced some exciting and innovative ideas. People in the center were pleased with the changes and optimistic about the future. Mathie's career with the company looked promising. However, when a conservative marketing strategy failed to market new products as aggressively as Mathie expected, he became frustrated and critical. In corporate meetings, Mathie began to push angrily for a change in marketing strategy. He became quite critical of managers in other departments and skeptical of their methods of operation. His friends warned him that he was taking big risks in antagonizing his counterparts in marketing and production, but he said that he wasn't going to "play politics." His job, he said, was to help the company develop new, profitable products and to see that the company benefited from them. Mathie had trouble getting his best supervisors promoted into positions in other divisions, but he was highly regarded and respected in the center.

After 13 years, a new president was appointed who brought in a consulting firm to recommend how to improve the company's performance. The consultants interviewed a number of people, including the managers of all the divisions. Several said that Mathie was the problem. They said that he was causing major conflicts between the research and development center and production, marketing, and personnel. The new president acted on this information, and Mathie was told one Friday afternoon at 4 o'clock that he should clean out his desk by 5 o'clock. Everyone at the center was shocked and saddened at the loss of a capable manager and by the way Mathie had been treated.

Lynn Mathie was personally one of the most attractive men that we came to know. He was bright, articulate, and highly principled. He was bold, straightforward, and admired by his subordinates. He had an excellent technical background and a strong technical record in the company. But he failed, no, refused to acknowledge that his power to get his people's new products marketed, to promote the careers of those he sponsored, or even to protect his own position, was limited by the power held by his counterparts in other divisions of the organization. In this respect, he was like a number of other professionally trained people whom we met in organizations. To acknowledge this limitation and to act on that knowledge was, in his mind, stooping to "play organizational politics." As this limitation became more apparent and he could not find attractive positions for his capable people in other parts of the company, he became more angry and lashed out harder. In the process, he formed a coalition against himself, and his own power became even more limited.

Organizations are complex places and are made up of a complex interwebbing of a variety of systems: economic, technical, and political. To fail to understand the properties of these systems is to limit one's ability to act effectively in organizations. As Mathie moved into a Stage IV role, where the exercise of organizational power was critical to his effectiveness, his failure to understand and respect others' power limited his own power to act. We met other individuals in other organizations, equally principled, who accepted the fact that their power was limited by and dependent on that of others, and used that knowledge to increase their own effectiveness and power. One highly respected university dean told us:

> You have to be ready to respond when someone is talking nonsense, even if it is a superior. You must be seen as respectful but not deferential. You tell them that you have complex problems on issues they see differently. You work to educate them.

This same dean told us that there were many people who had power and influence in that large and complex university system. His ability to get things done and to obtain the resources that his college needed was dependent on the power and cooperation of others.

> You have a lot of networks that you have to work. In the military service, I found the platoon sergeant had almost all the power. If I failed to take his power into account, I was dead in the water. There are a lot of people who

are like that for me in this job. One of them is the dean of admissions. He is tough. If a parent calls the president about an admissions problem, the president calls the dean of admissions, who gives him the rule and that is the end of it. But I have worked on our relationship; if I have a parent call and I go to the dean of admissions with the problem, he can tell me lots of different rules that apply. I need his help at times, and I work to get it. I have also worked out a solid relationship with the financial vice president. I taught him to trust me by turning in my surpluses at the end of the year instead of rushing to spend them all. You have to be careful whom you do that with, but over time our mutual trust has given me a lot more power over financial resources.

One division chief we interviewed explained how he always treated with deference and respect a staff employee at headquarters that many other executives treated with contempt. When asked why, he replied, "I know I will need his help some day."

A new president of a wholly owned subsidiary learned, when he was given the position, that there was one person who had strongly opposed his appointment. He went to that person and told her that he had heard of her opposition, wanted to understand her concerns, and earn her support in his new position. After several frank sessions and working together on issues and projects, she became one of his most solid allies.

The reader may well be asking, "If the management of dependencies is critical, why do some of the insulting, imperial people with whom I have to deal have any vestiges of power left?" Our only response is that an individual's power is derived in large part from being viewed by those upon whom he or she is dependent as contributing importantly to organizational goals. Take a careful look at these individuals. Upon whom are they, in fact, dependent, and how are they perceived by these people?

MARCHING INTO LOSING BATTLES

James Marley, vice president of purchasing, read a report of the recommendations of the committee set up by the president to expand international sales. Marley had had international sales experience himself, and he disagreed with the recommendations. He wrote a strong memo, outlining his objections, and sent a copy to the president and committee members. He also asked that it be placed on the agenda of the next meeting of the executive committee, of which he was a member. At the executive committee meeting, Marley raised his objections. The vice president of marketing, who was chairman of the committee on international sales expansion, responded to Marley's points briefly and said that his committee would be willing to meet with Marley to consider the issues that he had raised. However, he pointed out that he would need to bring in the final recommendations to the executive committee for approval the next week if they were to meet the deadlines necessary to get the program into place that year. At the next executive committee meeting, the marketing vice president brought back the original recommendations, explained why his committee chose not to take Marley's suggestion, and asked for approval of the plan to implement the recommendations. His request was granted, over Marley's objection. After the meeting the financial vice president said to the president, "I had no trouble voting against Marley this time. This is the second time he has blind-sided a program when it was almost set in concrete. He knew that committee was meeting; if he wanted to have an input, he should have talked to them early when he could have made a difference. He swings after the bell."

Marley's experience was similar to that of a number of individuals we observed, heard about, or interviewed. He chose to enter battles that he had little chance of winning. Stage IV individuals who exercise power effectively tend not to take stands where the issue seems already decided. As one Stage IV scientist put it, "You don't throw yourself in front of a juggernaut." We are not saying that successful Stage IV people do not get involved in controversial decisions or take on tough problems. However, we have noticed that they will not "openly" take on an issue or confrontation until they have carefully lined up enough support and resources to ensure a high likelihood of winning.

Some managers of professionals get in trouble by unnecessarily promising more than they are sure that they can deliver.

Jack Mann, the division manager of a high-tech firm, was admired for his ability to develop innovative strategies. However, he sometimes failed to see that all the parts of the strategy were fully executed. He went to Germany and persuaded a designer with an international reputation to head up a new project. He promised the designer that he would hire six new technical people for the project and provide the needed resources. But he found later that he could not obtain the resources nor hire the six people. The designer resigned and joined a competitor. This was a major setback for the project and placed Mann in an unfavorable light. The event triggered a careful study of Mann's division by the president. Mann, disturbed by the pressure and the scrutiny, handed in his resignation.

We learned about three individuals in Stage IV roles and a number more who were blocked from Stage IV, who had their power to accomplish things eroded by making promises they couldn't keep. Like those who went unprepared into losing battles, they undermined the confidence others had in them. James Quinn, in his study of strategy management, also observed managers get themselves in trouble through "announcement-itis." He describes one C.E.O. who in other ways performed admirably under difficult circumstances, but was eventually forced out because he promised a 10 percent increase in profits that did not materialize (17).

Conversely, a number of those operating successfully in Stage IV told us of the care they took never to promise anything that they were not sure they could deliver. One of the most problematic areas for many of them was profit or budget projections. Typical of the strategies for coping with the vulnerabilities of this process was the approach taken by the managers of a division of a large manufacturing firm. Like the other divisions, they had been making annual projections, updated semiannually, and reviewed results with top management annually. In a year when raw material costs took unexpected turns, however, they chose to take a more active stance. Since they were the largest division, they asked for brief quarterly and, when needed, monthly operational reviews with top management. In these reviews, they presented revised financial projections, the reasons for the revisions, and the steps that they were taking to ensure the new projections. Their more active stance increased their credibility and influence at both headquarters and inside the division.

There are times, of course, when each individual, for issues involving principle and integrity, must chose to fight, even in a losing cause. There are also times when individuals must be ready to put their careers on the line, but they should carefully pick the time and the place.

UNSHEATHING THE SWORD

Machiavelli's writings imply that the more one acts on one's power the more one is apt to lose it (18). Rex Matkin, the Waste Containment Program manager described at the beginning of this chapter, was one who got caught in this trap. He retaliated angrily when others did not comply with his demands. He frequently rejected their work and did not hesitate to pull rank to step up production. Matkin essentially stripped himself of his informal power by appealing too often, and too quickly, to his formal power. But this is said too easily, too glibly. We have not come close to understanding this pitfall in the exercise of power until we do better than that. For help, we turn to the excellent study by Neustadt on the exercise of power by those holding the office of the President of the United States (19).

Neustadt initially distinguishes between the formal powers vested in the Presidency and what he defines as "power"—the power to persuade. He quotes Harry Truman:

> I sit here all day trying to persuade people to do things they ought to have sense enough to do without my persuading them. . . . That's all the powers of the President amount to (20).

Neustadt next examines instances where Presidents used the formal powers of the office of the Presidency, such as President Truman's recall of General MacArthur from command during the Korean conflict. In each, he describes the high cost and, sometimes, inconclusiveness of the formal action. The price Truman paid for MacArthur's dismissal was public exposition, at the Senate hearings, of his administration's innermost thoughts about the further conduct of hostilities—to Peking, Moscow, and the American public. These costly "last resorts" could be justified only because the costs of continued inaction would have been even higher. In MacArthur's case, says Neustadt, "Truman could no longer have retained MacArthur without yielding to him the conduct of the war." Neustadt completes this part of the analysis by concluding that Truman was quite right in saying that presidential power is the power to persuade. Command is but a method of persuasion, not a substitute, and not a method suitable for everyday employment (21).

Neustadt then turns to examine what he considers the real power of the president—the power to persuade. He begins with the task:

> The essence of a President's persuasive task is to convince such men that what the White House wants of them is what they ought to do for their sake and on their authority.

Then Neustadt moves on to the power:

> Presidential "powers" may be inconclusive when a President commands, but always remain relevant as he persuades. The status and authority inherent in his office reinforce his logic and his charm. . . . few men—and exceedingly few Cabinet officers, are immune to the impulse to say "yes" to the President of the United States. It grows harder to say "no" when they are seated in his oval office at the White House. . . . With hardly an exception, the men who share in governing this country are aware that at some time, in some degree, the doing of *their* jobs, the furthering of *their* ambitions, may depend on the President of the United States (22).

Neustadt is talking about an extreme case of someone holding power in an organization—the President of the United States. But let us not allow the example to prevent us from understanding his point. Organizational power is the power to persuade. Articulate presentation of a persuading argument can be a source of power, of course, but the articulateness of the suggestion is only a part of the power to persuade. The status and authority of the persuader, as well as the present and anticipated dependence of the person being persuaded, are critical elements in the power to persuade. This power, you will note, is exercised within real limits; the President is trying to persuade them to do what they "ought to do for their own sake and on their own authority"—to do what he thinks will be best for the country (23).

The power available to the President may be different in quantity, but not in kind, from that which was available to Rex Matkin and anyone attempting to play a Stage IV role in organizations. There are some things available to those holding formal management positions that are not available to nonmanagers, which we will discuss later, but the main sources of power are available to both.

One source of power—to persuade—is the use of one's time to focus attention on some objective. If the individual has status and respect, if the individual's time is perceived to be valuable by others, so much the better. Rex Matkin had time to prepare, to plan, to present, to persist. Part of the power of his role as program manager was that he had control over 100 percent of his time to focus attention on the accomplishment of the objectives of that program.

Another source of power is the ability and effort expended to provide direction, to map the environment, to reinterpret history, to present that vision in the light of the organization, and to manage the process by which steps are taken to respond to or reveal new information. This can be done in many ways: face to face, in small groups, or in public statements. Rex Matkin had the authority of knowledge. He was one of the world's authorities on waste containment. He could collect and interpret information to which no one else in the company, even in the world, had access.

Power comes from asking questions. Questions can focus attention and persuade. Questions can enlighten, instruct, and signal concern. The same questions, asked over and over again, can draw attention to fundamentals and instill in others the determination to be prepared to answer that question next time.

Part of the power to persuade lies in the example of the persuader. "What you do speaks so loudly, I cannot hear what you say." We mimic, we learn from, we are inspired by models.

Power is also exercised by being attentive to behavior desired in others, and praising and reinforcing that behavior.

All of the above sources of power are available to managers and nonmanagers alike. Managers with formal positions have other means of persuasion at their disposal. They can set the agenda at meetings. Within limits, they can select who comes to meetings. They can decide on the location of the meetings. If they want better coordination with production, they can hold meetings at plant locations. They can focus attention by asking that all presentations follow a certain format or include an analysis of certain fundamental assumptions or issues. They can signal their attention by the way they utilize their staff(24). These and a thousand other devices form the arsenal of those who exercise power in organizations. To use them well requires energy, planning, will, and determination. To ignore them and to leap too quickly into formal commands is a form of self-impoverishment. To unsheath the sword of formal commands before it is necessary and without it being a part of a web of other forms of persuasion is to lose power.

In this chapter on exercising power, we have found ourselves forced to talk about the management of organizations' interfaces and networks. We now turn our attention to the Stage IV function of representing the organization to those inside and outside its boundaries.

9

Representing the Organization

While interviewing at a large national CPA. firm, we asked a regional director to tell us the most common blocks to moving into Stage IV that he had observed in his organization. He responded by saying:

> When I was regional director over an area that included the San Antonio office, the partner-in-charge in that office had to retire suddenly for health reasons. It was my job to choose the new partner-in-charge. It turned out to be one of the hardest things I had to do that year. I had known one of the partners, Mark Bone, from my previous visits there. He and I had graduated from the same school, and I thought that I had my man. As I began talking to the other partners and principals, I found that they all liked and respected him as a manager. He was bright and had scored second in the country on the CPA exam, only two points away from winning the gold medal. But after I had looked at the records and talked with the retiring partner-in-charge, I knew that I couldn't put Bone in charge. As able as he was on other dimensions, he was weak in practice development (i.e., bringing in new clients or new business from current clients). He barely did the minimum each year. The retiring partner-in-charge said that they had made Bone a partner hoping that he would improve in that area. The old partner-in-charge worked with him, and while Bone kept saying he'd go after it, he never did. I had to pass him over. If a partner-in-charge is weak in the area of practice development, I can't see how he could run an office. He can't teach others to do something that he doesn't do, and the partner-in-charge usually has to pick up more of the practice development than any other partner.

A member of the board of directors of a medium-sized retail firm told us about a man who had been hired as C.E.O., one who was in danger of losing that position:

When our president retired, we decided to go outside to bring in some new marketing ideas and know-how. We brought in someone who seemed to have plenty of both. But it doesn't seem to be working out. He brought in someone from his old firm to be his second-in-command. They sit in the corporate office and draw up what look like good marketing plans, but not much seems to happen. They claim that the division directors are resistant to new ideas; the division directors say those two live in an ivory tower without knowing what our business is all about. I get the impression that the C.E.O. and the executive vice president he brought in don't know what's going on in the trenches. I don't think he will last.

The similarity in these two situations is that these two men were being scrutinized to see if they could skillfully represent the company to critical groups, and both were failing. The CPA was seen as not performing the vital function of representing the firm to outside groups. He was not developing a network of relationships with individuals and groups through which he could bring resources and information into the organization. The C.E.O. was viewed as having failed to build a network of relationships with individuals and groups inside the firm through which he could gather the information that he needed and also communicate a map of where the organization should be going.

A significant factor of the novation into Stage IV is demonstrating the capacity to build and maintain networks of relationships both inside and outside the organization. It is through these networks that an individual represents the organization: a president meets with stock analysts or a manager negotiates with a union. Sometimes the representation is formal, though more often it is informal or semiformal. A partner from a CPA firm may give a talk on the effects of a new tax law on investments, or a manager may have a conversation with his old friend in the production department. When a bank manager serves on the United Fund committee, he or she not only performs a civic service but is also getting to know members of other organizations who may need information that the bank manager can supply and who may someday need banking services. If the banker is able to supply services or information, a relationship is likely to develop, which can be mutually beneficial to both of the individuals involved as well as to their respective organizations. Likewise, serving on a task force or committee within one's own organization can perform the same functions internally. Organizations have powerful needs for resources and for information. Therefore, those individuals who can build relationships that bring resources and information into the organization and at the same time present an accurate picture of the organization's strengths are highly valued.

For much of its history, the literature on management and professionals focused almost exclusively on superior–subordinate relationships. One of the first exceptions was Melville Dalton. His data came from inside "informers" reporting what was actually determining events in the company. These informants emphasized the powerful influence that informal networks and relationships played in the firm (1). More recently, Kanter found that the managers who failed to establish informal relations with their peers were rendered powerless and ineffective (2). Mintzberg found that top executives spent 44 percent of their time talking to individuals outside their own organization (3). Pfeffer noted that managers form coalitions to acquire influence with groups outside the organizations, as well as with groups inside, whose support they needed (4). Kotter found that general managers spent over 75 percent of their time talking and listening to others, including many who were not their direct subordinates or superiors. It was not unusual, Kotter reported, to find a general manager talking to a subordinate's subordinate, a boss's boss, a customer or supplier, a competitor, a union or government official (5). He even found that "one typical G.M. [general manager] was alleged by those who worked with him to personally know well over a thousand people in his company and industry." (6) Kaplan concluded, after reviewing a number of studies, including his own, that managers' lateral relationships inside and outside the organization were often their most valuable asset in getting their work done (7).

EXTERNAL REPRESENTATION

We have already stressed the organization's need for parties who can "read" what is going on outside the organization. It is also vital that an organization's interests be well represented to a wide range of entities. Direct contact with customers, clients, and suppliers comes to mind immediately, but the complex network of other important individuals and institutions is equally important. There are "recommenders," such as bankers and accountants, investors and financial analysts, government regulators, media representatives, and trade association representatives. Why is it so important that the organization be well represented to these entities and what functions do the representatives perform?

BRINGING IN RESOURCES

Clearly, one of the important functions of anyone who represents an organization to the outside is to bring in resources even in settings where that seems less logical or necessary. Most people would not associate sales or marketing with public accounting, but Mark Bone's poor record in "practice development"—bringing new clients and increased revenues into the firm—was enough to prevent his appointment as partner-in-charge. One of a university president's major responsibilities is to see that the necessary funds flow into the university. A scientist with an outstanding reputation can attract other strong researchers and research funding.

When we travelled through the Dallas airport, we would often see Hugh McNulty, the chairman of the board of a small computer firm that we studied. We finally asked him why he was always on the road. He explained:

> The only way to survive in this industry is to go out and get the money to keep us alive. I have to go out and find contracts and investors. A growing start-up is a big mouth to feed. We can't just sit in Dallas and expect people to come to us.

Hugh McNulty was *expected* to represent his firm. The investors demanded it of him. As chairman of the board, one of his formalized tasks was to bring in resources. Most individuals who represent organizations are in a similar position. Organizations need people with the capacity to deal effectively with the institutions or publics that supply resources. Demonstrating promise as a representative is often a critical milestone in making the novation into Stage IV.

There are many others who assume these responsibilities from a position outside mainline management roles as well. In our study, one of the most dramatic movements into Stage IV concerned an engineer who had left his company twice to start up new ventures. Each time he had come back to the large aerospace firm where he had worked before. Somewhere in the process of these entrepreneurial experiences, he came to understand the importance of building up networks. A colleague told us this story:

> An individual contributor in an aerospace firm, Harry Baine, was finishing up a project and was looking for something challenging that would have substantial benefit to the company. He became interested in torpedoes and was convinced that even though the firm had never built torpedoes, it had the basic technological capacity to do so. He presented his suggestion to his supervisor and received no support. Undaunted, Baine went to the president, a former classmate of his, and explained the opportunity he saw for the company. The president told him he would get him a budget of $25,000 to come up with evidence that the idea was feasible. As Baine began to talk to people inside and outside the firm, gathering more data, the president was advised to stop him before he created a situation that could cost the company many times the $25,000 to rectify. Baine was called in, as well as the people responsible for engineering and contract procurement. He surprised them by answering all their questions, by being able to identify the areas of electronics, guidance systems, and aerodynamics where their firm

could make unique contributions to this field of weaponry. Baine came out of the meeting with a larger budget. For the next year and a half, he visited and became acquainted with people in every organization that designed, manufactured, or bought torpedoes. He especially worked on relationships with Remington Corporation, a company that had many years' experience and a reputation in developing and manufacturing torpedoes. He persuaded Remington to make a joint proposal with his aerospace firm to build two torpedo systems. Baine's contacts at Remington helped him put together a strong proposal for the Navy. Both contracts were funded, and Harry's firm now had $100-million worth of new business, as a result of both the strong network of relationships that Baine had set up, and the technical know-how that he had been able to bring into his organization through that network.

We also found that bright researchers and idea innovators were often adept at this function.

When the federal government made the decision to provide funding for a program to develop methods of extracting fossil fuels from oil shale, a highly respected geologist from one of the research laboratories we studied was asked to come to Washington, D.C., to help lay out the program. When we were at the laboratory several years later and were asking people to point out Stage IV individuals, this nonmanager geologist was named by a large number of people. His acquaintance with the people administering the program, his intimate understanding of the program and its basic aims, and his personal reputation in the field had helped make him a key figure in developing a strong energy research program at the laboratory. Indeed, few people in the organization had played a more decisive role in bringing resources into the organization in the last decade than had this geologist.

BRINGING IN INFORMATION

So far we have talked about individuals whose representation of the organization to the outside resulted directly in additional resources. We also found a number of Stage IV individuals who brought in vital information. Most members of boards of directors are chosen because of their outside contacts and reputations. They are expected to represent the organization to outside parties to bring in information, as well as resources. Yet we were surprised to find the number of people in various positions—management and nonmanagement—who acted as information conductors for their organizations.

One of the most important decisions in most food processing companies is how much of the firm's anticipated product needs are purchased on contract before the growing season and how much is purchased later during harvest. That decision is one of the largest determinants of profit for the year since the prices can vary so greatly between those two times, depending on whether a shortage or a surplus of the produce develops later in the season. In one company we looked at, one manager was relied upon to make that decision each year because of the extensive network of relationships that he had developed among the farmers, the seed and fertilizer vendors, and the company's agricultural agents.

We often found that, particularly among the nonmanager Stage IV individuals, writing and publishing continues to be a means of representing the organization to other entities. In most fields of research, there is an inner group of researchers who know what is being done in the field before it reaches the professional journals. Access to such information, if it is centrally related to the company's major activities, can be vital to the organization's performance.

In studying two major universities, we asked individuals to tell us who they considered to be in Stage IV. In the first, we found very few people, except deans and university officials, whom anyone could identify as Stage IV individuals. At the second university, a number of nonadministrators were quickly pointed out to us. When we mentioned the difference to them, we were asked if the first university was strongly research oriented. When we replied it was not, they said:

> *That is the reason.* In order for someone other than an administrator to have that kind of influence or provide direction for any significant part of the organization, he or she must be doing something that strongly impacts the reputation of the organization and its ability to obtain resources. At a university, a nonadministrative faculty member can do research and publish, which falls into that category.

At the research-oriented university, the Stage IV nonmanagers all seemed to have strong, usually international reputations from their published research. (This was not always the case in the government research laboratories that we studied because some of the government-sponsored research could not be published.) The research and publishing of these Stage IV idea innovators was marked not only by high productivity but by the paradigm-shifting nature of their work. These people were usually described as having been effectual in moving their discipline or a major branch of their discipline in a new direction. But extensive publishing or inner membership in a technical field alone is certainly no guarantee of Stage IV status within the organization. Unless the publishing or the outside relationships are structured and focused in such areas where the organization has major interests, they are not likely to be viewed as valuable by others in the organization.

REPRESENTING THE ORGANIZATION TO OTHER CRITICAL ENTITIES

Another important entity the organizations must consider is the community in which they operate. One of the vice presidents of an electronics firm talked to us about the division manager of their operations in the west.

> Ted Sargent does a lot of things well and would have been considered a strong performer for other reasons, but the characteristic that has brought him the strongest recognition in the company is the way he has handled relationships with the community. Our company had brought a large operation into a fairly small community. Sargent, who is now the division manager, had done a lot of research on his own about the impact of adding 5,000 employees and an addition of 20,000 people to a community that was wary of growth. He had been very articulate in showing the community leaders the supply of jobs that it would create, the costs the city would incur, and the revenues that it would receive. He has worked with the city in getting technical and other assistance on their toughest problem, that of water. He has displayed many of the capabilities in working with the community that showed up only later in the company when he had become division director. Up to that point, he was primarily regarded in the company only as a strong technical man.

BLOCKS TO EXTERNAL REPRESENTATION

If this function is so important to both the organization and the individual's career, why do some fail to perform it? We found that some individuals simply did not understand its importance; others let a fear or dislike of "selling" prevent them from performing this function.

UNDERSTANDING IMPORTANCE OF REPRESENTATION

In an interview, a university faculty member talked about his disappointment with one of his colleagues. He told us that this man was capable, but that he just didn't seem to understand academic life:

> Nigel was invited to join one of the National Science Foundation committees, but he turned it down because he said he didn't like committee work. Then he couldn't understand why they declined his application for National Science Foundation grants. That didn't bother the rest of us as much as the

fact that he has passed up so many opportunities to provide openings for the junior faculty. He won't attend association meetings; yet other people with his abilities chair those meetings and provide places for their junior faculty members to present papers and get some visibility. He had the door open to him, and he could have opened lots of doors for others here if he'd given up some of his precious time and served on that National Science Foundation committee. We don't understand him. He could have established a national reputation and moved the university ahead in the field 10 years ago, to the point we are just reaching now.

We were told a very similar story in an electronics firm:

> A manager of human resources had been in his job for 7 years and had never been able to gain any influence with the top management, who were all technical people. He finally left the company in discouragement. A younger man took his place, who was fairly inexperienced in the field. But when he was asked by his superiors to get better data on future manning needs, contrary to what his predecessor had done, he went out and attended Human Resource Planning Association meetings. He met people there who were forming a consortium of companies to support an environmental forecasting effort at a university. With the data from the forecasting group and the information from other members of the consortium on how they coordinated their human resource planning with the business planning in their companies, the new human resource manager became an influential part of the strategic planning group in the company.

The opportunity to do those things had been available to the previous human resource manager, but he never used the outside support that was available to him. When he was asked if he was going to Human Resource Planning Association meetings, he always replied, as did the professor described above, that he was too busy.

FEAR OF "SELLING"

There are undoubtedly people who fail to move into Stage IV because they are not viewed by others as having the ability to present the image that other members of the organization expect of them. If universities are so concerned about the way their athletic coaches and presidents represent them, other organizations must also have the same concerns. We didn't find specific instances of individuals being rejected for assignments because it was feared that they wouldn't represent the organization well. What we did hear, however, were many instances in which individuals were uncomfortable, hesitant, and opposed to putting themselves in positions where they would be expected to promote the organization's services or products.

One director of engineering told us that when he started working as an engineer, he really had no idea of how important the presentation of projects, ideas, and results would be in engineering management. He had had to discipline himself to learn the necessary skills, and he was constantly disappointed that some of his able group leaders were unwilling to do likewise. He told us:

> Too many engineers and engineering managers have this abhorrence of anything that might be thought of as salesmanship. I wonder if they ever stop to think who sells their ideas and projects; other engineers do. Ideas, projects, and products don't sell themselves. A lot of very good ideas die because they don't have a champion who is willing to learn to present them in a way that others can understand and appreciate. There are some of my good group leaders who just won't use their brains to figure out how to make a good presentation to top management. It's emotional somehow. There's a lurking fear of being dishonest if they haven't buried someone in details. It sure has blocked some good people.

We repeatedly heard of individuals, particularly in public accounting firms, who were denied partner status or had limited influence in the office because they couldn't or wouldn't build new business for the firm. Mark Bone, whom we introduced at the beginning of this chapter, was only one of many who were failing in "practice development." We heard this term so often that we became intrigued and asked the partner-in-charge of an office of a large eastern CPA firm to tell us how he handled practice development:

> I go around and ask each of the partners how much they can commit themselves to in next year's budget. (I've already committed to national headquarters that we'd make 5 percent growth as an office). One may say that he'll get 1,000 billed hours; another 500. I usually make up the difference, but if it is not enough, I have to go back and ask for more. That is just something we have to have from our partners. We used to make people partners without their demonstrating that they can and will do practice development but that hardly ever happens now. They not only must do the practice development themselves but they have to be able to teach others to do it. They have to be able to show others how to build an industry specialization, establish a presence in the community, give speeches, write articles, and ask someone, "What business are you in?" and "Who is your accountant?" They have got to tell their people the day they come to work

for the firm, "Keep in touch with your classmates. You can forget, temporarily, the ones who went to work for public accounting firms, but stay in touch with the others. As you move up, so will they, and someday they will bring you big clients."

It is important for those who represent the organization to the outside to neither over-commit themselves to other organizations nor appear to have shifted their primary commitment away from their own organizations, if they are making the novation into Stage IV. Pfeffer, in his work on power in organizations, noted that the cost of building and using outside alliances is the risk of being viewed as disloyal to the organization and its goals. Pfeffer hypothesized, therefore, that the building of external alliances will be done circumspectly (8).

Before concluding our discussion on outside representation, let us note that this one function alone is seldom enough to move into and remain in Stage IV. The director of a division of a European research laboratory told us of a deputy director that he had had who did very well in making international contacts. The deputy director spoke five languages, had a good education, and had contacts in several universities. Everyone agreed that he did an excellent job of representing the laboratory to the outside by helping to bring in resources and information. However, when the decision was made to break the division into smaller divisions, the director and others he spoke to agreed that this deputy director was not likely to be able to provide direction for any one of the new divisions. He was asked to leave. We asked the director if the deputy director had learned to exercise power effectively in the organization or had been sponsoring people who promised to be key people to the organization in the future. He said "no" to these questions and added that it was because there was lack of confidence in his ability to perform these other requirements that he was not selected as one of the new division heads. Performing one of the Stage IV functions well can enhance performance in the other Stage IV functions. But if an individual becomes a strong outside representative and ignores all other functions, he or she cannot be ensured comprehensive Stage IV performance.

INTERNAL REPRESENTATION

We mentioned earlier that in the studies of Melville Dalton, Rosabeth Kanter, Henry Mintzberg, John Kotter, and Robert Kaplan, almost all the managers studied maintained a wide network of informal relationships with people at various levels inside the organization. We also noted that those researchers who looked for a relationship between these networks and management performance found that those who had built and maintained strong informal networks tended to be more effective and received higher evaluations than those who did not. Clearly, these networks and informal relationships are valuable to the managers who use them. But they are also vital to the functioning of the organization. Organizations need their leaders to have networks through which they can communicate a rationale for their actions.

In our interviews and observations, we also found not only effective managers, but also many influential nonmanagers operating within wide informal networks in the organization. They use these networks not only to dispense and gather information, but also to help provide direction for the organization and exercise power. If anything, the nonmanagers in Stage IV were more dependent on the informal system than were the managers; the formal system was not nearly as accessible to nonmanagers. But for both managers and nonmanagers, the informal system provides a vehicle to perform two major functions, both of which are vital to the organization: a vehicle for information transfer and a means of enlisting support.

TRANSFERRING INFORMATION

Individuals in Stage IV, if they are to provide adequate direction for the organization and exercise power effectively, must have good information. A great deal of the information they need is available from other members of the organization. Some of this flows through formal hierarchical lines or is transmitted in formal meetings, but much of it flows through informal channels. Formal directors often transmit a lot of their information outside formal meetings. Conversely, these informal networks give other members of the organization access to those who provide direction and make key decisions.

All organizations need this free flow of information and access to decision-makers. In fast growing high-tech organizations, this need is accentuated. That could well be the reason why the term, "management by wandering around" (M.B.W.A.) has been synthesized by some of the newer firms such as Hewlett Packard and Intel. M.B.W.A. legitimates and advocates the idea that a manager's time is often best spent out among the people who are performing the work that he or she is trying to oversee. It gives managers the freedom to ask questions of those doing the work. The workers gain access to someone who can wield power and has information about the direction the organization is taking. Such access can be particularly important to someone whose formal superior is not a good source of information.

The term, M.B.W.A., is nothing but a new term to describe how Stage IV managers (and nonmanagers) keep in touch with formal networks. One distinguished academic vice president of a large university, who refers to himself as a Victorian and who would be insulted if someone suggested that he was following some modern management approach, described to us what he did to make sure he stayed in touch with the faculty. After teaching an early morning freshman class, an important activity to him that confirms his position as a professor as well as an administrator, he walks all the way across campus, stopping to talk to faculty members that he meets. "I find that it's on these walks that faculty members talk to me about their accomplishments and their nagging irritations," he told us. "It's on the sidewalks that the faculty members can tell me about the grants they have received or the problems that concern them." This was a busy administrator, who works 12- to 14-hour days regularly. But he made it clear that the conversations on the sidewalk are among the most important things that he does each day.

LINING UP SUPPORT

Decisions are announced and votes are taken in formal meetings, but often the real decisions are made in informal discussions before the formal meeting occurs.

> At one large research organization, a division president told us how he had influenced a critical decision made at the group executive meeting. Because this decision was so important to his division, several days before the meeting, he took a draft of the proposal to every person who would be attending the meeting. After they had had a chance to read it, he went to see each of them personally. If they had reservations, he hammered out wording that would be acceptable to both of them. "In the process," he said, "I realized that I was using up some of my social capital. They will feel a little more free to come to me in the same way when they have something coming up that is important to them. But this was a key decision for our division. I was willing to call in a few social debts. I knew the president had no strong objections to it if everyone else felt all right about it."

This example illustrates how support was generated for a single decision. Next we'll look at a broader means for lining up support:

> Four years before George Davis was made vice president of research in a large chemical company, he was asked to be the executive secretary for the corporate executive committee. In this position, Davis came to know executives from all the divisions. He knew the research center, which had made some patentable discoveries in polymer chemistry during the previous two decades, and enjoyed considerable income from its patents. Much

effort in this division had been geared to create more patent income in order to keep their financial independence. Yet this emphasis generated negative side-effects. The other divisions felt that they were not getting the necessary support and attention, and began doing research for their own projects. Davis realized how negatively the research center was viewed. He knew how much easier it was to help other divisions when he understood problems from their point of view, when he knew the right people to call for information, and when others had confidence in him. Thus, when Davis was made vice president of the research center, he decided that what was needed most was the development of outside assignments. He began to obtain assignments in other divisions for those promising managers and professionals who had spent all their working lives inside the center. He also brought in managers from the operating divisions to head up departments in the research center. Before long, it became clear that to have influence in the center and in the company, a manager or a professional had to be able to work effectively and closely with people in other divisions.

Building and maintaining a supportive, informal network requires a certain amount of savvy. George Shultz, as treasury secretary and later as president of Bechtel Corporation, was known for his interpersonal skill. When he was asked by President Reagan to relinquish the presidency of Bechtel Corporation and become secretary of state, a reporter for *Time Magazine* gathered data about Shultz's operating style. The reporter wrote:

> He [Shultz] displayed an impressive talent for exercising authority and expanding turf without ruffling feathers or alienating colleagues. Says former Budget Director James Lynn: "He's one of the best base-touchers I've ever seen." An official who served under Schultz at Treasury explains, "he could make everyone, even those who opposed the action taken, feel an integral part of the process" (9).

BLOCKS TO INTERNAL REPRESENTATION

Failure to build and maintain informal networks can block individuals from making a successful novation into Stage IV. Some individuals are oblivious to the need to represent the organization in this fashion. Some fail to appreciate the reciprocity that is fundamental to maintaining relationships. Others find informal relationships uncomfortable and tend to avoid them.

UNDERSTANDING NEED

There are many people who, at least in their actions, seem to attribute all organizational transactions and arrangements to the workings of the formal system. Such individuals never realize that organizations are social systems as well as logical formal systems, and that people are responding to social obligations as well as to formal role definitions. Many capable individuals fail to build social ties and buttress formal arrangements with social obligations. They are first disappointed, then become cynical, never realizing that organizations are more complex than they appear on the surface. They fail to work with that complexity and are very frustrated by it.

The director of a European laboratory in a large international research organization told us of a highly disappointing experience that Garold Brun, chief of the automotive economics section of his laboratory had had.

> Brun had seen the opportunity to do a worldwide effectiveness study on auto safety devices. He sent a prospectus to two laboratories in the firm in other countries and asked if they were interested. Both replied positively and sent impressive descriptions of their capabilities. But when it came time to write the parts of the full proposal that each lab had agreed to do, one lab sent word that their key man was too busy, and the other lab sent something that appeared to have been thrown together hastily. In disgust, Brun ended up writing the whole proposal himself, primarily using his own time and discretionary funds to obtain funding for the project. A year later, when the final report was due, one lab's contribution again showed lack of adequate thought and care. The other lab's report was not only 6 weeks late but was seriously below the standard that the sponsor expected. The sponsors were unhappy and Brun was bitter.

In a recent study by one of our colleagues, it was found that half of all the formal decisions made in a large organization were never carried out (10). Results of the study surprised many students, but did not surprise any of the Stage IV people to whom we described the finding. They realize the complex forces that act on individuals and groups in an organization; not everything that is decided in á meeting will be carried out in the way they may anticipate. They know that if they want a certain outcome, they will have to use their time, their personal persistence, their understanding of the motives and pressures of others, and their relationships with others to make that outcome more likely.

Brun made the mistake of assuming that if he had the formal agreement of representatives of the other labs, they would do their part of the project that he had proposed. Brun, or some of his associates with strong contacts in the other labs, should have tried to ascertain important informal details beforehand: How committed were the other labs to this project. Who had the commitment? How much influence did those who had made the commitments have when a shortage of competent people arose? Competent and influential people at the other laboratories might have been willing to commit themselves to someone if they had felt a personal commitment to Brun and his associates whose opinions they highly valued.

There were a number of things that Brun, or those who worked with him, could have done *if* they had not placed too much reliance on the formal arrangements, *if* they had found how this project was viewed in the other laboratories, and *if* they had known the competence and power of the people that they were working with. But all these *ifs* are dependent on having a strong network of informal relations with people in other parts of the organization. Those *ifs* imply an understanding of the nature of complex organizations and the need for informal relationships and networks.

Ignorance of the need for internal representation can manifest itself through isolation. We saw how the entire research division of a large company had allowed itself to become isolated from the operating divisions. Only when George Davis from the research laboratories was made executive secretary to the executive committee of the company and then sent back as director of research that the management of the research lab realized the possibilities that were being foregone because they did not have rich informal ties to people in the operating divisions.

We also repeatedly heard stories of individual managers or outstanding professionals who had limited their influence and careers by "holing themselves up in their offices," and isolating themselves from others within and without their divisions. They allowed themselves to be entrapped and isolated by "busyness." Whether this isolation came from a lack of understanding of the importance of building ties with others in the company, an inability to build and maintain such ties, or interpersonal discomfort is very hard to determine.

UNDERSTANDING RECIPROCITY

We have discussed the principle of reciprocity at length as an issue in Stage III. Generally, those who are able to move through Stage III understand reciprocity and have no trouble with this issue in Stage IV. The likelihood that the move into Stage IV flounders on lack of understanding of reciprocity is much lower than in the move into Stage III. Nevertheless, the issue does arise in several ways.

A number of persons who were trying to move into Stage IV were described to us as "manipulative." They were suspected of working more to advance their own careers than working to solve the company's problems.

We also heard the term "self-centered" or a similar term that suggests certain individuals are focused so intently on their agendas and problems that they are relatively insensitive to others' needs or problems. When it is their problem that needs solving, they are very much in evidence, but when others have problems and are seeking help, they make themselves scarce.

In other cases, the individual in his or her own personal dealings is seen as warm and unselfish but seems unable to see the need for reciprocity between organizations. For example:

> A director of an engineering and technology center in a large company was viewed by the people in the center as very interested in others. In fact, he often suggested to the vice presidents of production and marketing that they promote some of his strong technical people to supervisory and management positions in their organizations. But when we talked to managers in production and marketing, they said that while he was always wanting them to take his promising people, he was never willing to consider taking any of their people. "He thinks that because of their graduate degrees, they can help us, but he can't see that our people with experience in the plants or in sales could help them do their work better."

Contrast what we have described above with Frank March, a former department manager in a research institute that we studied.

> March was known as a strong department chairman who had brought some capable people into the institute. His group had not grown rapidly, but it had an excellent reputation for being close to the state-of-the-art, and for being consistently well funded. March had been "loaned" by another laboratory to act as deputy director while the deputy was on an overseas assignment. A few years after March returned to his own lab, the laboratory director retired. According to the president of the institute, something really remarkable happened when he began considering individuals to fill the vacated position. The president indicated that he had never had so much unsolicited help in choosing a new laboratory director than he had had at that time. First, he had letters and then a visit from two of the "junior" scientists in March's department. One was a woman who had received her degree a few years ago and had come directly into March's department with no postdoctoral experience and no publications to back her up. The other was a man closer in age to March, joining the department without a Ph.D. but with extensive industrial experience. Both of them tried to convince the president that he should consider no one but March. When he asked why they felt so strongly, they both said that they had had trouble launching research during their first years while March was at the other lab. But when he came back, all

that changed for both of them. March had taken on projects with each of them, helped them put proposals together, helped them get funding and, when projects were complete, co-authored articles on their research to get a publication stream going. They both said that if March could do for the lab what he had done for their department, the lab would be in good hands.

INTERPERSONAL DISCOMFORT

We found another small group of individuals who fell in neither of the categories above. They seemed fully aware of the organization's need to have individuals representing the organization's leadership to other parts of the organization. They understood the nature of reciprocity; if anyone does something for them, they go the extra mile in return. But they find informal relationships with anyone other than a few close associates to be uncomfortable. A few were described as shy, others unapproachable, and still others as uncomfortable with peers. Most of the people described to us as shy were very competent, sometimes brilliant nonmanagers who, according to those around them, might have begun to perform Stage IV functions if they interacted with more people in the firm. Some have strong reputations outside their organizations, largely through publication, but keep to a small circle of people with whom they work. One of them told us that he would like to have greater influence over what happens, and he knows that he ought to work with others more. Any attempts, however, are so frustrating that he quickly retreats to his lab.

Those described to us as unapproachable included both managers and non-managers. Again, they were usually described as having unusual intellectual ability, but interactions with them have a standoffish quality, even in the most informal settings.

> One had graduated first in his MBA class and had an outstanding record in financial analysis, but he was not content to be a specialist. He had been in a number of firms when we met him. Because of his background and experience, he was placed in the chief financial officer's position, but he soon began to alienate himself from others by "putting them down" in his remarks to them. Even the president who hired him has been offended by the "unnecessary hostility" that marked many of his interactions. His influence has been limited to formal decisions. When we completed our interviews in the company, we were told that he was seeking a position with another company.

Those who were described as uncomfortable with peers were usually managers who seemed comfortable in dealing only with subordinates and direct superiors. They were usually described as very competent and well liked by those with whom they worked, but they seemed to avoid situations where they had to deal with people who did not fall into these two categories. When they were in such situations, they appeared stiff or ill at ease.

The common perception in the popular press is that "personality problems" are the major factor in derailing executives or preventing individuals from having greater influence. The number of people we found who seemed to be blocked from moving into Stage IV for interpersonal reasons is surprisingly small. Conversely, we were struck by the wide range of interpersonal styles of people in Stage IV. Some are quiet; some are stereotypical extroverts. The biggest difference between those who represent the organization well through informal networks versus those who don't seems to be an understanding of how things get done in organizations, and how information and power are obtained and utilized.

One caution must be noted in concluding our discussion of inside representation and informal networks. Formal *and* informal systems are very important in organizations and are highly intertwined. A great deal of the inside representation is done through the formal structure and hierarchical chain of command. The Stage IV people whom we observed and interviewed are fully conscious and respectful of the formal structure, and work to avoid undermining it. Stage IV managers, while using their wide network of relationships, are nevertheless careful to avoid undermining the positions of those who report to them. A fine line is observed between what could or could not be discussed outside formal channels. Any official information, as opposed to opinion and supposition, is usually distributed through formal channels. All effective managers see that their immediate subordinates are the first to be given that information.

10
Sponsoring

Roger Stein had been a successful scientist at a large research laboratory. His research had been well received, and he was asked to run some medium-sized projects, which also turned out well. In the late 1960s, he was chosen by the laboratory director to be deputy director, second in command at the lab. His appointment was popular at the time; Stein was held in high esteem by most of his colleagues. After a few years, however, support for Stein began to wane. Researchers started to complain about the administration of the lab. They particularly began to question his choice of appointees to key positions. As new appointments were announced, many of the scientists would shake their heads and ask, "Why was that person chosen for such a critical job? There are people here who could handle that job much better."

Moreover, many of the researchers and group heads felt that some of the division managers at the lab had lost their effectiveness and should be replaced by more competent managers. When concerns were brought to Stein, who had responsibility for internal administration at the lab, Stein either tried to convince them that they didn't understand the entire situation or after promising to look into the matter subsequently made no change.

After several years, concern about Stein's appointments became widespread among the researchers. Some of the scientists became quite outspoken about the problem. At about the same time that this concern reached its peak, a new director was appointed for the lab. The lab had a tradition of appointing directors from the outside, and this director was no exception. In his first month at the lab, the new director invited the employees to come and see him or write suggestions as to how he could best manage the lab. Dozens of scientists and managers accepted the new director's invitation. Their message shocked the director; they were unanimous in their suggestions to: "Remove Roger Stein as deputy director!" They complained that he had not appointed capable managers, and that the lab was suffering from it. They claimed that Stein, though himself a competent scientist, had caused serious harm to the lab by retaining and appointing people who neither respected scientists nor showed a fundamental understanding of what was needed to produce good science. The new director's first official act was an announcement of a reorganization, including the information that Roger Stein would return to his work as a scientist in 30 days.

Patricia Alden, national director of a large volunteer organization, called the new chairman of the board, Jim Spence, asking if he could meet with her a month before the annual meeting of the board. When they met, Alden surprised Spence by telling him that she had come to the conclusion that the board was going to have to go outside the present staff to get a new director. Alden explained that she was close to retirement age, and that many of the professional staff members at the national headquarters were within a few years of her age. Most of them had worked with her to build up the organization and had a great deal in common. But, the world had changed since they had all started working for the organization. Alden felt that the organization needed new direction but she honestly did not think that anyone in the national or regional offices could provide what was needed. After a careful review of the staff, Spence agreed that he could see no one in the organization who could provide new leadership. Alden proposed that she try to persuade as many of her associates as possible to retire with her, to make way for some new blood. Both knew that such a drastic change could be very hard on the organization, but they saw no other viable alternative.

Both Roger Stein and Patricia Alden had failed to perform the final Stage IV function: to assure that experienced and capable people were ready to play the key roles in the organization's future. Neither successfully filled the role of sponsor. Let us briefly define that role.

A sponsor must first select competent people and place them in key positions where they will make decisions affecting the organization's future. As we have pointed out earlier, not all Stage IV people we found were in management positions, but most were. The formal system in most organizations is such that if the people who are placed in the most responsible formal positions cannot, or do not perform the critical Stage IV functions competently, the organization suffers.

After these high-potential people have been identified to play the key roles in the future, they need to be given experience in key areas of the organization. Many large organizations now have formal key replacement planning systems to identify as early as possible those people with apparent high potential and to see that they are given assignments in various divisions with increasing responsibility. These systems are designed to assure that the organization will have an available pool of people who have had the wide experience and testing that the present top management wants their senior managers to have had. But the formal systems are merely an aid to the Stage IV managers who must see that capable people get the experience that they need to prepare them for the roles that they may be called upon to play.

In addition to identifying and training promising young professionals, a sponsor must work to assure that these individuals are not pigeonholed or left to stagnate in unchallenging assignments by a rigid seniority-type promotion system or by less-competent, insecure supervisors. Stage IV individuals must not only be constantly on the lookout for those who show promise for providing future leadership for the organization, but see that these promising people get the exposure and movement necessary to develop and demonstrate their capabilities. This is a signal to people throughout the organization that strong performance and strong capabilities will not go unnoticed. Where this signal is not present, organizations can lose a great deal of talent and energy through turnover and discouragement.

Finally, Stage IV individuals influence the future values that will be dominant in the organization by the people whom they sponsor. By sponsoring individuals who share and embody certain key values, Stage IV people can influence the extent to which those values will shape the behavior of individuals in that organization in the decades to come.

It is important here to reemphasize that we see sponsoring as a different function from mentoring. The two terms are often used interchangeably or are so closely co-mingled that they seem to be describing the same thing. It is not our wish to argue with the way others use these terms, as their right to use them as they wish is the same as ours. But, we want to be clear about what we refer to when we use these terms. We found two quite different and important functions being performed in the organizations that we observed. Table 10.1 may help to clarify the differences between the two relationships.

In the mentor relationships, we observed a strong teaching or training quality. The mentors had learned to operate in this complex professional-organizational world. They brought valuable knowledge to the relationship of how to operate effectively in this world. Along with this coaching relationship, there was often frequent contact. The mentor would provide assignments and then coach the

Table 10.1. Comparison of Sponsor and Mentor Roles

SPONSOR	MENTOR
Select—test	Coach—train
Infrequent contact	Frequent contact
More distant relationship	Tight social bond
Little outside activity	Common interests
Grandfather/grandmother	Older brother/sister

apprentice on how best to approach the task. There was often a tight social bond; many mentors shared some strong non-work interest or activity with their apprentices. It had an older brother/sister quality to it.

The sponsor relationship differed on all these dimensions. The sponsors we observed or had described to us were much less likely to be acting as teachers or coaches. Rather, they focused on seeing that their people had developmental assignments, which tested certain abilities. Contact between the sponsor and the individual being sponsored was less frequent. The older brother/sister metaphor didn't seem appropriate here. The familial metaphor that seemed better to characterize this relationship was that of the grandfather/grandmother, attempting to determine which of their grown sons/daughters, or grandsons/granddaughters, would best be able to perform key roles in the family business or in the tribe. Sponsors are not so much trying to teach or counsel as to select, test, groom, and bring forward those who show the promise that they can perform these roles well.

There are similarities in the two relationships, of course. Both mentors and sponsors are interested in the development of the individual(s) being mentored or sponsored. Advocacy and reciprocity were central in both relationships. But the two relationships are sufficiently different to be distinguished from one another and called by different names. Often, former mentors later become sponsors. But when they do, the relationship is different, even though the same parties are involved. In fact, if one party in a sponsor relationship signals that he or she expects the relationship to be the same as it was when the sponsor was a mentor, there is usually resistance, stiffness, or some signal that things are different now. Particularly, if the individual being sponsored shows any inclination toward the dependence of his or her former apprenticeship, the sponsor is likely to react negatively. Most frequently, if the sponsor tries to give the close direction that had once been so appreciated in the mentor relationship, there is likely to be a strong, sometimes angry pushing away.

The distinction that we are drawing can be illustrated by looking at a published series of interviews with Franklin Lunding, George Clements, and Don Perkins, who succeeded one another in the order listed as C.E.O.s of the Jewell Companies. Frank Lunding, when he was C.E.O., recruited Don Perkins, who had graduated earlier from Harvard's M.B.A. program, to the Jewell Companies. According to Lunding's report, he let Perkins know that he thought he had promise:

> Most people fear that they'll get stuck someplace, and no one will notice them. So, how did I get Don Perkins to come with us? Well, I think he was willing to believe me when I said, "If you have it, you'll make it. If you don't, you won't. And you can make it early. Look at my record (Lunding had

become president at 36 years of age)—I'm not going to deny anyone else the same chance(1).

Perkins must have known that he had a powerful sponsor. There is no mention of a close teaching relationship between Lunding and Perkins. Lunding took a strong interest in the assignments that Perkins was given. He first saw to it that Perkins was sent out to California to travel door-to-door for Jewell's Routes department to "learn the hard business of selling" and to know what it's like to be "face to face with the customer." Perkins soon found, however, that having a powerful sponsor was not enough. Perkins reported:

> I came to work for Jewell because I was very impressed with the fact that Frank Lunding, the chairman, would take the time to interview me. . . . I did not meet George Clements until I came back from my Routes training, and he debriefed me to find out what I'd learned. At that time I began to realize that the real challenge for someone like me at Jewell was to prove myself to George Clements. By the nature of what Frank thought the business needed, I felt I was more or less acceptable early; but in terms of what George felt might be needed, I had to do a lot of proving. I said to myself early in the game that I would only succeed at Jewell when I got George Clement's acceptance and support(2).

Apparently, a mentor relationship did develop between Clements and Perkins, at least for a time. Clements reports trying to teach Perkins patience and to "take some of the Harvard influence out of him," querying him, coaching him. In fact, Lunding reported that he thought a mentor relationship had developed between Clements and Perkins, but Lunding describes his own relationship with Perkins very differently. When asked if he encouraged Clements to look out for Perkins, Lunding responded:

> No, Clements' job was to take care of everyone in the business, and he did a first-class job of it, too. However, I think there was a direct mentor relationship between George and Don. . . . I knew what Perkins was doing, but I wasn't paying any unusual attention to him, only the same as I paid to everyone else(3).

From the evidence given, there may be some question about whether Clements had a mentor relationship with Perkins, but there is no question about Lunding's relationship to Perkins. Lunding was Perkins' sponsor.

SPONSORSHIP FAILURES

As has been true with the other functions, we feel that we can share more graphically what we are able to learn about the complex nature of sponsoring by first examining sponsorship failures and the negative outcomes that ensued for the individuals and the organizations. Of the four Stage IV functions, sponsoring seems to be the most difficult to predict. Failure to assume the role of effective sponsor is also the slowest to be made manifest. Individuals may appear to be able to select and develop good people to perform key tasks and play key roles for the organization, but subsequently fail to live up to that promise.

In some cases, the ability to perform this function is assumed without any serious question being raised. In other cases, it appears on the surface as if the individual is performing the sponsoring function adequately; failure in this area becomes apparent only after a considerable length of time. Consequently, the failure to sponsor sometimes does not appear to have had a negative affect on the career of an individual; only the organization suffers after the individual moves on or retires.

Despite this masking of effects, we were able to see a number of instances where individuals were failing to sponsor and to see the effects of these failures on the organizations, as well as on the individuals. The failures that we observed seemed to spring from four roots: poor selections, an inability to see the need for sponsoring, an unwillingness to make tough choices, and, finally, an inability to manage relationships.

POOR SELECTIONS

The case of Roger Stein, described at the beginning of this chapter, best typifies the failure to select individuals who can increase the organization's capabilities. Stein's own personal capabilities led most people to expect that he would develop and gather around him a capable group of people. In fact, even though his early choices surprised many people, there was a general willingness to believe that Stein saw capabilities in these individuals that were not apparent to everyone. Stein was not a former division manager; he had been chosen for his position on the basis of his strong individual performance. He had not, therefore, displayed the ability to select and develop others; he was given the benefit of the doubt. But, when several of the division heads whom he had chosen failed to gain the confidence of their subordinates and Stein subsequently supported, instead of replaced, the ineffectual division heads, others began to grumble about his choices. These came under particular question when he placed a very junior protégé over a division that he had created through a reorganization. When the protégé, whom Stein had been clearly sponsoring, showed little interest in managing the division and had to be replaced, many of the scientists and managers began to wonder if Stein was using his power to serve the needs of the lab or to meet his own social or psychological needs. As others began to more openly question Stein's ability to sponsor, he became defensive and distrustful. Finally, these dynamics led to the series of events described earlier, resulting in his removal.

Because the power to sponsor, and especially to appoint, is an entrusted right, the accusation of misuse of that power is a serious one. Everyone realizes that there can never be a complete separation of individual, social, and organizational bases for sponsoring, appointing, or promoting another individual. It is natural to have greater confidence in those we know and have had time to observe. We all are more inclined to choose people with whom we must work who have shown a propensity to be cooperative and supportive. But if it is suspected that an individual is sponsoring others *primarily* for personal ends rather than to further the ends of the organization, the trust granted that individual is seriously eroded.

One of the most damning statements that we heard about individuals who were seeking to make the novation into Stage IV was that they "surrounded themselves with weak people because strong people seemed to threaten them." Sponsoring or promoting only those who are psychologically more comfortable to work with, rather than those who have the greatest potential to contribute to the organization, is illegitimate. A dramatic instance of someone suspected of illegitimate sponsoring was the highly publicized furor that arose when William Agee, president of Bendix Corporation, promoted Mary Cunningham, an attractive 29-year-old recent Harvard Business School graduate, to the position of vice president, over the heads of a number of experienced potential candidates. The furor arose over the suspicion that Agee's decision was based on personal rather than organizational needs.

RECOGNIZING THE NEED

Many Stage IV individuals simply do not understand the importance of sponsoring. Patricia Alden, the president of the large volunteer organization, fell into this category. Although she had surrounded herself with people who adequately filled the needs of the organization in its early growth stage, she had neglected to continue the sponsoring process as time went on. She had not seen to it that new people were brought into the organization who were likely to be in tune with changes in the society. She had not been scanning the organization for those who showed promise in being able to read the environment accurately, and giving them broad experience and increasing responsibility. Until she was confronted with the prospect of her own retirement, she had not seen the importance of this kind of development. Nor had any other officers recognized this failure. Not even the volunteer board members, some of whom were corporate executives, were involved enough in the affairs of the organization to know that this function was not being fulfilled.

Two of our colleagues studied two privately held firms, which faced crises almost identical to Patricia Alden's. The founders and key people around them in these family-owned businesses had been so preoccupied with the problems of growth that they had neglected the sponsoring function. There were no individuals prepared to play the key roles in the organization's future. It is often this type of crisis that triggers mergers and buy-outs. We don't wish to give the impression that entrepreneurs and family-owned businesses, as groups, neglect sponsoring. Ed Roberts, who studied a group of entrepreneurs in an effort to identify factors that contributed to their effectiveness, reported the following:

> Entrepreneurs who regard people as one of their key problem areas are among the most successful. . . . Successful entrepreneurs have become successful in part, by manifesting their concern for their employees as the principal productive element of their technical organization (4).

There are some organizations that make the importance of sponsoring explicit. We interviewed a division manager of a firm well known for its history of innovation and growth. He explained to us that successful sponsoring was a specific criterion for advancement in that company. Division managers were told that any further advancement for them would be unlikely unless they were able to demonstrate that they could develop new businesses and business teams inside their divisions. A division manager who could successfully sponsor one or more teams to the point where they had the sales volume and the know-how to spin off and successfully manage new divisions was ready to be considered for promotion. This value was, of course, passed down in the organization. No one is considered for a responsible position, such as division manager, unless they have shown some interest in, and a high potential for, finding and developing able people.

The explicitness of this message in the firm mentioned above is uncommon, however. Most often, the importance of sponsoring or any form of employee development is far less explicit. Even where Stage IV candidates are evaluated on their ability to identify and develop good people, the messages that they receive from others about what is expected of them on this dimension are often unstated. Probably more than with other Stage IV functions, individuals have to learn about the importance of effective sponsoring by observation and experience.

In one of the organizations that we studied over several years, a group of first- and second-level engineering managers were given training on the importance of employee development. Many of them complained that they were being asked to spend time on something that they would not be rewarded for doing. Frequently, we heard the comment:

> It's not in my objectives to develop people. I am measured on bottom line items—on meeting time and budget objectives. You are asking me to take time away from accomplishing those goals and spend it on things I'm not being measured against.

But one of the senior managers in the organization disagreed with the comments:

> They may not think they are being evaluated on how well they develop people, but they are. Sure, they are expected to meet their time and cost targets, but they are expected to do that, plus develop their people. In fact, if they only knew it, they ought to be meeting their goals *through* developing their people. Most of them will probably never realize that, and they'd probably argue with me if I tried to tell them. The ones who do understand it will be the ones who will move into the senior positions. Of course, there will be times when short-term targets will conflict with long-run people development. You sometimes have to give up a good person who could help you meet current goals because that person needs another assignment in order to keep progressing. If you aren't willing to sometimes make things a little tougher for yourself and your sub-units in order to do what's best for the whole organization, you aren't ready to handle very much responsibility.

Sponsoring is not usually a sacrifice, but there are many who fail to see the reciprocal advantage gained for both the sponsor and the individual being sponsored.

MAKING TOUGH CHOICES

As we pointed out earlier, one of the important features of the sponsoring function is to see that capable people are not pigeonholed or left to stagnate in unchallenging assignments. Sometimes this occurs because those with the responsibility to prepare capable people to fill future key roles are unwilling to make the difficult choices that will change the situation.

In a medium-sized manufacturing and processing firm, we saw the failure of the president to take a difficult but needed step, which resulted in serious harm to the future of one of the largest divisions in the firm.

The division manager, Philip Grayston, had only 2½ years until his retirement. Some of the key managers under him became concerned about what was happening in the division. Grayston began to veto any changes or investments that would have possible effects on current operations. Moreover, he began to become much more aggressive in censoring information that might possibly reflect badly on the division. Anyone who brought up negative or disquieting information was harshly challenged. Word got around among his subordinates that it was not only the message but also the messenger as well that Grayston would go after.

An atmosphere of fear was described by several of the managers and supervisors in the department. Several people in the division shared their concerns with the controller and vice president of international operations. They, in turn, brought these concerns to the president and suggested that the division manager be given a different assignment, working on a special project that they outlined. The president, whose family was closely associated with Grayston's, admitted that the division wasn't being managed well, but he knew that Grayston was set on staying in that spot and that he'd fight a reassignment right up to the chairman of the board. He told the controller to tell people in the division that they'd just have to be patient for 2½ years.

During the next year-and-a-half, three of the key managers in the division left the company, two of them going to work for a competitor; two major accounts were lost, and volume and profits dropped. In addition, the division manager developed health problems. The president could find no one inside the division who was capable of managing the division and had to hire an executive search firm. The board of directors demanded to know why the president had not identified the problem and done something about it earlier.

We observed instances in a bank, an engineering division of a manufacturing firm, and a university, where individuals failed to make tough changes in assignments. Performance deteriorated, and many lost faith in the Stage IV individuals involved.

On the other hand, some of the people who were described to us as the best people-developers in their industry consistently found ways to move promising people into challenging assignments and poor performers into different assignments—where they often performed better. They looked for events that provided a rationale for necessary changes, even though the changes were often complex, involving a number of people. They took advantage of the shifting needs in their organizations and logical moves to see that very few promising people felt they were forgotten or neglected.

RESERVING JUDGMENT

Another problem we observed was that some sponsors determine very early who they think will be the strongest candidates for key roles in the organization's future and remained locked into that opinion. They develop such fierce loyalty to the individuals whom they are sponsoring that they are blinded to weaknesses. Probably more dangerous is their inability to see emerging capabilities in others whose strengths were not so obvious earlier, or who have come on the scene later. We observed two instances, one in a raw materials processing company and another in a research firm, where a powerful sponsor had fixed his opinion about two people very early in their careers and had decided that one was the more capable. In both cases, by the time it became necessary to choose one of these people for a key position, most other key people had come to believe that the one without the backing of the powerful sponsor was by far the better candidate. In one case, colleagues of the sponsor had to incite a near-rebellion to get him to reconsider his early prejudgment in the light of new data. In the other case, the powerful sponsor overrode the objections of others to his choice for vice president of manufacturing, only to decide later that he should have listened. Interestingly, in neither case did the initially overlooked individual leave the firm, even though both thought one very influential person had "written him off early." But it does show the importance of a sponsor's reexamining his or her early impressions in the light of later data.

TIMING

There is also the issue of timing. When are individuals ready for new responsibility? How much preparation and guidance do they need before they move on? One young manager we interviewed felt that his career had been jeopardized by an assignment for which he wasn't yet prepared. He had been given a supervisory position in the control department when he had only worked there for a month. He told us later:

> I guess I should have turned down the assignment, but Saul Cromwell had gone out of his way to get it for me. He encouraged me to try it, so I took it. Then we had some unusual things happen, and I couldn't stay on top of them and learn my job at the same time. It went from bad to worse. I can't blame anyone but myself, I guess. But I'd rather have not been put in that position when I'd had so little time to learn what they did in the department. I've got mud on my face and so has Saul. I learned a lot but at a great cost. Right now, I'm wondering if I'd be better off in another company where I could start out fresh.

On the other side, we met a 32-year-old employee in an oil company who felt that he had been held back by someone whose intention was apparently to help him. He told us:

> Frankly, I have done my best to get out of this division. Harold Crosby seems determined to have me go through every step that he went through to get to his position. He seems to forget that he started when he was 22 years old, and I started here at 28. Things were different then, and I have different goals than he did. I don't mean to sound ungrateful for his wanting to help me. He's a nice guy, but I feel like he's smothering me.

It is also extremely important what kinds of assignments a person is given.

> Abe Knowles had gone to work for a research organization for several years and then went back to graduate school to get a Ph.D., with partial financial help from the firm. The executive vice president invited him to come and work as his assistant for a year, then suggested that he go out to one of the labs and head up a department that had been having some problems. Knowles wasn't there long before he was brought back to headquarters again. He stayed there for 6 years working as secretary for two management committees. Several of his friends began to worry that the executive vice president wasn't letting Knowles have enough line experience. But the next year, he was appointed as director of the organization's largest laboratory. During his years at headquarters, he had gained the confidence of the president and all of the senior managers. Moreover, as lab director, Knowles was able to get some capital equipment, which the lab had been requesting for several years, as well as permission to expand the lab facilities.

What may have seemed like an inauspicious series of assignments to outsiders placed Knowles in a very strong position with several high-placed sponsors at an early point in his career.

In trying to describe the role that a sponsor can play in someone's career, let us hasten to acknowledge that there are very significant limits to what a sponsor can do. A sponsor can often provide opportunities, but unless an individual can convert those opportunities to successful performance, the sponsor becomes very limited in what he or she can do. We cited earlier the interviews published in *Harvard Business Review* in which both Frank Lunding and, later, George Clements had described acting as Don Perkins' sponsor. But Clements noted that Perkins was seen "as the bright boy out of Harvard Business School," and that he had to earn acceptance in the organization. "I knew he had to have a success," noted Clements (5). In the same article, Don Perkins made the same point: "Wes

Christopherson and I try to know the young talent in Jewell. But the organization is not going to let someone succeed just because either of us takes an interest in that person" (6).

UNDERSTANDING RECIPROCITY

We also observed people who could identify promising individuals, who saw the need to sponsor them, and who were willing to make difficult decisions when necessary, but who were ineffective as sponsors. Usually, the biggest problem was in understanding the reciprocity involved. What exactly do sponsors provide for the persons they sponsor?

RESPONSIBILITIES OF SPONSOR

A sponsor should stand up and fight for things that his or her people need, in meetings where they are not present. When someone submits a budget proposal or a new program, they can present their arguments in person or in writing, but they are not usually present in the meetings where the decisions are made and reviewed. A sponsor can greatly increase the probability that those proposals and programs will get complete attention if he or she is in that room fighting for them. In addition, a sponsor can offer valuable advice on what should be included in the proposal in the first place.

Sponsors help provide resources and assignments. They determine what new responsibilities their people can handle. Senior managers are often building toward the time when they will need a strong team to take on a critical assignment. It is the sponsor's responsibility to attract and maintain strong people by upgrading the job assignments and increasing resources. The sponsor will then have competent people when a strong team is needed.

Sponsors are also a critical source of information. Through them, persons they are sponsoring can obtain inside information, often in time for it to make a real difference in what they are able to do. Through sponsors, the sponsorees can short-circuit the formal chain of command and "drop by" the office of a sponsor at the home office to obtain information that is critical to them and their people.

As we mentioned before, persons in Stage III have greater credibility and influence as mentors if they themselves have prospects for promotion. Sponsors cannot single-handedly arrange promotions, but they can give input on behalf of someone they are sponsoring, placing his or her virtues above those of others being considered for advancement.

Finally, sponsorship itself signals to others that the person being sponsored has both promise and strong backing. If the sponsorship comes from a creditable source, it becomes easier to get the attention of others higher up in the organization and to develop support at several levels.

RESPONSIBILITIES OF THE SPONSORED

What does the individual provide a sponsor? In part, the individuals being sponsored fulfill their part of the exchange by providing some of the same things that form the basis for trust that Stage I individuals provide their mentors—accessibility, availability, predictability, and loyalty. But some new elements must also be added. A sponsor not only needs the efforts and support of those specific individuals whom he or she sponsors but the efforts and support of others as well. If the sponsor supports the funding of a project, he or she not only needs the personal efforts of the proposer, but also those of the entire team who must complete the project. If the sponsor asks someone to chair a committee or explore a new marketing approach, the sponsor needs the united efforts of the entire committee and not just those of the chairperson. It is the responsibility of the person being sponsored to engineer this broad support for his or her sponsor.

Sponsors, even more than mentors, need someone to cover their "blind sides." If sponsors are good at overall planning but weak at execution, they need Stage III supporters who can bring the plans into fruition. If sponsors are weak at communications, they will need someone in Stage III who can help them keep the lines of communication open. Contrary to popular stereotype, few managers are good at everything; strong management teams, like strong marriages, are composed of persons playing a constellation of roles in which one person's strengths complement those of another.

Finally, sponsors need information and ideas. Information and ideas are the sponsor's stock in trade. If the individuals being sponsored are going to make their sponsor look good, they must be constantly on the alert for unusually strong results and innovative ideas. They must also keep their sponsor aware of trends. The old cliché of management that "we don't want any surprises" applies doubly here. A sponsoree can save a sponsor serious embarrassment and valuable time in beginning counter-measures if the information is given quickly. Stage IV sponsors, who are usually deeply involved in issues of power, desperately need people in key spots who are constantly asking themselves, "Will this information affect my boss (or whomever the sponsor is) soon, and in what form should I pass it on so it will be most helpful?"

Those were some of the social goods that we saw exchanged between sponsors and those they sponsored. Unless individuals trying to act as sponsors could see what was needed and knew how to provide their part of the exchange, disappointments and misunderstandings arose. Moreover, those who chose to act as sponsors usually had expectations of those they sponsored, and when they were unclear in signalling their expectations, problems sometimes arose.

BENEFITS TO BOTH SPONSOR AND SPONSOREE

When both the sponsor and the individual(s) being sponsored fulfill their part of the bargain, however, mutually beneficial things can, and do, happen. There are many instances where the sponsoring "give and take" worked well. We have separated the situations according to the roles held by the sponsors.

TRADITIONAL MANAGERIAL ROLES

When we examined Stage III, we looked at the symbiotic mentor relationship between Sigmund Freud and Carl Jung—and their painful break-up. Now let us examine a similar relationship that did not end but matured into a mutually beneficial sponsorship.

> According to the "China-watcher," Fox Butterfield, a reciprocal relationship has existed for many years between Deng Xiaoping, China's predominant leader, and Hu Yaobang, whose appointment as Chairman of the Communist Party, the highest post in China, was engineered by Deng. From the 1940s on, the careers of Hu and Deng have closely parallelled each other. They served in the army together for 8 years. They were transferred to Peking together in 1952. And when Deng was purged in the Cultural Revolution as a "capitalist roader," Hu was toppled with him as a member of Deng's "club." After the Cultural Revolution in 1975, a re-ascendant Deng assigned his friend to try to restore shattered morale in the Chinese Academy of Sciences. Hu immediately won the sympathy of many of China's intellectuals. Hu helped write a controversial document for Deng on freeing China's scientists from Mao's demands for political study and manual labor. The report was assailed by the so-called "Gang of Four," and when Deng fell a second time, Hu again disappeared. But after Mao's death in 1976, Deng began to use Hu to rebuild his own power. Hu was installed in a series of key jobs: deputy director of the Central Committee, successively head of the party's organization department and its propaganda department, then general secretary of the party, a job that had been vacant since Deng occupied it before the Cultural Revolution (7).

Not only can we see the key role each has played in the career of the other, but we can see that Deng, who was 77 years old in 1984, was counting on Hu to preserve the changes that Deng had been able to bring about.

We came across dozens of symbiotic sponsoring relationships, which had had strong positive effects for the careers of both parties. One night, during a management training program for a large retail firm, Dell Nash, the corporate vice president of human resources, told us how his career had been intricately entwined with that of Merl Barnett, the executive vice president. Dell Nash reported that the relationship began soon after he came to work at Rayco Stores:

> When I first came to work with Rayco, I was just out of military service. I was supposed to be trained by the store manager and the area staff director, but with the experience I'd had in the service, I was farther along than either of them. The one I really enjoyed and learned from was Merl Barnett, an associate on the area staff. I only saw him every 4 months, but he trained the people in my functional area. After a while, he asked me to help in his training workshops. Barnett contacted a friend of his and arranged for me to move to my next job in Indiana. It was while I was there that I began to get into data automation. Then I became a store manager and then moved up to area staff. Several years later, Barnett, who was then over the Chicago office, asked me to come over and be his associate division director. It wasn't too long after that before he was promoted to be the number 3 man in the national office, in charge of field services. Later, I was brought to national headquarters to organize all the personnel records. I never really knew whether Barnett played any part in that move, but within 6 months of his becoming the executive vice president, I was appointed the corporate vice president of human resources. I have only worked directly under him two times, but we have stayed in touch. He'd drop by when he came to the office where I was. He'd tell me about the latest things in the company that he thought would interest me. I've tried to do the same for him. When he is thinking of trying something new, he often calls me to see how I think people will react to it.

Barnett had been a mentor to Nash early in their relationship. But Nash had gone on to be a mentor to others while Barnett became Nash's sponsor. It was clear that both men had benefited from the relationship. Nash had tried to keep Barnett informed about anything that he thought would aid him. Moreover, Nash had been a capable and loyal supporter in a position that was key both to Barnett's and the organization's success.

The organizations we studied are not unique. *Fortune Magazine* reports a similar relationship existed between Roger Smith, current C.E.O. of General Motors, and Tom Murphy, G.M.'s previous C.E.O. According to the *Fortune* report, Smith, 4 years after coming to G.M., at age 28, wrote a hard-hitting report suggesting that the company vigorously defend itself against an attack by the Senate Judiciary Committee, which was investigating G.M.'s dominance of its industry. The report not only influenced the upper management's response to the charges, but "it kindled an enduring friendship between Smith and Tom Murphy. Smith was one of those assigned to defend G.M. in Washington." Later Murphy called Smith to New York as a financial analyst, and Smith followed Murphy up the ladder from that point (5).

Both Tom Murphy and Merl Barnett were in formal positions with power to appoint promising individuals to key positions. Yet not all Stage IV individuals even carry any formal power. Some nonmanagers begin to perform the other Stage IV functions but fail to sponsor because they don't see the need or the opportunity for them to select and prepare others for future key roles in the organization. We talked to several highly respected scientists whose technical inventiveness was very important to the organization, but who had little influence in the decisions made. They all said that the Stage IV function that sounded most unlikely for a non-manager to fill was sponsoring. "That is a management function," they said. "I can't see a nonmanager getting involved in that stuff." Yet the nonmanager professionals that were described to us as being in Stage IV had been very deeply involved in sponsoring. The manager of a key division in a large research laboratory described one of the scientists whom he considered to be in Stage IV by saying:

> Jack trained me when I came into the lab. All the important people in the division have learned a lot from him. He has encouraged me to take each management job I have taken. I know he had a strong voice in my selection for this job.

Another nonadministrator Stage IV professional that we studied was a university professor. He was an active sponsor, not only inside his university but also for former students. This sponsoring of individuals in other universities benefits his own university and is intricately tied to the way he provides direction, exercises power, and represents his own organization. He is well connected and respected in the Office of Naval Research and obtains funding for his current doctoral candidates through that office. He writes with his students and helps them publish. While they are still students, he takes them with him to professional meetings and introduces them to the right people at the meetings. After they graduate, he still writes with them. He is the editor of a series for a publishing house, so he provides opportunities for his former graduates to write books in the series. He has a map on his wall and a pin for each graduate, keeping track of each one. If they are doing good work, he writes letters of recommendation for them when they come up for promotion, when they are applying to agencies for funding, and when they are applying for new positions. When he knows a university is looking for someone, he lets his people who are looking for a new position know of the opening. This kind of behavior feeds on itself. Some of the people he has sponsored are in funding agencies. They are editors and reviewers in professional journals. When he wants funding for his current students and wants to help them publish, he gets support. When he takes his doctoral students to the professional meetings to help them find jobs, it is the people he has sponsored and their colleagues to whom he introduces them. Consequently, the people he sponsors send him their good students, and good students want to work with him. In his own university, he brings in funding, good students, national recognition, and state-of-the-art information about what is happening in his field.

PROBLEMS FOR THE SPONSOR

We have tried to point out the benefits to the organization, the sponsor and the individual being sponsored when the relationship goes well. But, there are also problems that can arise. One of those, of course, is the suspicion and sometimes the reality of favoritism. When a Stage IV professional is impressed by someone who seems to have a great deal of potential, there are many factors that can go into making that impression. Propinquity, chance, personalities, etc., all have an effect. Once someone gets a good reputation, a sort of halo effect develops. Some are afraid to criticize this young rising star for fear that their judgment will be questioned or that they will be accused of being afraid of bright young people. Conversely, those who don't get on the fast track can perform well yet receive little recognition. Those without sponsors can justly feel that they are at a competitive disadvantage. For some sponsors, this never raises itself as an issue; they play the role of advocate for those they respect and with whom they have built reciprocal relations. For others, the question of equity is haunting. But in a world where they know that the information that they have is imperfect, the best that they can do is to "sin bravely" in an inevitably inequitable world.

Sponsors can also have their reputations harmed by those they sponsor. At an equipment company in the Midwest, a manager starting to make the novation into Stage IV took an interest in a promising young supervisor working at one of the plants. They came to know one another because they had both graduated from the same university, although a number of years apart. The sponsor at headquarters invited the supervisor from the plant to drop in and see him when he came to the home office. During those visits and when their families got together socially, company political alignments were discussed. The young supervisor began parading his knowlege of company politics back at the plant. Within 2 months, the supervisor had been fired, and his sponsor at headquarters had had his reputation badly damaged. Both had violated trusts and both paid heavily.

PROBLEMS FOR THE SPONSORED

Sponsors themselves are involved in competitive struggles and in the management of their own careers. Some lose out on those struggles and leave the organization. Some leave for other reasons. Those who have tied their wagon to a particular person's star may find themselves without the powerful sponsor in whom they had invested heavily. One manager, whose sponsor had left the organization when his rival had received a promotion he had wanted, found himself distrusted by his new superior. He confided in an anguished voice, "Can't he believe that I can be loyal to more than one man?"

In another situation, Harlow Kidder, a director of a development center, found belatedly that his sponsor had lost out in a power struggle in which the "showdown" was reached over the question of whether to follow the recommendation of a consultant that Harlow Kidder be dismissed. Kidder felt betrayed. He couldn't believe that his sponsor, who at one time had held his own particular job and who had become a group vice president and a member of the board of directors, could have let this happen. Three weeks after Kidder was dismissed and had spent many hours wondering how his friend could have forsaken him, Kidder learned that his sponsor had resigned and taken a position in the administration of a local university. The sponsor himself came to Kidder and told him that he had unexpectedly found himself confronted with Kidder's dismissal recommendation at a board meeting. As he began to challenge the recommendation, he suddenly found the board polarizing four to three against him, with the newly hired C.E.O. leading the opposition. The ensuing discussion and vote made clear to him that the vote was as much a signal that his own influence and future were gone as it was a vote to dismiss Kidder.

We did talk to some professionals and managers who followed their sponsors wherever they went or whatever their fortunes, much as we saw Mr. Hu following Mr. Deng in China. Yet more often when their sponsor left or lost power, most professionals and managers found new sponsors, carried on without a sponsor, or left the organization.

As a reader you have now explored with us the complex world that we discovered trying to answer the question, "What differentiates those who continue to be highly valued in their organizations throughout their careers from those who do not?" We have looked at four stages through which many people move during their careers, the functions they perform in each stage, the novations that they make in moving between stages, and the blocks that prevent many people from making those novations.

While the above question seemed simple, it called forth rich and often fascinating answers. However, it is only one question that individuals must answer for themselves in building a career, or in living out their lives. In the next chapter we shall look at some of the other questions involved.

Implications

11

A Different Drummer

Up to this point, we have presented data organized to answer one question: What distinguishes those individuals who continue to be highly valued by their organizations throughout their careers from those who do not? But as we have presented these data to individuals and groups over the past few years, we have been asked a number of other questions. One question that we are often asked is: Are you saying that everyone in an organization should strive to move into Stage IV? We would like to be clear that that is not our position. The career stages model is descriptive, not normative; it is an attempt to describe and explain what we see in organizations, not what we think people in organizations should do, nor the way organizations should be. But our descriptive model does raise some normative questions for us as well as for others. In this chapter we address ourselves to some of the normative questions that face those of us who are trying to build satisfying careers within organizations. In the chapter that follows, we shall address some of the questions that face those who manage and structure the organizations in which we work.

For those trying to build what Daniel Levinson calls a viable "life structure," (1) the question concerning whether or not they should strive to reach Stage IV is not the right question to ask. Asking oneself only what must be done to be highly valued by those who do the evaluating on behalf of organizations can have unintended and negative results. In one of the large companies that we studied, one of our junior colleagues was talking to a senior fellow on the company's technical ladder. He had been described to us as having moved up the technical ladder very rapidly. He told our colleague:

> I can tell you just how to get ahead in an organization. I have figured out the system and have made it work for me. First you have to work harder and longer than others. But that isn't enough. You have to figure out who the key people are and what they are looking for. Before I go into a meeting, I always have my boss brief me on who is going to be there, what they are interested

in, and how to deal with them. Then after every meeting, I go into my boss again and find out what went well, what I did right or wrong, and what needs to be followed up. I also do my marketing. When managers talk to me at the drinking fountain and ask me how things are going, instead of punishing them by talking about my problems or the details of my work, I give them a short 2-minute summary of what I have accomplished in the last month so they can report it in their meetings (pause). The only trouble is that while I was doing all this and giving it so much attention, my wife left me and took the kids. I am beginning to wonder what it's all about.

This individual was not alone in having focused on too narrow a question. But we met a number of people who seemed not to have asked themselves enough questions:

> Frank Dawson was an effective first-line supervisor in the research and development center of a large chemical company. He was enjoying his work when we first met him. His group was doing the development work on the company's highest volume product where he had developed strong expertise in the technical aspects of that product area. Members of the group liked him and enjoyed working with him. As time went by, he continued to receive promotions that took him further and further away from the technical work that he had enjoyed, and into forward planning and the coordination of marketing, production, and development in the company's headquarters. His role required him to perform many Stage IV functions. One day when we visited the company, he confided in us that he had allowed himself to get into work he didn't enjoy and was uncomfortable performing. He had lived frugally, saved his money, and had told his superior that morning that he was retiring in 3 months at age 50 and getting out of the "rat race." He was moving to a part of the country where he and his wife could live inexpensively and have a little peace for a change.

In retrospect, Frank Dawson felt that he had been unwise in accepting assignments given him without questioning whether they involved work that he would enjoy or perform comfortably. Perhaps the unquestioning acceptance of assignments is a problem with people of Dawson's generation and is less likely to occur among today's young professionals and managers. Nevertheless, finding answers to other career questions seems no easier for them. We interviewed Ralph Grimes, a 34-year-old executive in a large energy company who was described to us as being a "shooting star" in the company and very much on the "fast track." He was already just below the vice president level, which was unusual for someone of his age and experience. Three people had told us that he was one of the few in the company who had a good shot at someday becoming the president of the company. That possibility had been on Grimes' mind as well. Yet he voiced some concerns about it when he spoke to us:

> I know there is a possibility I could become president of the company if I were to really go for it. But I don't know if I want to become the kind of person I'd have to become to make it. It would mean working weekends and a lot of 14-hour days. It would mean I'd have to take some assignments I don't think I'd enjoy, just to get the experience. I'd probably have to live overseas for some time as a manager and eventually be president of one of the overseas subsidiaries. I'd have to change in the process, and I don't know if I want that.

We learned later that Grimes had decided he would "go for it," and that the question, "Could I have made it if I had really tried?" was one he decided that he needed to answer for himself.

If there were some individuals, like those just described, who were experiencing or fearing negative consequences by focusing too intently on doing what was valued by the organization, we also met a number of individuals who were finding many of their gratifications outside their primary work setting. After our interview with a 50-year-old Stage II chemist in a research laboratory, his face suddenly brightened as he told us that he was leaving the next week for 3 months' vacation. He and his wife were going to spend all that time exploring and studying the plant life in the Alaskan tundra. The animation that he showed in his discussion of the coming trip far exceeded anything that he had displayed when discussing his work at the laboratory. Similarly, when we were having a group interview with some design engineers in a large technology-based manufacturing firm, it came out that two of the senior engineers in the group were influential members of the state legislature and obviously enjoyed and were deeply involved in their political and legislative work. They had no such positive things to say about their design work or about the management of their division.

Are we saying that there are many rewarding things in the world—that you should balance your life and be careful not to sell your soul to the corporation? Unfortunately, it is not that simple either. One of the few longitudinal studies we have seen that examines both occupational and private lives of individuals suggests that high achievement and responsibility in one's occupation tend to accompany rather than preclude strong marriages and rich friendships. In his conclusions about the results of the Grant Study, in which 95 Harvard College graduates were contacted regularly from the time they were undergraduates until they had reached their late 40s, George Vaillant wrote:

> Contrary to popular belief, lucky at work means lucky at love. . . . Inner happiness, external play, objective vocational success, mature inner defenses, good outward marriage, all correlate highly—not perfectly, but at least as powerfully as height correlates with weight(2).

Vaillant reported that among those Harvard College graduates in his sample who went into business, those who did not reach the ranks of middle management had unstable marriages and did not make lasting friendships.

That was a small population studied over a long period of time. Let us look at some studies that examine larger groups. Lotte Bailyn of M.I.T. did a series of studies contrasting professionals and managers who said that family needs were primary to them (accommodators) with those who said career success was of most importance (nonaccommodators). In one of these studies, she found that the wives of the accommodators were more satisfied with their lives and with the options open to them than were the wives of the nonaccommodators. This was true whether the wife was choosing the role of homemaker or careerist (3). In another study of M.I.T. graduates who had left school only 10 to 20 years earlier, Bailyn found that the self-image of the accommodators was much different than the self-image of those who placed a high value on career success. The accommodators:

I. Had lower overall self confidence.
   A. Lower confidence in their ability to think creatively, identify and solve problems, continue to learn, induce change in others or the organization, or to exercise leadership.
II. Showed less interest in the character of their work.
   A. Less interest in challenging work.
   B. Less interest in gaining a sense of accomplishment.
III. Were less likely to have been given management positions.
   A. More were staff engineers.

Bailyn did find a small group of accommodators who had high overall self confidence, were fully as active as the nonaccommodators in leadership, and were just as confident in the areas listed above. But in general, a marked subordination of career interests to family interests among this relatively young population was accompanied by low self confidence, low interest in the nature of their work, and lower levels of responsibility at work(4).

For Bailyn's accommodators, who were largely not looking to their work for feelings of achievement, confidence, or more than minimal rewards, the focus on family had positive effects on the family. But in populations where participants still hoped for gratification in their work lives, lack of success at work had negative effects at home. Evans and Bartolome interviewed a fairly large sample of business managers and their wives from a number of different countries. Particularly among the managers who had not yet reached their mid-40s, Evans and Bartolome found a great deal of what they called emotional "spillover" from work life to family life (although they found very little spillover in the reverse direction) (5). These managers reported spending 62 percent of their time and 71 percent of their energy on their professional lives (6). What happened at work strongly affected home life in these families, according to Evans and Bartolome:

> What damages family life is the spillover of worry and tension: 40 percent of the wives saw that as the most negative effect of work life on private life. . . . "I don't mind the amount of work he has to do. That is, if he's happy in his work. What I resent is the unhappiness which he brings home." "As long as he's happy, I'm happy." This was the single most common phrase used by the wives. It captures the essence of the relationship between professional and private life for professional and managerial people. . . . To put it in the words of one manager: "If I'm miserable on the job, I'll be miserable at home. The reverse would not be true"(7).

As we will see later, Evans and Bartolome and other researchers found "a certain degree of disengagement from the career" among most managers and professionals beyond their early 40s. But available evidence suggests that unless professionals in the first half of their work life are willing to completely write off their work as a source of gratification and self worth, their work life will have a strong effect on their families and on other aspects of their life.

Consequently, it seems critical to have some criterion for selecting and evaluating one's own work—some criterion other than the zero-sum evaluations imposed by organizational officials. If we as individuals allow ourselves to be completely dependent on others to choose for us what tasks we had best undertake and to determine if we have done them well or poorly, we expose our sense of worth, naked and vulnerable, to a world of varying and even capricious standards. Each of us needs some basis for an inner locus of evaluation solidly rooted in our own goals, standards, and values. May we share with the reader some of the ways we find attractive to build and renew such a base?

THE REALIZATION OF ONE'S POTENTIAL

One of the touchstones each of us can use to decide where we will expend our energies—and against which to evaluate our achievements—is a sense of our own unique capability and potential. The folly of defaulting to some all-purpose generalized standard is best illustrated by a fable we heard first from Herbert Shepard, but whose authorship we have not been able to determine:

A School For Animals

Once upon a time the animals decided they must do something heroic to meet the problems of a "new world," so they organized a school. They adopted a curriculum consisting of running, climbing, swimming, and flying; and to make it easier to administer, all the animals took all the same subjects.

The duck was excellent in swimming, better in fact than his instructor. He made passing grades in flying, but was very poor in running. Since he was slow in running, he had to stay after school and drop swimming to practice running. This was kept up until his web feet were badly worn, and he was only average in swimming. But average was acceptable in school, so nobody worried about that except the duck.

The rabbit started at the top of his class in running, but had a nervous breakdown because of so much make-up work in swimming.

The squirrel was excellent in climbing until he developed frustration in the flying class, where his teacher made him start from the ground up instead of from the treetop down. He also developed charley-horses from over-exercise and then got a "C" in climbing and a "D" in running.

The eagle was a problem child and was disciplined severely. In the climbing class, he beat all the others to the top of the tree, but insisted on using his own way of getting there.

At the end of the year, the queer abnormal eel, that could swim exceedingly well and also run, climb, and fly a little, had the highest average and was valedictorian.

We each have unique capabilities and the potential to do certain things well—our genius. In David L. Norton's *Personal Destinies,* he articulates this idea well:

The Greek equivalent of *genius* is *daimon* and "eudaimonism" is the term for the ethical doctrine . . . that every person is obliged to know and live in truth to his *daimon,* thereby progressively actualizing an excellence that is his innately and potentially. . . .(8) According to self-actualization ethics it is every person's primary responsibility first to discover the daimon within him and thereafter to live in accordance with it. . . .(9) When an individual allows himself to be deflected from his own true course, he fails in that first responsibility from which all other genuine responsibilities follow. . . .(10)

In Norton's view, our prime responsibility is not to seek primarily or directly the esteem of others, but to "know ourselves" and to "become what we are." We each have a "personal truth" (what is right for us), and the greatest enemy of integrity is not falseness (honestly seeking but failing to know what is right for us), but—ironically—the attractiveness of foreign truths, truths that belong to others (what is right for them) (11). No easy doctrine this, but one that merits a lifetime of striving. It does provide an inner locus of evaluation.

Was the "shooting star," the young executive who decided he would strive to become the president of his company, following a personal truth or a foreign truth? Only he can know. But we have seen some individuals who seem to have been seeking to know their own "daimon" and to live in accordance with it:

> The director of a large and prestigious research laboratory, sensing that he could not make his greatest contribution nor find his greatest satisfaction in that position, stepped down from his job as director. He applied to do graduate work in international relations, hoping to return later and represent the laboratory to the government and the public. After the director stepped down from a position high in the hierarchy to that of an individual contributor, others in the formal chain-of-command felt freer to leave management positions to follow interests that they could best pursue as individual contributors.

> An engineer at a large research laboratory determined soon after he came to the laboratory that having a Ph.D. and the training that went with it would be critical to gaining greater responsibility at the lab. With the strong approval of management, he enrolled in a Ph.D. program, pursuing it while working at the lab. Not long after he had begun the program of study, he was called to be the lay pastor of the local religious congregation to which he belonged. Realizing that he could not pursue his studies if he accepted the call, he seriously weighed the costs and commitments. He concluded that his religious commitments were too great for him to turn down the call and withdrew from the Ph.D. program. As the years went by, he remained a bench engineer at the lab, well liked and admired for his personal integrity. He was greatly admired in his religious community for his leadership and highly principled family.

AN INTEREST IN ONE'S WORK

In Chapter 2, we quoted from Robert W. White, who spent a large part of his life studying the unfolding of individual lives over time. White attempted to identify what he considered the major trends of natural growth for individuals. Natural growth, according to White, does not just happen as one gets older, but involves a stabilizing of one's identity accompanied by a maturing of one's relationships and values. White's growth trends are "natural" in the sense that the potential for such growth is available to most of us. But when we see these trends in ourselves and others, we can't help viewing them as both admirable and remarkable. One of those growth trends is a "deepening of interests"(13).

An interest, according to John Dewey (who did so much to develop the concept) is always connected with some activity that engages a person in a whole-hearted way:

> Interest is not some one thing; it is the name for the fact that a course of action, an occupation, or pursuit absorbs the powers of an individual in a thorough-going way. . . . The person acting finds his own well-being bound up with the development of an object to its own issue (12).

White tries to describe the way natural growth is manifested along this dimension:

> Under reasonably favorable circumstances a person becomes increasingly capable of having his energies absorbed in the needs and properties of the objects with which he is working. . . . The trend we have in mind is away from a state in which interests are casual, quickly dropped, pursued only from motives that do not become identified with advancement of the object(13).

Incidentally, White notes that interests "often enough grow broader as well as deeper," but he focuses only on the increased capacity for absorption that comes with the deepening of interests.

White's and Dewey's notion of a deep interest in one's work provides another basis for an inner gyroscope, an internal locus of evaluation. Over time and in a thousand ways, we can make choices that lead toward work that interests us, and determine for ourselves whether we are doing careful or shoddy work.

We most often became aware of individuals with a deep interest in their work because of unusual circumstances:

> We interviewed a former engineering supervisor who had been returned to his status as an individual contributor during a reduction-in-force. The reduction in status had been very difficult for him to accept. It was hard for him to understand why he had been demoted when there were others who, in his opinion, were less competent than he but who were still supervisors. Very shortly thereafter, he had suffered a heart attack. He told us that while he was recovering in the hospital, he decided that he was not going to let

himself be bothered by what others thought about him. He recalled those times in his life that had given him satisfaction; in each case, it had been when he had created something new—solved a problem through his creativity that no one else had been able to solve. He swore to himself that he was going to take every opportunity to do creative work and not worry about how others evaluated his work, or who got credit for it. Since then, he told us, he had come up with a new and innovative fire retardant that was being developed and produced in another group. He had also come up with an idea for a new way to capture and store solar energy. He had described the idea in a meeting with a research group, whose members had then proposed and been granted a $1.2 million government research contract to test and operationalize the idea. His name had not been mentioned in the proposal, he said, and others would get to do the work on it rather than he. But he told us that he had worried about that for less than an hour. He was grateful to be alive and to be able to do creative work. That was enough for him.

An individual in his late 40s who worked for a large energy company was described to us by his former co-workers as "a good geophysicist and a helluva lot of fun." He was diagnosed by his physician as having terminal cancer. To the surprise of his co-workers, he continued to come into work each day until his death. When others remarked about it, he responded that, along with his home and family, this was where he had found satisfaction to this point in his life. He saw no reason to give up what he enjoyed.

Why do most of the instances that we heard about concerning a deep interest in work involve unusual circumstances? Perhaps it is because, in our society, a certain level of interest in one's work is expected among professionally trained individuals. But even if a certain level of interest is considered normal, we did not find that a deep and absorbing interest in one's work was a universal condition among professionals. There were not many who met the description of Maccoby's pathetic "Gamesmen"(14), but there were many who lacked the solid moorings of a deep and absorbing interest in their work and a self-calibrating sense of craftsmanship about the performance of their work.

Interestingly, both White's examples of "deeply interested" individuals and our own examples tended to be individuals performing individual tasks. Yet the nature of most work in an increasingly complex and interdependent world, certainly in organizations, is that the work is not done alone. Few products or services are produced by a single individual. Work is usually accomplished with and through other individuals and groups. Unless more individuals can develop a broad and deep interest in the process of working with other people and with organizations to accomplish work, the capacity for absorption and satisfaction in their work life will remain unavailable to them. If this book could do nothing more than to intrigue more professionals with that possibility, we would feel our efforts rewarded.

AN INVOLVEMENT IN THE DEVELOPMENT OF OTHERS

Over the years, as we have tried to understand how careers and lives unfold, we have found ourselves returning again and again to a short paper written in 1950 by Erik Erikson entitled "Growth and Crises of the Healthy Personality"(15). One has the right to suspect anyone with either the naivete—or the temerity—to discuss anything as grandiose and normative as "the healthy personality." But Erikson deals with the problem of normativeness in an interesting way. He examines the way individuals grow in their capacity to deal with the world, and with the crises that they encounter in moving from birth to death. The paper deals briefly with the issues of trust, autonomy, initiative, identity, and intimacy. These issues, each in turn, become central as the individual's increasing capacities meet the opportunities and limitations of his or her culture. During adulthood, according to Erikson, each individual faces the issue or crisis of what Erikson calls "generativity versus stagnation." Erikson deliberately took an adjective and made it into a noun, coining a new word for the issue that he wished to identify because:

> No other fashionable term, such as creativity or productivity, seems to convey the necessary idea. Generativity is primarily the interest in establishing and guiding the next generation. . . . The principal thing is to realize that this is a stage of the growth of the healthy personality and that where such enrichment fails altogether, regression from generativity to an obsessive need for pseudo intimacy takes place, often with a pervading sense of stagnation and interpersonal impoverishment. Individuals who do not develop generativity often begin to indulge themselves as if they were their one and only child(16).

Erikson points out that the most common means of dealing with this issue is through the rearing of offspring, but there are other forms of altruistic concern through which people become involved in the development of others. The emptiness of careerism, like other forms of self-centered activity in life, can sometimes be avoided by a genuine concern for others. It is almost a cliché for someone to say, when nearing retirement, "When I think back on all the things I have done during my years with the company, the things I feel good about are the people I have been able to help, the doors I have been able to open for young people coming along, and the growth I have seen in them." But cliché or no, the contribution of those feelings to a sense of personal worth cannot be written off as self-serving sentimentality.

> One of the authors was conducting a seminar for a group of senior managers in a large international bank where he presented Erikson's model of the eight crises in the human life cycle. An urbane senior vice president, approximately 60 years old, asked that the material on generativity be repeated. Clearly interested, he sought the author out after the seminar and asked where he could read more about Erikson's notion of generativity. "I have been trying to figure out what all these years I have spent in the bank have been about," he said. "I might have gotten a clue this afternoon."

> A university professor of public administration, recently deceased, kept track of nearly every student whom he had taught. He corresponded with many of them, wrote letters of recommendation for them, and found ways to visit them. Whenever he went into another city, in the United States or abroad, he would take out his bulky address book and call "his students," asking how they were doing. His wife said, "Stu never asked himself why he had gone into teaching—he knew."

We have said much in this book about the importance of informal relationships in an individual's career. They provide for many individuals an independent base for assessing one's self worth—apart from promotions, salary increases, and office size. But however important involvement with others may be, it is probably worthwhile recalling that Erikson said the most common means of dealing with the issue of generativity is through one's own family. He notes that "There are people who, from misfortune or because of special and genuine gifts in other directions, do not apply this drive to offspring but to other forms of altruistic concern and of creativity, which may absorb their kind of parental responsibility"(17).

Most of the studies with which we are familiar suggest that drawing satisfaction from family seems to be easier during the second half of male professionals' and managers' careers. Evans and Bartolome reported that after the managers they studied reached their mid-40s, their major preoccupation shifted to their children. In fact, they observed that a certain degree of disengagement from their career appeared functional and necessary at this stage in their lives. The older managers who reported being "very" active and interested in their careers were twice as likely to be dissatisfied with their lifestyle as were the managers who reported feeling only moderately active and interested in their careers(18). Wolfe and Kolb also found that, among the male professionals and managers they studied, emphasis shifted away from their careers and more toward family and self during the mid-life transition.

The women professionals and managers reported having had a different pattern. They reported having invested very heavily in families during their 20s, quite unlike the men. In their 30s, women reported investing more in career than family, although families still demanded considerable attention. The mid-life transition for women in their early 40s was characterized by a major reaching outward for career development and achievement. It was in their late 40s that women returned to a primary investment in family. But for both men and women, family, self, and generativity became more nearly equal concerns with career development in their 40s (19). These data correspond with our observations and interviews that an individual's marriage and family can provide an independent source of self-worth and an inner basis for assessing one's contributions. During the second half of one's working years, marriage and family can become an even stronger criterion for self assessment:

> One of the authors was interviewing a 55-year-old business consultant about his career. Before joining the firm with which he now worked, the consultant had had a successful career in the Air Force as a pilot, a professor at the Air Academy, and an international affairs specialist. He had received a Ph.D. from one of the country's most prestigious universities, had achieved the rank of colonel, and had represented the Air Force in relations with some of the country's most important and sensitive alliances. After answering our questions about his past and current career activities, the consultant offered a final comment: "Do you want to know what I have decided? If you want to do something that will make any real difference in the world, you do it by rearing good kids."

INTERNAL CONFLICTS

After having offered the reader the best criteria we have found for making career decisions and for making independent assessments of one's actions and performance, let us say a word about conflicts. We met few professionals and managers who didn't feel conflicted about the way they were responding to the many possibilities, expectations, and demands that they faced. The urge in many of us to have our contributions and abilities recognized is powerful. Most of us have a stronger need for some kind of visible status than we sometimes recognize. A supervisor in a design engineering department of a large manufacturing firm told us of an event that had occurred one Saturday in the department.

> I have an outstanding design engineer in the department named Ben Hafer. He has had a hand in designing some of the best products that we make.

Hafer has remained a designer for several reasons, I guess. He is good at it, and he likes his work. He has never asked to be considered for management, and the company is very happy with what he contributes. We pay him well. He makes a little more money than I do. He has a nice home out in the suburbs. But we have a policy that no one except managers have offices so, Ben has a desk out in the bull pen with the other designers. This is an old building, and it doesn't look too nice. One Saturday, I was in my office when Ben dropped by to pick something up from his desk. He had his young teenage son with him, who had apparently never been here before. When Ben stopped at his old grey desk, his son looked at him in disbelief, and said, "Dad, do you mean this is where you work?" As I looked at Ben's face and his boy's, I felt like crying.

We also have needs for money. It is hard to tell your daughter that you don't have enough money for her to have violin lessons. Many of us have a sense of a potential that we want to fulfill—our own "daimon." Some of us have deep interests that don't necessarily lead to some of the other things listed above. A young Ph.D. professor at a graduate business school told us:

I got a good offer from a strategy consulting firm when I graduated with my M.B.A. The starting salary and bonus, of course, were very good. A lot of my classmates envied me. I worked at it for over a year and was doing well in the firm. But when I got looking at what it would take—the travel—I just said that's not the kind of life I want to lead. I don't want to be in that "fast track." I don't want to compete in that way with those guys—I said that, intellectually, but in my heart I was still fast track. I rationalized it, but I've been a little defensive about it.

Some of us feel guilty that we don't spend as much time with our spouses, children, or aging parents as our neighbor seems to do. Dual career couples sometimes wonder if they are making the right choices. Sometimes women with careers feel guilty that they aren't spending more time at home and are angry that they feel guilty. Women or men who drop their careers for a time to rear families wonder if they are slipping behind.

Capable adults in a free, nontraditional society have many options, thousands of decisions to make, and many demands made on them by others and by their own values and interests. Some inner conflicts are felt by most of these people. We met no individuals who felt they had it all and were doing everything they felt they should. Conflict is part of the price that we pay for making our own decisions. There is some consolation in knowing that you are not alone. But conflict is also a fertile ground for creativity. Internal conflict, when handled with integrity and intellectual honesty, has been the source of some of our most important social innovations (20).

WILL ORGANIZATIONS CHANGE?

One of the things that we all ask is whether organizations will change. Will the things that frustrate us remain as they are? We believe and hope that organizations will change. We see some evidence that they are changing now. In particular, we believe that there will be greater opportunities in more companies for nonmanagers to play Stage III and IV roles. We believe this for several reasons. First, the combination of knowledge and entrepreneurial initiative are becoming more important to many organizations and their ability to compete. Capital is still an important factor in competing, but ideas and innovation are more important than they have ever been. Second, it has become easier for people with good ideas for new products or services to leave a company and start up their own firm—or work as an independent contractor. Venture capital for someone with a good new technical product has become easier to obtain. "Incubator" facilities and organizations are being set up to provide the facilities and services new ventures need to help them get started. Moreover, with the advent of the computer and its associated technology, a small firm can turn out technically sophisticated services and products with a much smaller capital investment than was needed in the past. Since most of the new jobs in the last two decades have been created by small companies, federal and state agencies have been set up to encourage new enterprises. Even the popular culture and the media has created a milieu in which more people are likely to be willing to attempt starting up their own small company. Indeed, the entrepreneur has taken on some of the trappings of a folk hero.

All these factors combine to make it more likely that the kind of people who are capable of making strong technical contributions—and who have the inclination, the capacity, and the drive to play Stage III and Stage IV roles—will leave organizations where the opportunities to play those roles are not present. If they find too little opportunity to exercise influence, to take initiative, and to be rewarded for what they have to offer, they are more likely to go out on their own. Finally, other companies, feeling the pressures just cited, will be working to create conditions where able professionals will not have to have formal management positions to gain influence over decisions where their knowledge is important.

We don't expect organizations to change fundamentally. In our opinion, the characteristics of organizations that we have described in the preceding chapters are unlikely to change dramatically. The functions performed by those in Stages I and II will be valued by organizations. But what we have called Stage III and Stage IV functions will continue to be more highly valued and rewarded. These latter functions are critical to the survival and growth of organizations, and the number of people who can perform them well is limited.

By saying that organizations won't change fundamentally, however, we are not saying that specific organizations won't change in specific ways. Perhaps many readers, like the authors, have ways that they want their organizations to change. But influencing organizations to change is usually slow work. And to have any chance of success, one needs credibility, trust, a knowledge of the organization and its key people. So if you want to change the organization, the place to begin is often by trying to change your situation and your influence in the organization. If you are not primarily trying to change the organization, but rather your own role in it, the strategy is likely to be quite similar. So let us turn to the kind of personal strategy that would grow from the ideas discussed in this chapter and preceding chapters.

A PERSONAL STRATEGY

UNDERSTANDING YOURSELF

In career planning, the place to start is with yourself. Before looking outward at the opportunities and barriers around you, look inward at yourself. What do you do well? What do you enjoy doing? Too few of us can answer those questions. Bartolome and Evans said they found that there were four main reasons why individuals found themselves in the wrong job: the strong attraction of external rewards, organizational pressure, an inability to say no, and a lack of self knowledge (21). Viewed another way, however, these are not four reasons, but one. If individuals don't understand their unique strengths or interests, they don't have any basis for deciding whether a job or an assignment makes sense for them. They are vulnerable to attractive external rewards or organizational pressures. They have little basis on which to form enough conviction to say no to an apparently attractive opportunity. Answers to career questions come from within one's self.

But how do we come to "know ourselves?" How do we determine what we enjoy doing and what we do well? One approach is to look at our histories. All of us have had hundreds of experiences that have tested our abilities, leading us to discover what we enjoy and what we find boring or distasteful. Not all the relevant experiences have been in work settings; most have probably been outside work. In our home life, in school, in teams, in clubs, in churches, at play, in a hundred settings, we have generated data with which to answer these two fundamental questions about ourselves.

A useful technique in gathering and analyzing these data is to write an autobiography. Pour out your experiences while growing up, serving in the military, going through school, working, and serving on the town council. Then go through your experiences; pull out consistent themes; look for the uniformities and implications of those themes. Above all, ask yourself these two questions:

I. What have I consistently done well?
   A. What has been the key to my successes?
   B. What has come easily and naturally to me?
   C. What has made me stand out?
   D. What have I been able to do that others have not?
II. What have I consistently enjoyed doing?
   A. When have I thoroughly enjoyed myself?
   B. What has given me the genuine satisfaction?
   C. What energizes me and keeps my interest?

In the process, try to understand your uniqueness, your potential, perhaps even your daimon.

Accept and enjoy your uniqueness. No one is good at everything, and you don't have to be. If you know what you do well and what you enjoy, you can look for jobs where those things will provide the key to success. Don't try to beef up your weaknesses. Look for assignments where your unique strengths are needed and critical. Look for tasks that interest you and intense effort will come naturally.

UNDERSTAND THE ORGANIZATION AND THE PERSPECTIVES OF OTHERS

Study your organization and your situation. Try to explain to yourself what is happening from the point of view taken in this book. Look at others from a career stages perspective. What functions are they performing? How do those functions reveal themselves in your organization and in your setting? Look at relationships and reciprocity. How have others broadened themselves and dealt with those outside the group for the benefit of others in the group? How do they get involved in the development of others? Who provides direction? How do they do it? Who is seen as influential and powerful? How do they exercise and gain power?

Talk to others about the critical tasks in your organization. How do they see things? Talk to them about functions and stages and relationships. What are they seeing that has been escaping you?

Look honestly at yourself. Are you in a job that utilizes your strengths? Can you do your job differently, in a way that uses your talents? Neither of the authors found that they were spell-binding lecturers, nor confrontive and electrifying case instructors. Each had to find a way to teach that fit their talents and interests. One of the authors does well in managing groups; his teaching improved when he planned how to manage the class, working with them in small groups.

Use the self-assessment questionnaire in the appendix of this book to help you think about the career stage that you are in. How well are you performing the functions and tasks in your stage? How are you handling the relationships? Have someone else fill it out concerning you. Don't be surprised if they see you in a lower stage than you see yourself. On average, individuals see themselves about a half stage beyond the way their manager describes them.

How are you blocking yourself from performing more effectively in this stage? What else is blocking you? Should you be grateful for the block? Will it force you to think harder about what you really want to do and can do?

Stop complaining about the organization. Organizations are not evil. Complex, yes; dangerous, yes; seductive, absolutely! But like the word processors we used to write this book, the better we understand, the more we can accomplish with them.

PERFORMING

Do well in the stage that you are in. Master it. Then move outside yourself, and ask what others need from you. What does your manager need from you? How can you help him or her be more successful? What do your co-workers need? Your mentor? Your sponsor? What does the organization need that you can provide? Peter Drucker claims that for individuals who want to be effective in organizations, the key question is, "What can I contribute that will significantly affect the performance and results of the institution I serve?" Drucker asserts that the individual "who focuses on contribution and who takes responsibility for results, no matter how junior, is in the most literal sense of the phrase, 'top management.'" (22)

EARNING MORE RESPONSIBILITY

If you want greater responsibility and want to move to the next stage, study what you must do to begin making the novation into that stage. What are the functions someone in that stage is expected to perform? How can you begin today to demonstrate to others that you can perform those functions? If those last two questions don't bring a flood of ideas to the reader, we have labored fruitlessly on the previous chapters and can say little at this point to redeem them.

LEAVING

After looking hard at yourself and your organization, you may decide you are in the wrong place. You may not be able to use your unique talents there. You may have needs that can be better met elsewhere.

David Meers was an engineering manager working for a large energy company. He managed a multi-million dollar government contract, received a good salary, and had a secure position. But the project no longer carried the urgency or the promise it had when he had taken it on. Government priorities had shifted toward other areas. No new people could be hired, and there were few prospects of growth. He inquired around the division about the possibility of transferring, but found that the likelihood of such a transfer was remote. He managed to get on some management task forces, only to discover how difficult it was to see the results of his efforts.

Then Meers was asked to join some friends in the company in the purchase of a fruit orchard that they would collectively operate on evenings and weekends. The orchard required hard work and long hours, but he found there an excitement and satisfaction that he no longer felt in his full-time work. He decided to look for a small business where he could use his engineering background. He finally found a small company for sale that was floundering badly. He got a loan from a bank in the new city, added his savings, resigned his position, and bought the business immediately. He worked long hours, finding new customers, changing the product and training the small workforce. For almost a year, the company operated at a loss, in spite of the fact that Meers took only bare living expenses for himself. At the end of the year, when the company had its first month in the black, Meers confided that he had felt more alive during the last year than he had since his work in graduate school. It was deeply gratifying to go to work each day, he said, knowing that the company stood or fell on his efforts.

Assure yourself, however, in determining to leave a job, that your lack of success or satisfaction stems from the nature of the job, the situation, or the organization. If it is a problem primarily stemming from your response to the situation, you are likely to carry the same problems with you to your next job.

But even if you have contributed to the problem, others' perceptions of you could be so fixed that it would be extremely difficult for them to see you differently—no matter what you do. If this is the case, make a deliberate decision whether to stay or leave. Think seriously before you allow yourself to remain in the vicious cycle that we have seen in so many cases: low evaluation and poor job assignments leading to discouragement and deteriorating confidence, which then lead to lower evaluation and more poor job assignments. In the early phases of this study (described in the introduction), we found that of all the engineers in a design center, the engineers who were *least* likely to leave voluntarily were the engineers with the lowest performance ratings. Many of them would have been better off leaving and starting anew somewhere else. In other settings, we have seen individuals get caught in negative cycles, which finally led to their dismissal. When we have met these individuals later, many have told us that they were grateful they had been forced to leave. They knew that they were doing poorly but were afraid to leave on their own. After being forced to leave, they had gotten another job where they had been able to perform better and feel better about themselves.

Some individuals use a disappointing and painful experience in organizational life as a stimulus for personal growth, an opportunity to move further in "becoming what they are."

> A research director was abruptly "fired" by management of the company where he had been employed for 25 years. His friends and those who worked for him were shocked at what they described as "rotten company politics." He was hurt and disappointed at this response to his many years of trying to build the company. But he used the break in employment to personally fill a need he saw in his city. He took a position as research director for a smaller company, but stipulated that he only work 3 days a week, for a reduced salary. The rest of his week he devoted to establishing and operating an organization to provide better housing for poor minority families in the inner city. He renovated decaying houses in the area, renting them to families at rates that they could afford.

ENJOYING

Our discussion of the larger questions facing individuals as they try to make decisions about careers has led to no simple or clear guidelines. Instead, it has left each of us with the daily task of finding our way as best we can on an uncharted course. But it is that daily task and the opportunity to perform it that impresses us as the central issue in our lives—inside and outside organizations. It is the issue that Thornton Wilder describes so well in *Our Town*. In the play, Emily, after having had a chance to revisit an ordinary day in her life, cries out:

> Good-by to clocks ticking . . . and Mama's sunflowers. And food and coffee. And new-ironed dresses and hot baths . . . and sleeping and waking up. Oh, earth, you're too wonderful for anybody to realize you. Do any human beings ever realize life while they live it?—every, every minute? (23)

12
Organizational Implications

Up to this point in the book we have focused exclusively on career issues from the perspective of the individual. It was a conscious choice, and we are optimistic that the ideas will be helpful to the professionals who read the book. In fact, those who are interested only in individual careers may choose to stop reading here. But since we first began to share with others our model of career stages, we have repeatedly been asked about the implications of the model for managing and designing organizations. Can the model help managers utilize more effectively the capabilities of professionals? This chapter will explore the possible uses of the career stages model by organizations. Note the following example:

The new vice president of research and development in a large manufacturing firm initiated a program to improve the effectiveness of his division. He held several meetings with the management team, and they decided to hold a 2-day off-site meeting with the 20 senior managers of the division. These managers identified 6 critical problem areas and appointed task forces to study each.

The managers agreed that one of the most serious of the 6 problem areas involved the careers of the scientists and engineers in the division. They reported that employees were concerned about their careers, and that many were frustrated because they were not making the progress that they desired in the organization.

The "careers" task force tackled the problem enthusiastically. They read articles on careers, contacted other companies to find out what they were doing, and interviewed over 120 professionals in groups of 12 to 15 people. They discovered that their professionals were intensely interested in the topic. The professionals wanted answers to questions such as:

- What is my job? (Why do priorities change so often?)
- How am I doing? (I get too little feedback.)
- What are the career paths in the division?
- How do I get ahead?

In response to the intensity of feeling on this issue, the task force recommended an ambitious program of career development. The management committee was impressed by the quality of data and recommendations in the report, but they didn't know quite how to proceed. Everyone agreed that there was a problem, but they were ambivalent about what to do. Some felt that it would be risky to start a career development program. They were afraid of raising unrealistic expectations, losing valuable people to transfers, and disrupting the organization. The management committee struggled with the problem for 18 months before approving a small pilot program.

The preceding example has been repeated many times in organizations throughout the country. A review of examples such as this one has led us to the following conclusions:

1. Employees are very interested in knowing more about factors affecting their careers.
2. Managers are reluctant to discuss career issues.
3. Most line managers and human resources professionals haven't found a way to explicitly approach career management issues in organizations.

If all three of these conclusions are correct, and there is considerable evidence to suggest they are, a great deal of frustration around the issue of careers is probably inevitable. Let us explore each one of these conclusions individually:

EMPLOYEES ARE INTERESTED IN CAREERS

In the example just cited, employees reported a higher interest in careers than in any other issue. We have found similar results in many different organizations. One of the authors helped to develop an organizational analysis questionnaire that has been administered to more than 200,000 employees in over 100 organizations. Respondents indicated a stronger desire for improvement in the way their organizations help employees manage careers than in any other area.

An overwhelming interest in careers permeates our society. This is not surprising considering the fact that a career is often a primary source of fulfillment and identity in an individual's life. What people do 8 hours a day, or more, has an immense impact on their sense of worth. Careers are also a direct connection to other basic needs—security, recognition, and a sense of control over one's life.

MANAGERS ARE RELUCTANT TO DISCUSS CAREERS

Given the high level of interest in careers, one might expect frequent discussions of the topic between managers and their subordinates. We have not found this to be the case. In the last 10 years, we have interviewed thousands of professionals about their careers. The vast majority indicate that they have had very few discussions about their careers with their supervisors. Most professionals indicate that although they have discussed their careers with an informal mentor at one time or another, discussions with superiors are rare.

Why are managers reluctant to discuss this topic with their subordinates? We have asked this question of many managers and have received the following responses:

- They want to avoid raising unrealistic expectations. Most managers assume that almost everyone wants to be promoted, and there are few opportunities for promotion in most organizations. They say: "If I discuss career opportunities with my subordinates, it will just get their hopes up and they'll end up being disappointed."
- They lack information about the needs of the organization. Many managers complain that they themselves don't know what's happening in the organization. They don't know where growth will be taking place, nor the plans for promotions, or transfers. They don't feel that they can realistically discuss future opportunities when they know so little.
- They want to keep valuable people. We have talked with managers who are reluctant to see their good performers go to other divisions. And they are fearful that if they accept a replacement from another division, they may get someone else's rejects; even if they get a good person, it will take a great deal of time for the person being transferred in to "get up to speed."
- They have too little time. Many managers say they are so busy "putting out fires" that they don't have time to *think* about next year, let alone take time to discuss it with their subordinates.

These reasons for managers' reluctance to discuss career issues are typically found in combination, making the reluctance even stronger.

Lack of Knowledge About How to Approach Career Development

In the last 10 years, we have talked to many managers and human resource professionals who are wondering what they can do in their organizations about career issues. Many express an interest in "career pathing" and training. Some focus on technical obsolescence and a desire to update professionals. Often they express frustration that their organizations do so little to help professionals manage their careers.

Many of these people recognize how critical career expectations can be to the company's ability to attract and retain top-notch professionals. Yet they are unsure about how to help professionals manage their careers. A major roadblock for many companies in deciding what to do about career issues has been the lack of a helpful theory or model. Several companies struggling with this problem have found the concept of career stages helpful.

There are several reasons why the idea that people progress through a series of stages with different responsibilities, activities, and adjustments provides a useful starting point for career development activities in an organization.

- The career stages model provides a new perspective and language that helps individuals and managers think about careers. It is often especially useful in helping individuals realize that, ultimately, they must take responsibility for their own careers. It also clarifies what may be expected of them at certain points in their career.
- Career development efforts can be less piecemeal if they are founded on a model that identifies novations that people face in their careers. This allows organizations to develop anticipatory programs, rather than "putting out fires" as they reach a crisis level or trying to take remedial action after it is too late to be of any help.

A central theme of this book has been that, to move from one stage to the next, individuals must demonstrate competence in performing the functions inherent in the next stage. In that sense, career development is an individual responsibility. However, organizations can do a great deal to either aid or hinder individual development efforts. Company policies and practices have the potential to substantially affect an employee's ability to work out a satisfying career.

For example, managers can either withhold or share information with employees about performance, anticipated organizational needs, and "how things work" in their organizations so that individuals can make intelligent choices about how to direct their efforts. Organizational practices can also have a substantial impact on an individual's willingness to contribute successfully to the company's efforts.

A COMPREHENSIVE APPROACH

Perhaps the best way to suggest what can be done about careers in organizations is to use examples. Let us begin by describing an organization that introduced a number of related changes that eventually had a major impact on the organization and the professionals involved.

Managers in the exploration division of a large multi-national oil company decided that they needed to address some critical career issues in their organization. One of the managers involved convinced the task force that the idea of career stages would be helpful to them in their efforts. The activities that the managers envisioned and began to promote were quite ambitious and could be classified in three distinct phases.

PHASE A: INITIATION

The first step in their program was to conduct a business and workforce diagnosis. The results showed that the turnover of geologists and geophysicists had reached alarming levels. Many older professionals and managers commented that the exploration division had become a training ground for the small oil companies in the region. By the time employees had 5 to 7 years of experience, they were prime candidates for one of the small companies, which offered them lucrative financial packages to entice them away. Turnover reached 18 percent among professionals with between 5 and 10 years of experience. The diagnosis confirmed a clear need for action.

The group of managers developed a matrix, using the stages concepts and language, that described the career progression of employees. A group of 20 managers of geologists and geophysicists attended a 1-day workshop, where they discussed how they might use the stages concept in career discussions with their subordinates. The workshop was followed by a half-day seminar attended by all of the professionals, where senior managers expressed commitment to, and support for, a career management effort. The concept of career stages was also introduced and the implications discussed. In the next 6 months, managers and professionals attempted to use the model in discussions about performance, compensation, and career development. They found it provided a useful language that enabled them to discuss difficult issues more effectively.

The effectiveness of this initial phase became apparent as geologists and geophysicists were finally able to describe some of their aspirations and frustrations. Together they, with their superiors, explored possibilities whereby they could, with effort, achieve their aspirations within the framework of their own company. Managers came to understand the frustrations of the professionals and took steps to eliminate some of the counter-productive practices in the company, which caused those frustrations. These measures brought a decline in the turnover, and the objectives of the original program began to be met.

PHASE B: INNOVATION

In retrospect, however, the most significant effect of this initial effort, which we have called Phase A, was the creation of a context for managers and employees in the division to make major changes in the organization, moving from human resource concerns to a focus on business productivity.

The exploration division might not have moved beyond their initial program if the economic situation in the oil industry had remained stable. However, in 1981, profits declined rapidly in the corporation and a decision was made to reduce the staff in the exploration division by 20 percent. Rumors circulated that management commitment to the career program was over. The initial business need for the career program had been to reduce turnover; there was now a need to reduce the number of employees.

At this critical point, a senior manager took an interest in the program, and he pointed out a new business need. He had been involved in a project analyzing successful oil companies in which some interesting data had been found. The research indicated that successful oil finds were often the result of professionals spending several years in the same geographical area, which enabled them to better understand the business and technical challenges in the area. The exploration division had not used this approach in the past and typically moved professionals between geographical areas on a regular basis. By linking this finding to the career management effort, a new business need was identified. Rather than laying off employees, the department instituted an early retirement program that was so attractive that almost all who were eligible took advantage of it. However, the large number of early retirements, along with the high turnover of experienced staff previously described, left an inexperienced workforce; 70% of the remaining professionals had less than 5 years service. An additional business need had been created. When this information was presented to the vice president, he authorized funds to continue the career development program. A key objective was to retain the remaining Stage III professionals, and to assist those in Stage II with high potential to move into Stage III as soon as possible.

With an increased emphasis on taking individual responsibility for one's own career, some of the nonmanager Stage III professionals started taking more initiative and began using their contacts in other departments to do more cooperative projects. It was during this period that a few of the nonmanager Stage

IV professionals recognized the link between career stages and the literature on innovation. They read about product champions with executive champions to sponsor them.

A series of workshops was conducted to discuss product champions and encourage more risk-taking. Many of the Stage III professionals responded enthusiastically, and the number of new ideas and projects increased substantially. Unfortunately, this brought about an increase in conflict between Stage III nonmanagers and a number of the supervisors in the department. One of the areas of conflict revolved around resources. A professional would request resources for a project, and the supervisor would turn it down. In the past this would have effectively killed the project. Under the new climate, the professional would take it on to other Stage III and Stage IV professionals hoping to rally support and continue working on the idea. The supervisors called this process "end running" and didn't like it. Others considered this kind of initiative a sign of success.

Phase C: Institutionalization

It was the lack of agreement between the various levels of the organization that provided the impetus to move into Phase C. Many managers in the formal system were quite traditional and only felt comfortable when decisions were made in the formal hierarchy. Those pushing the ideas about career stages and innovation wanted to place more emphasis on the informal system of doing business. They wanted to encourage mentor relationships and the pushing of new ideas through the system to "beat the bureaucracy."

The general manager supported the new direction and initiated a meeting with several key people. At the meeting, they first attempted to envision what was critical for the future success of the division. They asked questions concerning the ideal future: "What would be the role of professionals and managers? How would jobs and work be different?" In the meeting, they decided to restructure the division along the lines of a professional team concept. It was agreed that a change of structure would signal to everyone that senior management wanted to move in new directions. Teams were organized around geographical business areas. Each team was assigned professionals from Stages I through III. Support people such as business analysts and computer specialists were assigned to teams on a full-time basis. The teams were given a budget with full responsibility to manage it. If they were "successful," they could get additional resources from a division-wide "slush fund." Perhaps the most controversial issue concerned supervision. Some district managers elected to set up project teams where no formal leader was assigned. Where this occurred, the team either shared the administrative load, or someone emerged to provide leadership. In either case, the teams usually felt that the process was effective and preferred it to having an assigned project leader.

All of these organizational innovations were triggered by allowing career stages concepts to take root and impact the organization. Upper management and professionals alike were pleased with the results. Productivity increased and employees were strongly in favor of the new entrepreneurial climate. The chief geologist said: "This is what I've been trying to convince management to do all along. These ideas have minimized bureaucracy, and it keeps managers off the backs of professionals. It avoids the problem of managers making technical decisions they don't really understand anymore."

By describing the experience of this organization in detail, we do not suggest that all organizations that start discussing career stages will end up completely restructured or have any of the experiences that we have described here. We present this example because it includes the application of a variety of different elements of the career stages model. We want next to look at those elements in more detail, including organizational diagnosis, job assignments, training, compensation, and career discussions.

THE ORGANIZATIONAL DIAGNOSIS

One of the most critical steps in implementing any career development program is to conduct a careful analysis of the organization's business, its workforce, and its practices. We observed that organizations start career development efforts for a variety of different reasons. Some embark on them because they want to be considered a humane organization or because they believe that career development is a "good thing." Other organizations start career development efforts because they have gotten feedback from interviews or employee surveys that demonstrate a concern in this area. Still others implement programs as a measure to reduce turnover. However, these are all "fair weather" justifications. Organizations whose career efforts are developed to meet a business need are less likely to have their efforts cut off or ignored during company "bad times." The exploration division is an example of a career program designed to address business needs.

The career stage model can be a useful tool in providing an accurate and insightful profile of the workforce because it looks at more than just formal titles and pay scales. The career stage model can shed light on other helpful information such as who's contributing, who's blocked, and what's causing the lack of progress. The workforce analysis in the exploration division, for example, identified a serious problem of turnover among the professionals.

Some may feel that such detailed diagnosis is unnecessary because it will merely generate information already widely known in the organization. Managers often respond to such proposals with comments like: "I know the workforce; I've been with the company for 25 years." However, situations can change so gradually that managers may not be aware of developing problems.

> In one large technical organization, management ignored career issues for years. As time passed, engineers became more frustrated and outspoken about issues impacting their careers. Nothing changed. Finally, these engineers began to talk about forming a union. At that point, management became concerned enough to look into the concerns of the engineers.

> They found that many engineers felt stuck in their job assignments. The company, they said, had a "product cycle mentality." Engineers were assigned to a particular product and kept on it until both the product and the engineers working on it became technically out of date. When that product declined and ended, the engineers' careers were suddenly in jeopardy. Managers on projects requiring up-to-date technology preferred hiring recent graduates whose salary costs were lower. The experience of the older engineers did not offset their higher salary costs, because their technical experience was, in large part, irrelevant. Those who requested transfers to get a chance to learn new technology were seen as disloyal. In some cases, engineers reported having to quit their jobs in one division in order to get hired in another.

> The engineers recognized that the company was not growing at the time, so they weren't expecting promotions. But they felt that the company could do much more to foster employee development.

In this case, the organization's failure to pay attention to career issues generated a great deal of hostility and frustration among the professional workforce. An earlier diagnosis of the situation could have helped to prevent or alleviate the serious barriers to many engineers' careers, and the anger and frustration that grew out of them.

HOW TO DO AN ORGANIZATIONAL DIAGNOSIS

Diagnosing the career issues in an organization involves several steps.

BUSINESS DIAGNOSIS

Begin with a clear understanding of the strategy or business plan of the organization. Focus on such questions as:

- What human resources will be needed to implement the strategy or business plan?
- What career issues are critical to assure that the organization will have the committed efforts of individuals with the training and experience needed to implement the organization's strategy?
- What would be the impact of having Stage III and IV people who really knew how to use the system to make things happen?

Another way to explore the organization's needs is to compare your organization against your best competitors. Look for any competitive advantages that these organizations enjoy because they have more loyal, dedicated or long-service employees. Many recent books on culture and excellence point out that a common factor in companies like I.B.M., Proctor and Gamble, and Hewlett Packard is that they have committed, long-service employees and generally promote from within. These companies consider keeping people in their organization to be a strategic business advantage.

WORKFORCE DIAGNOSIS

Information regarding demographic aspects of the employee pool such as age, seniority, length of the job assignment, education level, and field of degree should be obtained first. Recent educational activity such as evening classes and company courses is also relevant. Performance data and salary information can be very useful.

A different picture of the workforce, which will reveal information not available from the other data, can be obtained by examining the current career stages of the organization's professionals. This information is relatively easy to obtain. Our method has been to put the name of each individual in a department (50 to 75 professionals) on a 3×5 card and then arrange a meeting with the manager. We discuss with the manager a 1-page description of the 4 stages (see Figures I.5 and I.6) asking him or her to take the cards and place each member of the department in the stage that most nearly describes the contributions that person is making. Most managers can complete that exercise for 50 people in about 30 minutes.

It is also helpful to ask employees about their career concerns through interviews or questionnaires. The task force described in the oil company at the beginning of this chapter accomplished this by dividing the total workforce into three groups:

1. Less than 5 years of service.
2. Service for 5 to 15 years.
3. More than 15 years of service.

The task force then selected 45 people from each group and interviewed them in groups. Groups of 8 to 10 people can generate a great deal of useful information in a short time.

The interview format need not be complex. Some questions that could be used to start this discussion include:

1. What does the organization do to help people grow?
2. What does the organization do that hinders career development?
3. What does it mean to be a high performer in this job?
4. Who has been most helpful to you in your career?
5. What could the organization do to improve career development?

Managers can also be interviewed to see how they feel about employees' careers. Are people being transferred too often? Not often enough? Do employees have adequate training to do their jobs? If managers report being too busy to be concerned about helping their people, that can also be useful information.

The final step involves analyzing the data. That analysis could be conducted at a fairly simple level (looking at a change in age distribution at two points in time), or it could involve a fairly sophisticated analysis. Much can be learned by conducting a straightforward analysis of a few variables. Some simple but often useful analyses include:

- Age and performance rankings.
- Age and salary levels.
- Age, performance, and career stage.
- Education level and performance.
- Age and length of job assignments.
- Stage and length of job assignments.

These are a few ideas to begin the data analysis. Once a person gets into the data, most people can formulate questions that will increase their understanding of the workforce.

Signals that may indicate problem areas include:

I. A large proportion of employees in one age or seniority group.
   A. One company had 40 percent of its managers in the 55 to 65 age group.
   B. In another company, 35 percent of the employees had worked with the company for 3 years or less.

II. An overabundance of employees in one stage.
   A. One company had most of its employees in Stage II with very few identified as being in Stages III or IV.
III. A low correlation between stage and salary.

After the preliminary analysis, it is important for whomever has gathered the data to work closely with the line managers to understand the data. Managers can answer questions such as why so many professionals over age 40 are still in Stage I, or why there are so few professionals in Stage III. Managers need to be involved at each step because they will eventually determine and implement whatever action is taken.

ISSUES IN DIAGNOSING AN ORGANIZATION

While the process of organizational diagnosis has the potential to help the organization a great deal, it is critical that those from whom data will be gathered understand why the information is being collected and what will be done with it. A decision needs to be made before the data are collected about how results will be shared with respondents. Finally, care should be taken not to raise expectations that dramatic changes will follow as a result of the study.

Performing an accurate organizational diagnosis is just the first step to an effective career development program. The knowledge gained from the diagnosis can aid the organization in knowing how to facilitate the development of its professionals through specific practices: job assignments, training, compensation, and career discussions. These workforce practices are building blocks for creating change in the organization. To understand these building blocks, we will need to discuss each component separately.

JOB ASSIGNMENTS

The notion of career stages can be helpful in determining which job assignments will be most helpful in an employee's career at a particular point in time. In Stage I, challenging assignments are critical to the development of the employee. In Stage II, the variety of job experiences is more important. As employees move into Stages III and IV, issues around job assignments take a new twist. Employees who are clear about the way careers develop in that organization may well choose an assignment that allows them to open new options rather than electing to be promoted in a more narrow field. Some may even want to recycle through an individual contributor phase to gain skills or pursue interests. Let us examine some of the job assignment issues that typically arise in each stage.

STAGE I

Professionals in Stage I are often concerned about their first job assignment. They want an assignment that will allow them to test themselves, make a meaningful contribution, and learn new skills. At this stage, the amount of challenge in the first assignment can have a significant impact on the employee's entire career. Research has shown that challenging job assignments are critical to good performance rankings. In a longitudinal study of AT&T employees, Berlew and Hall found that those who had more challenging assignments in their first year were more likely to be evaluated as effective even 7 years later (1).

But a high level of challenge is usually not built into initial job assignments, despite its powerful effects on individual careers. One study of 22 research and development organizations by Hall & Lawler showed only 2 in which employees felt that they had been given moderately or highly challenging first job assignments. This common practice of cautiously starting new recruits on simple projects can be frustrating to graduates and wasteful for the company. Organizations usually err in providing too little challenge for competent new employees (2).

STAGE II

When professionals begin to seek independence, take responsibility for projects, and broaden their experience, is usually the time for making a variety of job assignments available.

The amount of time that employees spend on one assignment can make a big difference in their effectiveness and satisfaction. Many employees indicate that after 3 to 5 years on the same assignment, little new learning or challenge takes place. If professionals are not learning, growing, and gaining greater competence on their jobs, they become bored, frustrated, and eventually less effective.

Many professionals note this phenomenon in their own careers:

> In the first year I am just getting used to the job. I work hard, but I am not at the peak of performance. In the second year I know what I am doing, and I am still interested so I'm pretty productive. By the third year I begin to lose a sense of challenge, and I am not as productive.

Research by Katz supports the notion that the length of time in a position can influence employee effectiveness. Katz suggests that there are three periods in any assignment: socialization, innovation, and stabilization. During the socialization period, employees become familiar with their environment in preparation for the highly involved innovation stage when they are most effective. As the individual becomes accustomed to the demands of the position, he or she may enter a less productive stabilization stage. Katz recommends moving employees periodically into new groups or positions to maintain an optimal level of productivity (3).

Katz has also found that project groups are most effective if they work together between 2 and 4 years. After 4 years, they begin to cut themselves off from valuable sources of information outside of the group, and the productivity of the group declines (4).

Companies that ignore their employees' needs for providing a breadth of job assignments take the risk of losing those employees.

> In the computer department of one company, programmers were hired to work on three distinct types of projects. Although each project required specialized training, many of the skills were transferable across projects. Several employees at various times expressed an interest in transferring to one of the other projects to broaden their experience. But the supervisors refused to let their valuable people go. One of the reasons was that there was no program or model in the department that clearly articulated the value of developing employees. Management talked about the value of developing people, but supervisors were not sure how to go about it. They did not share information about openings with people inside the department. Instead, they hired from the outside to fill openings. Turnover skyrocketed among programmers who felt that they had to go elsewhere to broaden their career experience.

Contrast this example with the sales manager in a Fortune 500 organization who kept a chart for the career development of each of her subordinates.

> She had developed a system of listing each person's name along with the assignments under her jurisdiction. By checking who had held each assignment, she could easily see which people might need new assignments to round out their experience. She actively developed her people by literally trading them in and out of jobs and transferring them to other areas to broaden their backgrounds.

One of the dilemmas that organizations face is not having enough developmental positions to go around. Even though top employees may need to broaden their experience, there is sometimes no place in that part of the organization which will provide them with the development they need. This problem can be solved in part by arranging interdepartmental transfers or job rotations. (The team concept used in the exploration division was an attempt to accomplish this result.) It is important to recognize that the final responsibility for determining assignments for professionals should not be left to the immediate supervisor. First, the supervisor often has little knowledge of other available positions throughout the organization. Secondly, supervisors also have a vested interest in keeping good performers in their departments. Losing competent people, no matter how beneficial to the individual, is seldom easy for the immediate supervisor.

One way of facilitating developmental interdepartmental transfers is to set up a board of managers, two or three levels removed, to review potential candidates for positions that open up. One organization holds a semi-annual review attended by second and third level managers. At that meeting, the managers review the career progress of each professional in the division. If it is decided that a person needs a transfer to develop new skills, the personnel manager is directed to work out the arrangements for such a move. Because all the managers are involved in the meeting, they have information about the developmental needs of individuals and available opportunities in the organization. There is also more pressure not to hold on to one's best people when doing so would be detrimental to an individual's career. When the exploration division, discussed earlier, was in full swing with the professional team concept, teams were encouraged to "recruit" people from other teams with little managerial involvement. There was a strong value placed on people working in areas that interested them.

STAGES III AND IV

While everyone agrees that good job assignments are important to employees early in their careers, they don't always recognize the importance of job assignments for people in Stages III and IV. Often, they too need the benefit of a new job assignment. Some of these over-age-40 employees are very susceptible to boredom, to the itch to start over in another career, or simply to leave the frustrations of the organization to start their own companies. These "happy dropouts," as a recent article in *Forbes magazine* describes them, still have the "guts, imagination and ability" to throw themselves wholeheartedly into new and sometimes vastly different positions (5). Unfortunately, these top performers are often limited by "up or out" attitudes. They are likely viewed as having gone as high as they can go in the organization. Unless managers broaden their thinking about the feasibility and acceptability of lateral moves or even "demotions" in facilitating career development, they will lose a valuable resource in these senior employees.

Beverly Kaye, author of *Up is Not the Only Way*, suggests that alternatives to the "moving up" option—such as moving across, moving down, or staying put—can be attractive to both the organization and to the employee (6). Moving across, for example, has the advantage of providing a "way of demonstrating adaptive abilities and broadening skills, learning about other areas of the organization, and developing new talents." One computer company facilitates "moving across" by requiring each professional employee to spend 2 weeks of every year working in another division. This way employees are exposed to other areas of the company and are better able to explore their interests and open doors to possible transfers.

Moving down can also provide an opportunity for those who seek fulfillment in outside areas to free themselves from time-consuming positions. One 50-year-old manager who had successfully supervised 300 employees for 8 years felt that he had reached a dead-end in his career until he was given an opportunity to make a unique career shift.

> I was asked to do a major study for the president that would require my full time effort. I was reluctant to accept the assignment if it meant giving up my position as department manager because I didn't know where it would lead. In order to do the study I had to go back and learn a lot about surveys, interviews, analyzing questionnaire data, and so on.
>
> After I finished the study, the president asked if I would take a position in which some of the things proposed in the report would be implemented. He invited me to become his assistant and work out of the office of the president. I decided to take the new position, and it has been a very good experience. It has enabled me to have an impact on the whole organization and to work with issues and people I've genuinely enjoyed.

Although this kind of move can carry the stigma of failure with it, the benefits to be gained for both the individual and the organization can be so great that the fear of that stigma should not paralyze efforts to make changes that make sense on all other levels. By entering into honest dialogue, using imagination, and creating new roles that may differ from the organization's normal bureaucracy, moves can be made that use everyone's talents more fully.

A final option for those in Stages III and IV is to explore new dimensions of their current jobs. Jobs can be broadened by creating opportunities for employees to deal directly with customers, supervise increasing numbers of employees, or take on new areas of responsibility. Organizations that ignore the developmental needs of their professionals risk losing their competitive edge. Unless management keeps a watchful eye over the job assignments given to their professionals, productivity and innovation may suffer.

TRAINING

Training is considered by many to be the most valuable part of a career development program. In fact, in some organizations, training is the whole program. But despite the billions of dollars that American organizations spend each year on training, the results are often disappointing. Some of the characteristics of training programs that contribute to this problem include:

1. Same training for everyone. Many organizations decide what topics should be covered in this year's training and then run everyone through the same programs.
2. Repetition of subject matter. In many corporate training programs we've heard people complain, "This is the fourth time in the last 5 years that I've been told about McGregor's Theory X and Theory Y. Why don't they do a better job of coordinating what's covered in these training programs?"
3. Last minute "planning." Many organizations specify the amount of training that a person should receive each year (i.e., 5 days each year). Unless managers are careful, these policies can lead to poor planning of training activities. As the year draws to a close, managers may begin to send their people to whatever courses happen to be offered at that time, with little consideration for what would be most useful to the employee.

To avoid these problems, those responsible for developing training programs, as well as those seeking training, need a way to think about what training individuals need at various points in their careers. Some organizations have used the concept of career stages to provide a framework for their training activities. It has helped those responsible for designing training programs to develop training modules that will aid individuals as they approach critical transitions in their careers. Managers and individuals have been able to select training programs that are better suited to the needs of each individual at that particular point in his or her career. It has been useful to identify holes in the overall training program. One organization realized that they had programs for new hires, new supervisors, and those about to retire, but lacked programs for all of their managers between new supervisors and retirees.

COMPENSATION

One of the most interesting findings in our career research is that many organizations have compensation systems that do not reward the most productive employees. Many organizations use pay systems that reward individuals primarily according to the number of subordinates they supervise, rather than on the value of their contribution to the firm. Such systems discriminate against the highly contributive nonmanagers. In recent years, several organizations have revised their compensation plans to recognize nonmanagers who contribute as much to organizational performance as managers:

> At Analog Devices, a computer components company in Norwood, Massachusetts, managers are not the only ones who receive top perks, salaries, stock options, and autonomy. Purely technical engineers called corporate fellows, division fellows, and senior staff engineers are compensated very much like management. Division fellows can have the same perks and salary as a division or general manager.

> Senior staff engineers at Analog are given flexibility around working hours and the option of working at home or in the office, in addition to the same salary as senior-level managers. Senior engineers are given a great deal of leeway on the types of design projects that they tackle and are encouraged to suggest improvements on current products.

Most compensation systems could be improved greatly by a conscientious attempt to reward those who make significant contributions while remaining in technical work, rather than managing people. Such modifications would help organizations attract and keep top quality professionals.

CAREER DISCUSSIONS

In the introduction, we briefly discussed several reasons why managers are so reluctant to discuss careers. Ironically, career discussions between employees and supervisors are one of the most critical elements of an effective career development process. There are several reasons for this:

I. Organizations cannot develop people's careers. Managers must be interested in their employees' current performance level. Because managers are often rewarded for a short-term focus, they cannot be expected to always be thinking about what's best for each individual in the long run. Even if they had the time and the inclination, managers do not have the omniscience to know what each individual desires, nor what will be best for him or her. Individuals must take responsibility for deciding what they would like to do and for seeing that they are not stuck in jobs below their capacity. Career discussions allow individuals to communicate what they want to do to become more valuable to the organization, and to learn how they are perceived by others.

II. Careers are not linear or static. Individuals must recognize the dynamic, complex nature of organizational careers. Careers are not simple ladders, nor are organizations clear-cut hierarchies. People move in and out of jobs constantly, and individuals continually have opportunities to take on new tasks. Discussions between managers and subordinates can help keep employees abreast of emerging opportunities and managers aware of their own employees' emerging interests.

III. Individuals who understand the organization can contribute more effectively to it. Often, managers can help their subordinates a great deal by sharing with them "how things work around here."

IV. Even though immediate supervisors usually do not, and, in our opinion, should not make ultimate decisions on significant assignment changes for their subordinates, it is through the supervisor that information about an individual's interests and capabilities are usually transmitted to those who do make those decisions. Therefore, one of the most useful things that a company can do to help employees manage their careers is to give both managers and professionals some training in holding fruitful career discussions. We have found that the three blocks to holding productive career discussions, which can be removed by training, are:

A. Lack of an adequate language or vocabulary to discuss careers.

B. Failure to distinguish the responsibilities of both the manager and the professional in career discussions.

C. Inadequate preparation by the professional for a discussion of his or her career.

Let us note briefly how training has helped overcome each of these blocks. Where both managers and professionals have been introduced to one or more career models and given an opportunity to discuss it, the vocabulary problem has been resolved. They are then able to approach their discussion from a common ground. The failure to distinguish the responsibilities of each party in a career discussion can best be understood by examining Table 12.1, on the following page.

Only individuals can decide what they like to do or where they want to go. The manager cannot decide that for them. If managers allow themselves to be seduced into making plans for individuals, they implicitly promise, "If you do this, you'll get that assignment (or promotion)." If employees ask, "Where should I try to go?" the manager must gently but firmly respond, "Only *you* can decide that for yourself." On the other hand, managers have information that would be of value to their subordinates. Managers can share with an employee how that individual is

Table 12.1. A Realistic Division of Responsibilities in Career Discussions

DIMENSION	PROFESSIONAL EMPLOYEE	MANAGER
Responsibility	Assumes responsibility for individual career development.	Assumes responsibility for employee development.
Information	Obtains career information through self evaluation and data collection. What do I enjoy doing? Where do I want to go?	Provides information by holding up a mirror of reality. How manager views the employee. How others view the employee. How "things work around here."
Planning	Develops an individual plan to reach objectives.	Helps employee assess plan.
Follow through	Invites management support through high performance on the current job, by understanding the scope of the job and taking appropriate initiative.	Provides coaching and relevant information on opportunities.

perceived. "You haven't had enough experience to assure me that you could handle that assignment," or "The people in that department see you as hard to work with and would resist your being given that role."

In addition, while managers can critique a plan and point out omissions, the individual must implement it, starting with his or her performance in the current assignment. When managers and employees have been trained to keep their responsibilities separate and have been able to see themselves on videotape as they role-play career discussions, the fear of raising unrealistic expectations diminishes. When they have actual discussions where they are able to keep those responsibilities separate, their fears disappear.

The last block is inadequate preparation by employees before a career discussion with their manager. Unless employees have given serious thought to what they enjoy doing and what they do well, they are not ready to carry out their part of the discussion. Workbooks to assist them in exploring those questions can be helpful.

Much of this chapter has focused on such topics as: job assignments, training, compensation, and career discussions—specific programs that can help managers to improve the way they manage professionals. But well-designed programs are not enough. The important ingredient to success in the management of careers lies with the managers themselves. An organization can have quality programs and competent people in human resources and still do a poor job of career development. The greatest need is for managers to take this issue seriously and devote adequate time to its implementation. When that condition is met, organizations are well on the way to more effective management of their professional workforce.

Appendix

Career Stages
Self Assessment Guide

INTRODUCTION

One way to think about individual development is to use the notion of *Career Stages*. Many professionals find this notion useful in helping them think more clearly about their current performance. You'll find the type of work you do is probably distributed across each of the stages. Your job more than likely requires a certain amount of attention to routine detail. On other occasions you are called upon to perform tasks that demand the integration of resources, information, and problem solving skills. You probably spend more of your time in certain activities than in others. To help clarify your thinking about which stage is most characteristic of you, answer each of the questions on the *Career Stages Self Assessment Guide* as you really think you are now.

The *Career Stages Self Assessment Guide* is designed to help you determine what career stage you are in at this time and what skills you should be working on to improve current and future performance.

HOW TO COMPLETE THE GUIDE

A. Select the stage that you feel most closely fits where you are now. Respond to the ten statements for that stage. Then respond to the ten statements in the preceding and succeeding stages (if any). This means that you will respond to a maximum of thirty statements.

B. There are two boxes—Box A and Box B—where you mark your responses.

Box A asks you to determine whether or not the statement is central to your current performance. Once you have determined this, you make one (✔) in the appropriate space.

Box B asks you to determine how important it is that this skill be improved in two areas—
(1) to do well in current assignment,
(2) to earn greater responsibility.
Once you have decided, you make two checks in the appropriate spaces—one for each area.
Example:
Situation—Assume you are a new supervisor. You decide that since you are a first-line supervisor you are probably in Stage 3. The first statement reads:
"Have broadened your perspective and technical understanding to the point that others can trust you to guide tasks greater in scope than any one person can accomplish."

NOTE: Reprinted with permission of The Center for the Management of Professional & Scientific Work.

Step #1: Look at Box A and determine whether or not this statement is central to your current performance.

You decide that this is central. Now you are asked to determine how often you perform competently—seldom, often, almost always.

You decide that you have had some difficulty adjusting to your new supervisory position and you realize that one of the problems you have is not knowing how to let go of specialized technical work. Therefore, you put one (✔) under *sometimes:*

Step #2: Look at Box B and determine how important it is that this area be improved.

You decide that it is *critical* that you improve in this area. To be a supervisor requires a broader perspective than doing just your own work well. This is true in your current assignment and especially true if you want to go on to become a senior technical consultant or a manager.

Therefore, you mark two (✔ s) as follows:

STAGE III: WOULD YOU SAY YOU . . .

Have broadened your perspective and technical understanding to the point that others can trust you to guide tasks greater in scope than any one person can accomplish?

A. Determine how central this activity is to your performance: (mark one)						B. How important is it that performance in this area improve: (mark two)					
NO LONGER CENTRAL but you:		CENTRAL to performance / You perform competently			NOT YET CENTRAL TO PERFORMANCE	To do well in current assignment			To earn greater responsibility		
Still do it when appropriate	Continue to focus on	Seldom	Sometimes	Almost Always		Critical	Important	Not important	Critical	Important	Not important
			✔			✔			✔		

Now, following the same steps as in the example, fill out the *Career Assessment Guide* on the following pages.

STAGE I: WOULD YOU SAY YOU . . .

Follow directions willingly, intelligently, and enthusiastically?

Carry out assignments carefully, following through on important details?

Do a good job of keeping the project leader informed on the status of the project?

Appear to be able to see things from the project leader's point of view?

Are making the project leader look good through your efforts?

Appear to be anticipating needs and doing something to meet them?

Appear to be learning quickly how to get work done in the organization?

Ask good questions and try to implement suggestions?

Are learning when to proceed with a task the best you can and when to check with a project leader?

Maintain detailed documents on the part of a project which you are assigned and organize them so you can support details for the project leader at any time?

A. Determine how central this activity is to your performance: (mark one)

NO LONGER CENTRAL but you:		CENTRAL to performance / You perform competently			NOT YET CENTRAL TO PERFORMANCE
Still do it when appropriate	Continue to focus on	Seldom	Sometimes	Almost Always	

B. How important is it that performance in this area improve: (mark two)

To do well in current assignment			To earn greater responsibility		
Critical	Important	Not important	Critical	Important	Not important

STAGE II: WOULD YOU SAY YOU . . .

Can be counted on to perform individual professional work without close supervision?

Can perform individual professional tasks as well as or better than anyone else?

Ensure that you master the new technologies necessary to carry out your work in the best way possible?

Can take on a one-person project and be trusted to utilize the relevant technology to solve problems that arise, and to do so intelligently and within deadlines?

Can be counted on to manage your own time wisely to see that the work for which you are responsible moves forward in a way that best meets organizational needs?

Keep others, who might be affected, informed about the progress of the work for which you are responsible and its possible implications for them?

Are supportive and cooperative with peers, superiors and technicians, operators and administrative personnel?

Have developed the capability to do some type of professional work unusually well?

Are seen as having good professional judgment?

Are seen as someone who applies professional knowledge creatively and intelligently to the solution of problems?

A. Determine how central this activity is to your performance: (mark one)						B. How important is it that performance in this area improve: (mark two)					
NO LONGER CENTRAL but you:		CENTRAL to performance			NOT YET CENTRAL TO PERFORMANCE	To do well in current assignment			To earn greater responsibility		
			You perform competently								
Still do it when appropriate	Continue to focus on	Seldom	Sometimes	Almost Always		Critical	Important	Not important	Critical	Important	Not important

Have broadened your perspective and technical understanding to the point that others can trust you to guide tasks greater in scope than any one person can accomplish?

Provide technical ideas and advice to the members of your group to initiate and complete significant projects?

Are entrusted to head up groups and projects because of your breadth of technical, human, and economic knowledge?

Deal with persons outside the group for the benefit of others inside the group?

Deal with persons outside the group to obtain resources for the group (contracts, budgets, raises, assignments, etc.)?

Involve yourself in the development of others in the group?

Have significant contacts with other groups inside or outside the organization which benefit the performance of your group?

Bring information into your group which enhances its ability to solve problems?

Have formal and informal relationships with others which result in their learning how to structure and solve problems, and deal with the organization?

Help others obtain developmental tasks and opportunities?

A. Determine how central this activity is to your performance: (mark one)						B. How important is it that performance in this area improve: (mark two)					
NO LONGER CENTRAL but you:		CENTRAL to performance			NOT YET CENTRAL TO PERFORMANCE	To do well in current assignment			To earn greater responsibility		
			You perform competently								
Still do it when appropriate	Continue to focus on	Seldom	Sometimes	Almost Always		Critical	Important	Not important	Critical	Important	Not important

STAGE IV: WOULD YOU SAY YOU . . .

Provide direction for a significant part of the organization through management and policy determination, direction of major programs and/or through technical contributions that have a substantial impact on the direction and growth of the firm?

Have a substantial impact on the direction of the organization based on a clear understanding of the organization's distinctive capabilities and limitations?

Exercise influence over important decisions in the organization through your management of the process by which the organization meets challenges and implements objectives?

Exercise strong influence in the organization on the basis of your demonstrated ability to assess trends and lead the firm to take advantage of those trends?

Exercise significant influence in the organization on the basis of your demonstrated ability to deal effectively with external entities for the benefit of the firm (bringing in business information, dealings with the government, etc.)?

Exercise strong influence in the organization on the basis of your demonstrated ability to get information from and affect the behavior of key individuals and groups in the organization?

Are involved in the sponsorship (providing key assignments, responsibility and visibility) of individuals capable of playing future key roles in the firm?

Have wide and varied interactions with key persons inside and outside of the firm?

Are able to exercise power effectively on behalf of the groups, ideas, and projects which depend on your advocacy to achieve important organizational objectives?

Work with able people in a way that helps them develop and demonstrate whether they have the ability to play future key roles in the organization?

| A. Determine how central this activity is to your performance: (mark one) | | | | | | B. How important is it that performance in this area improve: (mark two) | | | | | |
| NO LONGER CENTRAL but you: | | CENTRAL to performance / You perform competently | | | NOT YET CENTRAL TO PERFORMANCE | To do well in current assignment | | | To earn greater responsibility | | |
Still do it when appropriate	Continue to focus on	Seldom	Sometimes	Almost Always		Critical	Important	Not important	Critical	Important	Not important

ANALYSIS

A. Did I Pick the Right Stage?

As you look at the center three columns in Box A—*Central to performance,* many of the checks (✓s) should be in the *sometimes* and *almost always* columns, if you are actually in this stage. If there are not very many checks in these columns, then you should consider carefully whether or not you are really in this stage.

Try to answer these questions.

1. In what stage do you think your supervisor/others place you?

2. What things would they suggest you need to work on if you want to perform solidly in this stage?

3. What would they suggest you work on if you want to move to the next stage?

B. Developing and Improving Performance in Current Job

I. No longer central (Box A)

Turn to the page which describes the stage you think you are now in. Look at the checks in Box A under *No Longer Central* and *Continue to Focus On.* Make a mark beside each statement that has a check in this column. The statements identified by these marks represent the areas which you feel are no longer central but on which you continue to focus on inappropriately.

Write down your responses to the following questions:

1. Do you see any trends or similarities?

2. Can you think of some areas that you do not seem to have time for which are central to your performance in your current assignment because you are still paying too much attention to these inappropriate areas?

3. Can you identify barriers or constraints resulting from the work itself, your supervisor or subordinates, or anything else that keeps you from cutting back on these areas? What can *you* do to deal with these constraints?

4. Where/to whom could you delegate these activities? If you do not have formal authority to delegate, who could you influence to do these things?

5. What else can you think of doing to cut back on these inappropriate activities in order to free yourself to pursue those activities which are more critical to your success?

II. Improvement areas—to do well in current assignment (Box B)

Continue to work on the page of statements which describe your current stage. Look at the checks in Box B under *To do well in current assignment* under the columns *critical* and *important.* Make a different mark beside each statement that has a check in either column. The statements identified by these marks represent areas which you feel are either critical or important to improve in your current assignment.

Answer the following questions:

1. Are there any trends in these statements?

2. Can you identify any organizational constraints/barriers keeping you from making changes? What can you do to change or go around these barriers?

3. What ideas do you have which might help you improve in these areas? (meeting people, exposure to something or someone . . .)

4. Who else might have ideas on how to get what you need to improve in these areas? (managers, peers, friends . . .)

5. Do you need to influence anyone to put some of these ideas into action? Who/How?

6. What can *you* do now?

C. Not Yet Central (Box A)

Consider the statements with checks in Box A under the column *Not Yet Central* to current assignment. These areas may or may not be problems. Answer the following questions as honestly as you can:
1. Are you neglecting areas that are central to current performance because you are attempting to get into activities that are not yet central?

2. Can you identify factors pushing you to perform these activities before you are ready *or* are you doing these things because you want to stretch and develop yourself?

3. Generally, do you see your performance in these areas as helping or hindering you now? What can you do to make sure that you can continue/stop performing in these areas?

D. Earning Greater Responsibilities (Box B)

We do not wish to imply that you should seek additional responsibility. However, if this is important to you, then some further analysis will be worthwhile. As we have stressed before, it is imperative to do well in your current assignment before considering additional responsibilities.

Talking with your boss or your peers or someone who knows your work well is an important *reality test,* so don't shortchange yourself by assuming you know *all* of your strengths and weaknesses better than anyone else.

Turn to the page of statements describing your current stage. This page should have two or three different marks on it. Look for the checks in Box B under *To earn greater responsibility* and *critical* or *important.* Think of another mark or find a colored pen or pencil and make your mark beside the appropriate statements. The statements identified by this mark represent the critical and important areas to improve on for earning greater responsibility.

Write down your responses to the following questions:
1. Do you see any trends or similarities?

2. What kinds of experiences would help you develop these skills?

3. Who could give you more ideas on where to get these experiences? Are there steps you could take to develop these skills yourself?

4. Do you need to influence anyone else? How can you?

5. What can you begin to do differently to earn the opportunity to take on greater responsibility in this area?

265

Notes

Introduction

1. Gene W. Dalton, Paul H. Thompson, and Ray Price, "The Four Stages of Professional Careers," *Organizational Dynamics* (Summer 1977), pp. 19-42.
2. *Webster's New World Dictionary* (The World Publishing Co., 1978), Second College Ed., p. 974.
3. "Baby Boomers Push for Power," *Business Week* (July 2, 1984), pp. 52-62.
4. Earl C. Gottschalk, Jr., "Many June Graduates Are Still Hunting Hard for a First Career Job," *Wall Street Journal,* Vol. CIX, No. 76.
5. Derek C. Bok, "A flawed system," *Harvard Magazine* (May-June 1983), p. 41.
6. *Earned Degrees Conferred 1979-80,* National Center for Education Statistics, United States Department of Education, pp. 6-20.
7. James O'Toole, *Work, Learning and the American Future* (San Francisco: Jossey-Bass, 1977), p. 38.
8. "ACLI Analysis Shows Effect of Maturing Members of Baby Boom," *National Underwriter, Life and Health Insurance Edition,* Vol. 85 (August 24, 1981), p. 5.
9. *Statistical Abstract of the United States,* U.S. Department of Commerce, Bureau of the Census, 1981, p. 401.
10. "A New Era for Management," *Business Week* (April 25, 1983), p. 52.
11. Gene W. Dalton and Paul H. Thompson, "Accelerating Obsolescence of Older Engineers," *Harvard Business Review* (September-October 1971), p. 59.
12. Paul H. Thompson, Gene W. Dalton, and Richard Kopelman, "But What Have You Done for Me Lately—The Boss," *IEEE Spectrum* (October 1974), pp. 85-89.
13. Thompson, Dalton, and Kopelman, *IEEE Spectrum,* p. 87.
14. Dalton, Thompson, and Price, *Organizational Dynamics,* p. 23.
15. Dalton and Thompson, *Harvard Business Review,* pp. 57-67.
16. There is also the expectation or hope from others that as individuals gain experience in the organization, they will begin to perform more highly valued functions. If an individual, 25 years of age, after 3 years with the organization is competently carrying out two individual projects that had been assigned by his or her manager, the individual could easily be seen as doing well. If that same individual were doing the same thing 15 years later, others are likely to be asking, "What's wrong?"

Chapter 1

1. Edgar H. Schein, "The First Job Dilemma," *Psychology Today,* Vol. 1 (January–March 1968), pp. 26–37.

2. Elton Mayo, *The Social Problems of an Industrial Civilization* (Boston: Graduate School of Business Administration, Harvard University, 1945), p. 120.

3. Homer, *The Odyssey,* contained in Great Books of the Western World (Chicago: William Benton, Publisher, University of Chicago Press, 1952), Vol. 4, p. 190.

4. Daniel J. Levinson, Charlotte N. Darrow, Edward B. Klein, et al., *The Seasons of a Man's Life* (New York: Alfred A. Knopf, 1978), p. 333.

5. E. E. Jennings, *The Mobile Manager* (New York: McGraw-Hill, 1967), pp. 47–48.

6. William Oncken, Jr., and Donald L. Wass, "Management Time: Who's Got the Monkey?", *Harvard Business Review* (November–December 1974), p. 79.

7. Jennings, *The Mobile Manager,* pp. 47–50.

Chapter 2

1. Mignon McLaughlin, *The Neurotics Notebook* (New York: Signet Books, 1970), p. 88.

2. P. E. Leathers, "Staff Retention in Public Accounting Firms," *Journal of Accountancy* (January 1971), p. 37.

3. J. DePasquale and R. Lange, "Job Hopping and the MBA," *Harvard Business Review* (November–December 1971), p. 5.

4. D. Sommers and A. Eck, "Occupational Mobility in the American Labor Force," *Monthly Labor Review* (January 1977), pp. 3–18.

5. Sommers and Eck, *Monthly Labor Review,* pp. 9–10.

6. Edgar H. Schein, "How 'Career Anchors' Hold Executives to Their Career Paths," *Personnel* (May–June 1975), pp. 11–24.

7. Edgar H. Schein, *Career Dynamics: Matching Individual and Organizational Needs* (Reading, Mass.: Addison-Wesley Publishing Co., 1978), p. 125.

8. Robert W. White, *Lives in Progress* (New York: Holt, Rinehart and Winston, 1952), pp. 348–349.

Chapter 3

1. Harriett Zuckerman, *Scientific Elites: Nobel Laureates in the United States* (New York: The Free Press, 1972), pp. 96–143, 176–189.

2. Leonard J. Arrington, "Historian as Entrepreneurs: A Personal Essay," *Brigham Young University Studies* (Winter 1977), pp. 200–204.

3. William Foote Whyte, *Street Corner Society* (University of Chicago Press, 1943), p. 260.

4. Technical ladders are most common in research laboratories and engineering organizations. The typical technical ladder has from two to four levels. Professionals on the technical ladder are paid salaries comparable to those received by first level supervisors. For more information see D. C. Moore and D. S. Davis, "The Dual Ladder—Establishing and Operating It," *Research Management* (July 1977), pp. 14–19.

Chapter 4

1. Sterling Livingston, "Pygmalion in Management," *Harvard Business Review* (July–August 1969), p. 82.
2. George E. Vaillant, et al., *Adaptation to Life* (Boston: Little, Brown and Company, 1977), pp. 202, 218–219.
3. Daniel J. Levinson, et al., *The Seasons of a Man's Life* (New York: Alfred A. Knopf, 1978), pp. 100–101.
4. Carl G. Jung, Memories, Dreams, Reflections (New York: Random House, 1961), pp. 146–157.

Chapter 5

1. Edgar H. Schein, "The Individual, the Organization, and the Career: A Conceptual Scheme," *Journal of Applied Behavioral Science,* 7 (1971), pp. 401–426.
2. Erik H. Erikson, "Identity and the Life Cycle," *Psychological Issues* (New York: International Universities Press, Inc., 1959), Vol. 1, No. 1, p. 97.
3. Fritz J. Roethlisberger, "The Foreman: Master and Victim of Double Talk," *Harvard Business Review* (Spring 1945), Vol. XXIII, No. 3, pp. 283–298.
4. Robert L. Kahn, et al., *Organizational Stress: Studies in Role Conflict and Ambiguity* (New York: John Wiley and Sons, 1964), p. 149.
5. Roethlisberger, *Harvard Business Review,* pp. 294–295.
6. Daniel J. Levinson, Charlotte N. Darrow, Edward B. Klein, et al., *The Seasons of a Man's Life* (New York: Alfred A. Knopf, 1978), p. 91.
7. Abraham Zaleznik, Gene W. Dalton, and Louis B. Barnes, *Orientation and Conflict in Careers* (Boston: Harvard Graduate School of Business Administration, Division of Research, 1970).

Chapter 6

1. We asked a group of executives in one of the largest banks in the world to help us understand what Stage IV people in their bank did. They produced a statement that they found to be so useful that they reproduced it and sent it to the other officers of the bank. They began by pointing out that "the scope of his or her job extends beyond that of the bank itself to the external business environment." They emphasized that Stage IV people are and must be "institutionally oriented," and are "engaged in linking institutional capabilities and potential across organizational lines." They are involved in "strategy formulation and implementation, establishing budget goals, and allocating resources." Another major function they stressed is "people evaluation and development, with emphasis on institutional interests."
2. When we talked to the directors of one of the largest management consulting firms in the world, they produced their document on staff advancement that had been developed through regular usage over a period of many years. The document specified the issues that were to be dealt with when someone was considered for election as a director. The directors pointed out that the process of using the staff advancement document was highly subjective, though the document did a good job of stating the central

issues that had to be considered. The first criterion set forth in the document required the individual to "have demonstrated that he or she can deal effectively with *top-management* executives in leading enterprises on their most important and often their most intimate problems." The next criterion specified that the individual had made "contributions to the firm for a significant period of time that were substantially greater than those required of a principal." The individual "will typically (a) make recognized contributions to the firm's policies and programs, (b) provide substantial leadership for the consulting staff, (c) serve outstandingly in an administrative capacity in the firm, and (d) represent the firm in an important way in the business community."

3. In discussing the functions of Stage IV people with the academic vice president of one of the largest universities we studied, he brought forth a statement of those functions a dean of a major college must perform (which had been drafted by the university president): "He or she represents the faculty to the administration, as well as represents the administration to the faculty and the college to the professional world. Most importantly, the dean gives imaginative leadership to the direction the college will take and the contributions it will make. The dean's role in setting direction for the college, in using resources, and in giving professional leadership to our efforts, is of great consequence to the entire university."

4. James D. Thompson, *Organizations in Action* (New York: McGraw-Hill, 1967). Thompson points out that in organizations where there are a number of sources of uncertainty and several bases for exercising power, we are likely to find these dominant coalitions. He makes it clear that although the "rational model" view of organizational structures might call for the "omnipotent individual" directing the organization, any of the following prevailing conditions negates the use of that model in practice:

1. When the complexity of the technology or technologies exceeds the comprehension of the individual.
2. When the resources required exceed the capacity of the individual to acquire.
3. When the organization faces contingencies on more fronts than the individual is able to keep under surveillance (p. 133).

The organizations we studied, and most modern organizations, operate under one or more of these conditions. Each of these conditions requires that there be individuals who have an understanding of the technological complexities, an understanding of the organization's capacities and needs, and the power to influence organizational decisions by making informed judgments that are consistent with, and contribute to the organization's strategy.

Thompson further postulates that, "The more numerous the areas in which the organization must rely on the judgmental decision strategy, the larger the dominant coalition" (p. 136). Thompson's theory on coalitions certainly found verification in our research. In some of the organizations we studied, which deal with very complex technologies, as many as 11 percent of the professionals and managers were in Stage IV.

5. John Kotter, *The General Managers* (New York: The Free Press, 1982).

Chapter 7

1. Chester I. Barnard, *The Functions of the Executive* (Cambridge, Mass.: Harvard University Press, 1958), p. 231.

2. Philip Selznick, *Leadership in Administration* (New York: Harper & Row, 1957), p. 37.

3. Michael McCaskey, *The Executive Challenge* (Boston: Pitman, 1982).

4. H. Edward Wrapp, "Good Managers Don't Make Policy Decisions," *Harvard Business Review* (September–October 1967), pp. 91–99.

5. James Brian Quinn, "Strategic Goals: Process and Politics," *Sloan Management Review,* (Fall 1977), pp. 21–37. For a fuller explication, read Quinn's *Strategies for Change: Logical Incrementalism* (Homewood, Ill.: Richard D. Irwin, 1980).

6. McCaskey, *The Executive Challenge,* pp. 14–33.

7. Theodore H. White, *In Search of History* (New York: Harper & Row, 1978), p. 194.

8. Solomon Asch, *Social Psychology* (Englewood Cliffs, N.J.: Prentice-Hall, Inc., 1952), pp. 450–500.

9. Peter L. Berger and Thomas Luckman, *The Social Construction of Reality* (New York: Doubleday, 1966).

10. Karl Weick, *The Social Psychology of Organizing* (Reading, Mass.: Addison Wesley, 1969); R. Duncan, "Characteristics of Organizational Environments and Received Environmental Uncertainty," *Administration Science Quarterly,* Vol. 17 (September 1972), pp. 313–327; Alan L. Wilkins, "Organizational Stories as Symbols Which Control the Organization," in *Organizational Symbolism,* Louis Pondy et al. eds. (Greenwich, Conn.: JAI Press Inc., 1983), pp. 81–92.

11. Walter Kiechel III, "Tom Vanderslice Scales the Heights at G.E.," *Fortune,* 30 July 1979, p. 82.

12. John Naisbitt, *Megatrends* (New York: Warner Books, 1982).

13. McCaskey, *The Executive Challenge,* p. 27.

14. White, *In Search of History,* p. 197.

15. "Harry Cunningham Didn't Play for Safety," *Fortune,* July, 1977, pp. 148–154.

16. Melville Dalton, *Men Who Manage* (New York: John Wiley and Sons, 1959); James D. Thompson, *Organizations in Action* (New York: McGraw-Hill, 1967).

17. James G. March and Johan P. Olsen, *Ambiguity and Choice in Organizations* (Bergen, Norway: Universitetsforlaget, 1976).

18. McCaskey, *The Executive Challenge,* p. 6.

19. Selznick, *Leadership in Administration,* pp. 42–55.

20. Herbert Dreyfuss, Public address entitled "Decision Making: Minds of Machines," recorded by station WOI, Iowa State University, Ames, Iowa; rebroadcast on Options, National Public Radio (Fall 1979)—tape 790914.

21. Richard P. Rumelt, *Strategy, Structure and Economic Performance* (Boston: Harvard Graduate School of Business Administration, 1974).

22. Selznick, *Leadership in Administration,* pp. 17, 62.

23. R. D. Laing, *The Politics of the Family and Other Essays* (New York: Vintage Books, 1972), p. 78.

24. Case written by John A. Seager under the supervision of Jay W. Lorsch, *First National City Bank Operating Group (A)* (Boston: Harvard Graduate School of Business Administration, 1974).

25. McCaskey, *The Executive Challenge,* pp. 61, 167, and 170.

26. Quinn, "Strategic Goals: Process and Politics," pp. 21–37.
27. Selznick, *Leadership in Administration,* p. 68.
28. Quinn, "Strategic Goals: Process and Politics," pp. 27–28.
29. Raymond E. Miles and J. Bonner Ritchie, *"Participative Management:* Quality and Quantity," *California Management Review,* Vol. XIII, No. 4 (Summer 1971), pp. 48–56.

Chapter 8

1. One of the authors of this book had previously co-authored a book that discussed authority: Gene Dalton, Louis B. Barnes, and Abraham Zaleznik, *The Distribution of Authority in Formal Organizations* (Boston: Division of Research, Harvard Graduate School of Business Administration, 1968).
2. Richard Neustadt, *Presidential Power,* originally published by Wiley in 1960 but a revised edition has been published (New York: John Wiley and Sons, 1980).
3. John Kotter, *Power in Management* (New York: Amacom, 1979), pp. 1–2.
4. Abraham Zaleznik and Manfred R. F. Kets de Vries, *Power and the Corporate Mind* (Boston: Houghton Mifflin, 1975), p. 3.
5. Kotter, *Power in Management,* p. 1.
6. Kotter, *Power in Management,* p. 16.
7. Rosabeth Kanter, "Power Failure in Management Circuits," *Harvard Business Review* (July–August 1979), p. 65.
8. Rosabeth Kanter, *Men and Women of the Corporation* (New York: Basic Books, 1977), p. 168.
9. Kanter, *Men and Women of the Corporation,* p. 165.
10. Jeffrey Pfeffer, *Power in Organizations* (Marshfield, Mass.: Pitman Publishing Co., 1981), p. 137.
11. David McClelland, "The Two Faces of Power," *Journal of International Affairs,* 24 (1970), pp. 29–47. See also David McClelland, *Power: The Inner Experience* (New York: Irvington Publishers, 1975), pp. 257–259.
12. McClelland, *Power: The Inner Experience,* pp. 5–29.
13. McClelland, *Power: The Inner Experience,* pp. 5–29.
14. John Underwood, "We're Going to Win, You Better Believe It," *Sports Illustrated* (July 28, 1969), pp. 18–19.
15. Theodore H. White, *Breach of Faith* (New York: Antheneum Publishers, 1975), p. 408.
16. Morgan McCall, Jr., and Michael M. Lombardo, "What Makes a Top Executive," *Psychology Today* (February 1983), p. 28.
17. James Brian Quinn, *Strategies For Change: Logical Incrementalism* (Homewood, Ill.: Richard D. Irwin, 1980), p. 71.
18. Nicoló Machiavelli, "The Prince," contained in *Great Books of the Western World* (Chicago: William Benton, Publisher; University of Chicago Press, 1952), Vol. 23, pp. 3–37.
19. Neustadt, *Presidential Power.*
20. Neustadt, *Presidential Power,* p. 9.
21. Neustadt, *Presidential Power,* p. 25.
22. Neustadt, *Presidential Power,* p. 27.
23. It is on this issue that we have trouble with the definitions of power used by such writers as Pfeffer, in Jeffrey Pfeffer, *Power in Organizations* (New York: Pitman Publishing Co., 1981), p. 3.

Pfeffer draws from an earlier article with Salancik by saying, "Power may be tricky to define, but it is not that difficult to recognize: the ability of those who possess power to bring about the outcomes they desire." Gerald R. Salancik and Jeffrey Pfeffer, "Who Gets Power and How They Hold onto It: A Strategic Contingency Model of Power," *Organizational Dynamics* (Winter 1977), p. 3.

Although we cannot disagree with the words, per se, the "definition" suggests that power in organizations is the ability to bring about whatever outcomes the power possessor desires. The definition, and its context, fails to take into account that organizations are purposive, voluntary associations whose members are entrusted to use the power given to them to advance the interests of the organization. Such a definition provides no basis for distinguishing between use of power and abuse of power (where the outcomes desired are not in the interests of the organization).

John Kotter's definition has some of the same problems: "Power is the measure of a person's potential to get others to do what he or she wants them to do, as well as to avoid being forced by others to do what he or she doesn't want them to do." But his book makes clear the distinction between the use and abuse of power in organizations. John Kotter, *Power in Management* (New York: Amacom, 1979), [found on unnumbered page preceding page 1].

24. For a thoughtful discussion of the means managers have at their disposal to focus attention and elicit action, see Thomas J. Peters, "Symbols, Patterns, and Settings: An Optimistic Case for Getting Things Done," *Organizational Dynamics* (Autumn 1978), pp. 3–22.

Chapter 9

1. Melville Dalton, *Men Who Manage* (New York: John Wiley and Sons, 1959), p. 31.

2. Rosabeth Kanter, *Men and Women of the Corporation* (New York: Basic Books, 1978).

3. Henry Mintzberg, *The Nature of Managerial Work* (New York: Harper & Row, 1973), p. 45.

4. Jeffrey Pfeffer, *Power in Organizations* (Marshfield, Mass.: Pitman Publishing Co., 1981), pp. 154–55.

5. John P. Kotter, *The General Managers* (New York: The Free Press, 1982), p. 67.

6. John P. Kotter, "General Managers are Not Generalists," *Organizational Dynamics* (Spring 1982), p. 8.

7. Robert E. Kaplan, "Trade Routes: The Manager's Network of Relationships," *Organizational Dynamics* (Spring 1984), pp. 37–52.

8. Pfeffer, *Power in Organizations*, p. 158.

9. Walter Isaacson, "Schultz, Thinker and Doer," *Time* (July 5, 1982), p. 15.

10. J. Bonner Ritchie, "We Need a Nation of Scholar-Leaders," *Exchange* (Published by the School of Management, Brigham Young University, Provo, Utah, Fall 1980).

Chapter 10

1. G. C. Collins and Patricia Scott, "Everyone Who Makes It Has a Mentor," *Harvard Business Review* (July–August 1978), p. 92.

2. Collins and Scott, *Harvard Business Review,* p. 96.

3. Collins and Scott, *Harvard Business Review,* p. 92.

4. Edward Roberts, "Entrepreneurship and Technology," *Research Management,* Vol. II, No. 4 (July 1968), p. 235.

5. Collins and Scott, *Harvard Business Review,* p. 95.

6. Collins and Scott, *Harvard Business Review,* p. 101.

7. Fox Butterfield, "China Alive in the Bitter Sea," (New York: Times Books, 1982), pp. 242–293.

8. "A Tried and True Model for GM," *Fortune,* October 6, 1980, p. 15.

Chapter 11

1. Daniel J. Levinson, Charlotte N. Darrow, Edward B. Klein, et al., *The Seasons of a Man's Life* (New York: Alfred A. Knopf, 1978).
2. George E. Vaillant, *Adaptation to Life* (Boston: Little, Brown and Co., 1977), p. 373.
3. Lotte Bailyn, "Involvement and Accommodation in Technical Careers," *Organizational Careers: Some New Perspectives*, John Van Maanen, ed. (London: Wiley International, 1977), pp. 120–121.
4. Bailyn, *Organizational Careers: Some New Perspectives*, pp. 121–128.
5. Paul A. Lee Evans and Fernando Bartolome, "The Relationship Between Professional Life and Private Life," *Work, Family and the Career*, C. Brooklyn Derr, ed. (New York: Praeger Publishers, 1980), p. 276.
6. Paul A. Lee Evans and Fernando Bartolome, "Professional Lives Versus Private Lives—Shifting Patterns of Managerial Commitment," *Organizational Dynamics* (Spring 1979), p. 6.
7. Evans and Bartolome, *Work, Family and the Career*, pp. 287–289.
8. David L. Norton, *Personal Destinies, a Philosophy of Ethical Individualism* (Princeton, N.J.: Princeton University Press, 1976), p. ix.
9. Norton, *Personal Destinies, a Philosophy of Ethical Individualism*, p. 16.
10. Norton, *Personal Destinies, a Philosophy of Ethical Individualism*, p. 9.
11. Norton, *Personal Destinies, A Philosophy of Ethical Individualism*, p. 9.
12. John J. Dewey, *Interest and Effort in Education* (Boston: Houghton Mifflin Co., 1913), p. 65.
13. Robert W. White, *Lives in Progress* (New York: Henry Holt and Co., 1960), pp. 348–349 (Copyright, 1952).
14. Michael Maccoby, *The Gamesman* (New York: Simon and Schuster, 1976), p. 111.
15. Erik H. Erikson, "Growth and Crises of the Healthy Personality," *Identity and the Life Cycle* (New York: International Universities Press, Inc., 1959), Vol. 1, No. 1. (Psychological Issues), pp. 50–100.
16. Erikson, *Identity and the Life Cycle*, p. 97.
17. Erikson, *Identity and the Life Cycle*, p. 97.
18. Evans and Bartolome, *Organizational Dynamics*, p. 22.
19. Donald W. Wolfe and David A. Kolb, "Beyond Specialization: The Quest for Integration in Midcareer," *Work, Family and the Career*, C. Brooklyn Derr, ed. (New York: Praeger Publishers, 1980), p. 276.
20. Abraham Zaleznik, Gene W. Dalton, and Louis B. Barnes, see "Comments on Conflict and Innovation," *Orientation and Conflict in Careers* (Boston: Harvard Graduate School of Business Administration, Division of Research, 1970), pp. 409–431.
21. Fernando Bartolome and Paul A. Lee Evans, "Must Success Cost So Much," *Harvard Business Review* (March–April 1980), p. 144.
22. Peter Drucker, *The Effective Executive* (New York: Harper & Row, 1966), pp. 52–53.
23. Thornton Wilder, *Our Town* (New York: Harper & Row, 1938), p. 100.

Chapter 12

1. D. Berlew and D. T. Hall, "The Socialization of Managers," *Administrative Science Quarterly*, 2 (1966), pp. 207–223.

2. D. T. Hall and E. E. Lawler III, "Unused Potential in Research and Development Organizations," *Research Management*, 12 (1969), pp. 339–354.

3. Ralph Katz, "Job Enrichment: Some Career Considerations," in *Organizational Careers: Some New Perspectives*, John Van Maanen, ed. (New York: John Wiley and Sons, 1977), p. 141.

4. Ralph Katz and T. J. Allen, "Investigating the Not Invented Here (NIH) Syndrome," *R and D Management* (1982), Vol. 12, No. 1, pp. 7–19.

5. "Happy Dropouts," *Forbes*, January 17, 1983, pp. 78–85.

6. Beverly Kaye, *Up is Not The Only Way: A Guide for Career Development Practitioners* (Englewood Cliffs, N.J.: Prentice-Hall, Inc., 1982), pp. 103–125.

Index